A WILD COWBOY

Heidi Bigler Cole

Rocky Comfort Press
1992

First Printing, December 1992
Second Printing, January 1993
Third Printing, October 1993

On the cover: Chris Anderson takes a chilling January ride on the Snake River breaks. (Photo by Doug McKinney.)

Rocky Comfort Press
12500 Hill Road
Payette, Idaho 83661

DEDICATION

To three of my favorite people:
Bryan Hixon, Ben Warner, and Sam Warner.

Bryan's family now owns the OX Ranch, and Ben and Sam's family has lived in Bear, Idaho for over 100 years.

Eight-year-old Bryan was sitting behind the wheel of his dad's brand-new pick-up when the boys met last summer. Wanting to establish his territory, he rared back in the seat and announced, "I can drive this truck."

Without missing a beat, four-year-old Ben piped up, "Well, I can clean a chicken."

The future of the OX Ranch could rest in their hands. Today's business climate requires ranchers who are sharp enough to finance a new truck, yet have the common sense and practical skills needed to clean a chicken.

If these boys do play a role in the OX's future, this book's sequel should be well worth the read.

A stroll around Horse Heaven provides a spectacular view of the country surrounding the Seven Devils mining district. (Photo by Heidi Bigler Cole.)

Idaho

Snake River

O
X
Ranch

New Meadows

McCall

Council

Weiser

Boise

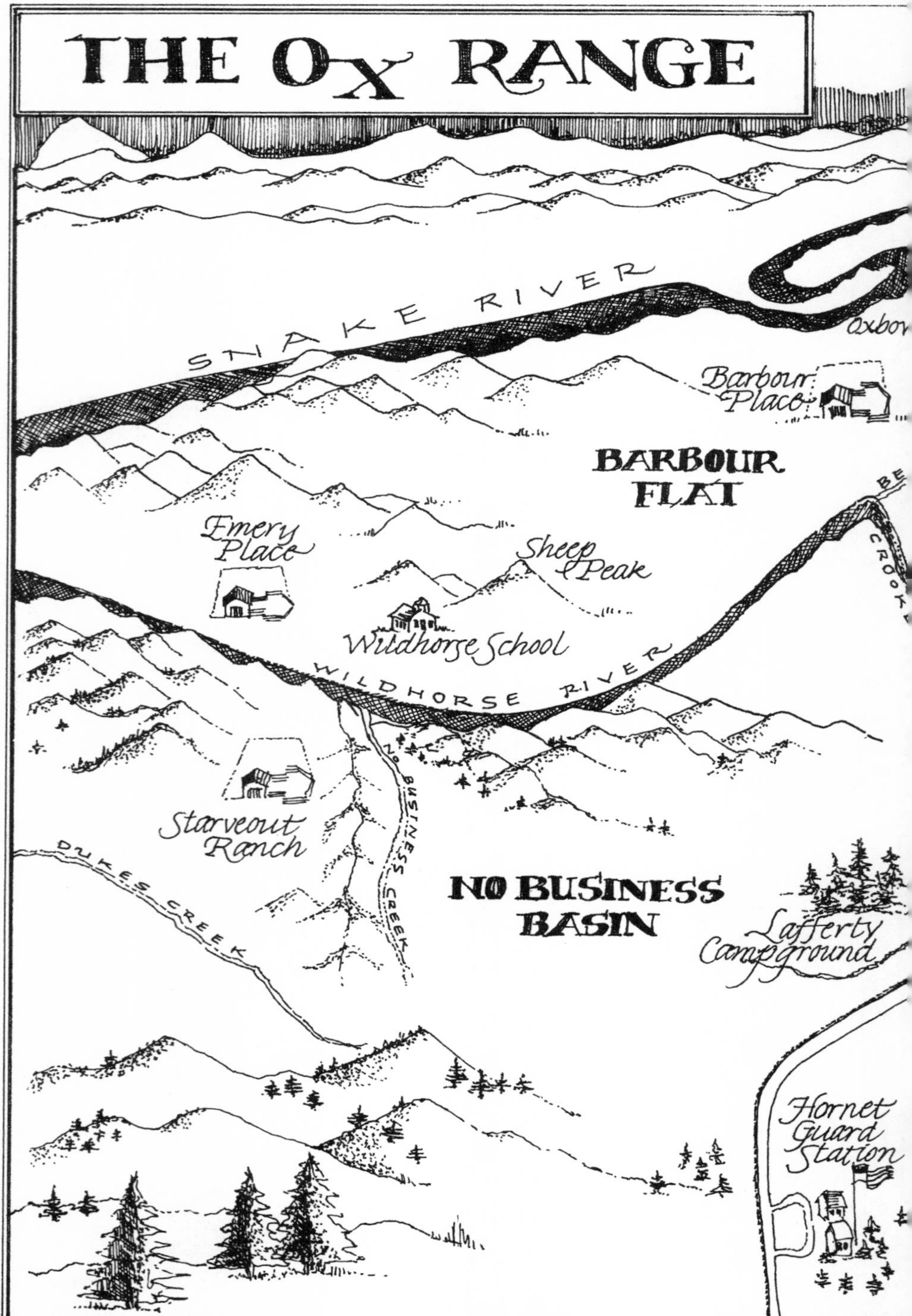

THE OX RANGE

SNAKE RIVER

Oxbow

Barbour Place

BARBOUR FLAT

BE CROOKE

Emery Place

Sheep Peak

Wildhorse School

WILDHORSE RIVER

NO BUSINESS CREEK

Starveout Ranch

DUKES CREEK

NO BUSINESS BASIN

Lafferty Campground

Hornet Guard Station

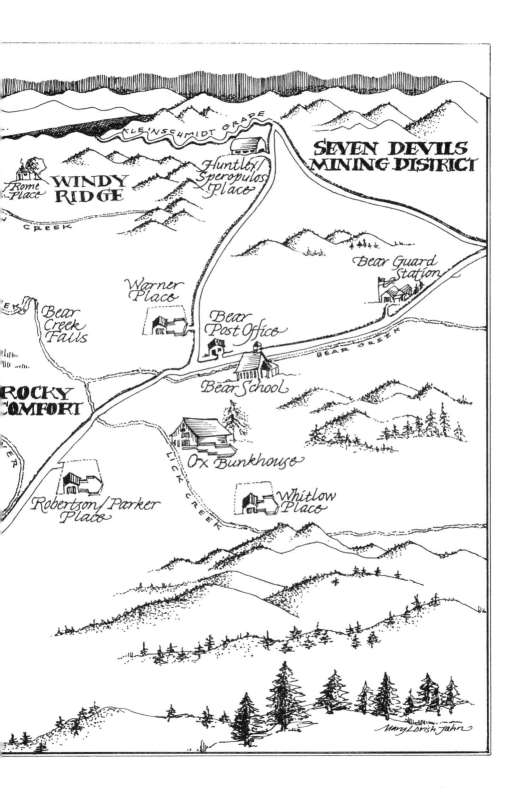

TABLE OF CONTENTS

Born and raised in Estes Park, Colorado, Heidi Bigler Cole is a graduate of Trinity University in San Antonio, Texas. She and her husband, Tony Cole, live on the site of an old peach orchard near the OX Ranch. Since coming to Idaho, she has learned how to preg test heifers, rid her home of pack rats, and can vast quantities of produce. (Photo by Noel Walsh Fletcher.)

Albert Campbell was just about fed up. He and a couple of his cowboys were trying to sort cattle, but an inexperienced hand was always in the wrong place at the wrong time. Wily cows kept slipping past him, slowing up the entire operation.

Finally Albert halted work, and rode over to the hand. "You know that gate five miles down the fence?" he asked.

"Yes," the hand said eagerly.

"I want you to ride down there, and check it. If the gate's open, leave it open. If it's closed, leave it closed."

The hand rode down the fence line without saying a word. Albert and his remaining crew finished the job.

More than ten years after his death, the name Albert Campbell still evokes strong emotions. Some people hated the cattleman, and others admired him. Either way, almost everyone respected him.

Albert showed a prodigy-like knack for the cattle business while he was growing up on the Circle C Ranch in New Meadows, Idaho.

In 1910 he borrowed $3,000 from his dad, and he started his own ranch, the OX. He was twenty-one years old. When he started, he held only 222 acres, but after thirty-two years of shrewd dealing and persistence, he controlled nearly 70,000 acres in the rugged country around Bear and Wildhorse, Idaho. His range stretched into the Seven Devils mining district, whose tremendous copper boom had played out shortly before he arrived.

He managed to keep the place together for sixty-nine years in spite of a near-fatal car accident in 1953, and the new wave of nutritionists who scoffed at his favorite slogan: Eat beef for health.

Albert's successor is John Dyer, who currently manages the OX ranch. He and four other men formed a partnership which purchased the OX in 1980, a year after Albert's death.

The partnership sold the ranch to the San Antonio, Texas-based Hixon family in 1982, but John was retained to spearhead ranch operations.

John and Tim Hixon let me tag along while they were gathering cattle a few summers ago. Tim took one side of the ridge, and John and I circled down toward Barbour Flat.

I started plying him with questions. How did Barbour Flat get its name? Where was the homestead situated?

As we rode by the Barbours' old well, John grew reflective. "A lot of the old-timers who remember the ranch's history are dying off," he said. He talked about Dick Armacost, who worked and neighbored with Albert Campbell for nearly half a century. Dick was one of the area's best storytellers, and he had died a few years earlier.

"Why don't you ask Tim to underwrite a history of the ranch?" he asked.

Tim was enthusiastic, and an incredibly involved project was launched.

Two weeks later, my mind was overrun with ideas and questions as I drove the twenty-two miles of dirt road and ten miles of pavement into Council, the nearest town. During the course of the summer, I had been into town only three times, and I didn't know a soul.

My first stop was the *Adams County Leader* office. Ancient linotype machines were churning out newspaper copy as I stepped in the door and met Shirley Rogers. She eyed my skirt. "Are you one of the new schoolteachers?" she asked curiously.

I explained my project and she eagerly offered to put a notice in the paper.

"Do you know anybody who I should interview?" I asked.

She thought. "Yes," she said slowly, "but they're all dead."

Her answer was prophetic. Many people who could have provided fascinating information are gone: prospectors, the men who worked for Albert in the early days, the moonshiners, and homesteaders whose places now make up the OX.

A little investigation and a lot of help from the local population provided me with plenty live people to interview. Unfortunately several of my sources died while I was writing the book.

The mining chapter was the most difficult to research, since the miners and even their children have long since died. Written documentation of the period is spotty—the mining district's weekly newspaper, *The Seven Devils Standard*, would have been a vital resource, but few of its issues have survived.

Most of this chapter's anecdotes came from Winifred Brown Lindsay, who chronicled the mining highlights in a research paper. She grew up in Cuprum and Landore, and witnessed their booming growth and eventual death. Mrs. Lindsay has been dead for several years now, and I'm thankful she had the foresight to perserve her insights.

One of the most lively interviews was with Albert Campbell's ninety-six-year-old sister, Carrie. Before we began our visit, she interviewed me. Satisfied, she settled back and reminisced about her incredible childhood. After she finished, she leaned forward and peered at me intensely. "Young lady," she said, "I don't know if you're wise or a fool. But I know people who do know, and I'm going to ask them."

I haven't had nerve enough to go back and learn the verdict.

Albert's daughter, Charlotte Campbell Armacost, was another invaluable source of information. After her mother died, she had the bittersweet task of sorting through her parent's belongings. Hoping to preserve some of her family's history, she methodically read drawersful of old correspondence, tossing the keepers into a bushel basket. Someone grabbed her basket and threw its contents into the fire. Charlotte discovered the mistake, raced to the fire, and plucked out most of the documents. Some of the book's most character-revealing stories came from the charred papers she rescued.

Charlotte also had the foresight to tape several interviews with her father. Albert wasn't too keen on the idea. Tape recordings caused President Richard Nixon plenty of trouble, he grumbled during one taped conversation. Since his interviewers were his young granddaughters, Tina and Anita Armacost, he agreed to do it.

Albert is a legend in this part of the country. Hearing him talk about his life helped me see the man, rather than the legend. It was a much needed insight.

More than 100 people told me stories about the OX and its neighboring ranches. Sometimes they had to search their memories for little events that happened fifty or sixty years ago. Major difficulties surfaced when two people told the same story—with different, highly embellished viewpoints. Stories naturally become better with age, but it makes nailing down the facts a tough job.

Some skewed facts have probably worked their way into the manuscript, but my proofreaders and I have tried to keep things factual.

Bud McGahey gave me that charge when I first started the project. He was helping his neighbors, the Bill Jordans, crank up their old sawmill. Eager to meet my neighbors, I wandered down, borrowed a pair of gloves and learned how to pull green chain, or take the sawed boards off the mill.

We shared one of Mavis McGahey's lemon meringue pies before Bud offered to drive me home. As we crept up the road in his four-wheel-drive Chevrolet pick-up, he voiced some apprehensions about my project. Other outsiders had written slip-shod articles, full of errors. If I'd take the time to do a thorough, factual job, he would help me in any way he could.

Bud and his wife, Mavis, have gone beyond their promise. Whenever I needed to verify a story, find a new source, or organize a difficult chapter, I walked the mile to their house where I could always find encouragement and a cup of tea.

Writing is solitary, lonesome work. A wonderful group of neighbors helped me forget the lonesome part by including me in Bear schoolhouse dances, brandings, and family gatherings. They pulled my rig out of several snowbanks, and called me to make sure I was eating my vegetables. The younger ones even shared their lemon drops with my dog, Storm.

I don't want to put the people I've researched and interviewed on a pedestal. Like the rest of us, they do and did have their share of human flaws. But I respect them. They're good, down-to-earth people who know how to work. If the rest of the world would slow down long enough, these people could teach it some valuable lessons about patience, perseverance, and character.

The men and women who lived on and around the OX Ranch made a solid contribution to history and the community. I thank Tim and Karen Hixon for recognizing this.

Whenever the author got stuck, Bud McGahey and his power winch were always close at hand. (Photo by Heidi Bigler Cole.)

Acknowledgments

Those Who Offered Insight and Encouragement

Dean and Janee Adams
Chris Anderson
Frank Anderson
Bertha Armacost
Erma Armacost
Gary Armacost
Vic and Charlotte
   Campbell Armacost
Bob and Lois Bigler
Randy Bigler
Wendy Bigler
Mike Bledsoe
Troy Bond
Leo Braun
Lloyd Bradshaw
T. Ray Bridges
Mary Brooks
Ralph and Dodie Brown
Bob and Eva Bureau
Amos Camp
Jim and Laura Camp
Darrell and Donna Campbell
Loyal Campbell
Rollie Campbell
Frank Carroll
Dick and Margery Clay
Larry and Hazel Clay
Tommy Clay

Darrell Cole
Debra Cole
Fred and Ruth Cole
Lee and Dee Cole
Tony Cole
Vicky Cole
Phyllis Cranor
Bob Davis
Leland and Louise Davis
Chuck Degitz
Bob Dunnington
John and Jeanne Dyer
Tom Ellison
Arnold and Ruth Emery
Paul and Ruth Ernst
Joan Ferguson
Dale and Anna Fisk
Michael Fisk
Tim and Noel Walsh Fletcher
Dougie and Beth Fout
Jim and Joanne Fry
Kathy Gaudry
Cary Davis George
Ginger Getusky
Dave Gipson
Gordon Gipson
Jim Gipson
Ron Gipson

Patty Gross
Becky Dunnington Hall
Linda Hall
Frank Hendricks
Chris and Lucy Chronic Hinze
Bryan Hixon
Joe and Renata Hixon
Tim and Karen Hixon
Timo Hixon
Dawn and Joe Holmes
Dianna and Phil Holmes
Howard and Leigh Hultgren
Ray and Caroline Hunt
Phil and Mary Lorish Jahn
Pat Jordan
Henry and Anna Kathrine
    Kamerdula
Georgia Killebrew
Bob Keith
Harold Kelly
Zoe Kelly
Ed Kesler
Larry Kingsbury
Morris Krigbaum
Bud and Marsha LaFay
Dale Lake
Vonda Lawrence
Colleen LeClair
Scott Lemberes
Margaret Lindgren
Hugh and Gayle Lydston
Berniece Martin
Clarence and Marie McFadden
Bud and Mavis McGahey
Ruth McGuiness
Doug and Lori McKinney
Kayla McKinney

Kendra McKinney
Kerri McKinney
Jan Mees
Herb Mink
Jeremy Mink
Norval Moritz
Clark Neeley
Paul and Maxine Nichols
Holworth and Marthabelle
    Nixon
Gay Lyn Olsen
Don and Kay Page
Dick and Georgianna Parker
Dennis Pattee
Ken and Shirley Pecora
Jay and Lori Quilliam
Mabel Ray
Bonnie Whiteley Reid
Susan Reinhard
Cheryl Ringering
Bert and Shirley Rogers
Toots and Louise Rogers
Neil and Mary Rosener
Darrel and Bobbie Sawyer
Helena Schmidt
Opal Shelton
Frank Shirtcliff
Vern and Helen Sinclair
Heitho Speropulos
Dale Smith
Frank and Betty Smith
Gale Stillman
Fred and Penne Stovner
Glenn and Barbara Stout
Sherwood Strickler
David and Debra Tate
Dixie Taylor

Bill Walsh
Becky Ward
Gail Ward
Robert and Teri Ward
Ben Warner
Bert and Tina Warner
Clarence Warner
Joe and Sue Warner
Lawrence and Millie Warner
Sam Warner

Bub Whiteley
Darline Whiteley
Don and Mabel Whiteley
Bob Whiteman
Carrie Campbell Whiteman
Don and Pat Whiteman
Dan Wilson
Jean Wilson
Mona Wright
Frank Youngblood

A Special Thanks to the Editors:

Tony Cole
Vic and Charlotte Armacost
Troy Bond
Dee Cole
Bob Dunnington
John and Jeanne Dyer
Becky Dunnington Hall
Lucy Chronic Hinze
Tim and Karen Hixon
Bob Keith
Bud and Mavis McGahey
Ronna Simon Monte
Maxine Nichols
Don and Kay Page
Dick Parker
Helena Schmidt
Bert and Tina Warner
Joe and Sue Warner

Miners Collis Lynes, Stewart Rug, and Charles Anderson gather at a cabin on Deep Creek. Besides prospecting, Anderson home-steaded 160 acres on Lick Creek in 1899. After three years he sold the parcel, which now houses the OX Ranch headquarters, for $1,213.96. (Photo courtesy of Becky Dunnington Hall.)

Prologue

THE MINERS: 1862–1916

"We never got down to Decorah very much when we was kids. We went to school with the kids from down there, but didn't go there much. There was too many saloons and sportin' houses there, you know. You mustn't go there—the devil is in them places. We always wanted to know what the devil looked like, so we wanted to look in."

—Anna Adams, former Landore resident

Of all the clapboard towns that sprang up during the Seven Devils copper boom, Decorah had the most scandalous reputation. Its founder, C.W. Jones, had every reason to believe his bawdy, young town would make him a rich man. Turn-of-the-century newspaper articles gushed about the area's financial prospects. One account, printed in the *Boston Daily Advertiser*, boasted there was enough copper in the Seven Devils to satisfy the national debt.

The area's discovery and subsequent mineral development occurred during the last phases of western expansion. The remote, rugged terrain had discouraged early exploration.

Fur trapping drew the first white men into the Seven Devils country, which fringes upon the OX Ranch. The first recorded expedition was sponsored by John Jacob Astor, owner of the American Fur Company. The group, led by Wilson Price Hunt, left St. Louis, Missouri in March, 1811. The party split and Donald MacKenzie led his group through the Seven Devils that winter. The journey was treacherous. Weighing travel difficulties against the relatively scant number of furs, the men deemed the Seven Devils a place to avoid.

MacKenzie returned to the area eight years later to determine whether the Snake was navigable. He reported that travel could be made between the Seven Devils and the Salmon River, but his findings were ignored.

Entrepreneurs again became interested in the area around 1862. The Oregon Steam Navigation Company sent Levi Allen with a crew of twelve men to evaluate navigation possibilities upstream from Lewiston. Icy conditions in Hells Canyon made the river impassable, so the group made a permanent camp next to some friendly Nez Perce on Pittsburgh Landing.

They decided to use their time prospecting, and that decision was to spark the Seven Devils mining boom. According to accounts given by Allen and another member of the party, Edmund Pearcy, their discovery was almost by accident.

Allen left six men to guard the boat and supplies. Borrowing or purchasing some horses from the Nez Perce, the seven prospectors attempted to travel up the Snake River. The horses couldn't gain footing on snowdrifts blocking the trails, so the men were forced to return the animals and continue on foot with 100-pound packs on their backs. Their days started at 3 a.m., since the snow crust often froze hard enough to support a man's weight. On the average, they traveled six miles before warmer daytime temperatures made the snow impassable.

With a great deal of difficulty, they climbed the walls of the canyon on the Idaho side, traversed the Snake River/Little Salmon divide, and dropped down to the Little Salmon River. They followed it to its headwaters and dropped over into Lower Payette Lake. After paralleling the Payette River until it came to Horseshoe Bend, they stopped to assess their situation.

Each day for the previous two months, the men had fished their gold pans out of their packs and tromped around in the streams trying to find some color. They didn't find anything.

While they were rearranging their packs, patching holes in their shoes, and making venison jerky, they debated whether to continue prospecting or find a shorter route back to Pittsburgh Landing. Frustrated with the bickering, Allen and another man left for Pittsburgh Landing. Within three days, the expedition party was reunited; the men were reluctant to continue exploring without Allen's wilderness knowledge.

The return route took them northwest from Meadows Valley along the ridge leading to Smith Mountain, which now marks the edge of the OX Ranch's summer range. They camped at White Monument, at the head of Copper Creek, on July 1, 1862.

In a letter to William Winkler, Allen described what followed:

> One night we camped in the Seven Devils close to the summit on the Snake River side. The next morning we could look down the mountain and see the Peacock mine, a copper property. We all went down the hill and looked it over. I told the boys we should take it up, but they all said they didn't want anything to do with it, as it was too far from transportation.

The men helped Allen both measure the ledge, which was one yard wide by 100 yards long, and locate his claim.

The prospectors celebrated the discovery on the Fourth of July in a snowstorm. Diminishing supplies of salt and other provisions spurred their decision to hurry back to Pittsburgh Landing.

The ore's brilliant color inspired Allen to name his claim the Peacock. This first claim of the Seven Devils mining district was filed in Hailey, Idaho Territory in July of 1862.

After gathering several ore samples, Allen set off for Montana in search of investors. Isaac Ives Lewis and Houser Lewis, both superintendents of several Montana Territory mining properties, were enthusiastic about his find. The samples Allen showed them yielded an amazing eighty-five percent copper.

It wasn't until 1877 that Allen convinced Lewis to inspect the claims personally. They chose a risky time to travel, as the Nez Perce and Sheepeater conflicts were in full swing. One portion of the trail was littered with empty whiskey bottles and tin cans. They later learned that it was the site of the Birch Creek massacre, and that they were following a group of Nez Perce who had hijacked a wagon train hauling whiskey and supplies.

In an attempt to avoid a conflict, they took a detour through the Hailey/Ketchum area. Ironically, they were traveling through what would become one of Idaho's richest silver mining areas.

Another difficulty awaited them at the Peacock claim: claim

jumpers. Lewis described what they found in his 1892 autobiography:

> Two log houses that had been occupied by four placer miners for some four or five seasons, (who had been) working the creeks below, and up to the copper mine. They had even sluiced off the surface of the mine; it appeared that the gold found in the stream below had all come from the Peacock mines. They had brought water from the creek above on it and had evidently spent considerable time sluicing down the decomposed surface of the lode.

Investigation revealed that brothers Billy and John Simpson and their partners had filed a placer mining claim on the land. Period law allowed two different types of claims to be filed on the same land. Allen agreed to pay the men $2,500 for full mining rights.

Lewis was enthusiastic about the mine's potential. He estimated there were 500 tons of loose ore, and of that, about 200 tons was first-class copper ore.

The men immediately marked the claim's corners with permanent posts and claim notices, and they took samples of the lode. Allen and Lewis formed an equal partnership and staked three additional claims called the North Peacock, the Helena, and the White Monument.

Word of the copper bonanza soon reached the ears of Montana investors. Granville Stewart and S.T. Hauser wanted to be in on the ground floor. Stewart had made his fortune after acting on a tip from a half-breed Indian. His cabin became the center of the placer mining boom town of Virginia City, Montana. Hauser later became the territorial governor of Montana. With $1,500, they bought a quarter interest in the Peacock, Helena, and White Monument mines.

Other miners sensing the activity began to file claims. Charles Walker, Arthur "Frenchie" David, and Charles Anderson proved to have accurate hunches. They filed on the Blue Jacket, Queen, and Alaska mines in 1879.

The Kleinschmidt brothers' interest in the area ignited the mining boom in 1885. Albert, Reinhold, and Carl were immigrants from Gorlitz, Germany, who owned a large merchandizing business in Helena, Montana. They had subsidized their income by grubstaking, or lending money, to successful gold miners. The possibility of a big strike in the Seven Devils especially appealed to Albert.

The Kleinschmidts purchased an interest in Levi Allen's claims and they bought the Blue Jacket, Queen, and Alaska mines outright. Exploratory testing began in 1885 and continued for the next two summers. Work focused on the Blue Jacket, since it was closest to the road and assay tests revealed high percentages of copper in the ore.

The miners formed a makeshift community of tents at the base

Walter James, Joe Salsberry, Arthur "Frenchie" David, and Pat Kane take a break in front of ore sacks at the Arkansas dump. James was Landore's butcher and a hotel proprietor. Frenchie was a long-time prospector in the area who gained fame when he tested his new "autermatic" pistol . . . inside his cabin. After the test, his wash basin and several pans wouldn't hold water. (Photo courtesy of the Idaho State Historical Society.)

of the Peacock mine. Before long, tents housing saloons and a hardware store were erected. There was talk of naming the community Annie Bristow, after the first white woman to set foot in the Seven Devils. The suggestion never took hold.

As mining activity continued, a more permanent community began to take shape farther below the mine along Copper Creek. It was named for Helena Smith, the first white baby born in the area. Eventually, the town featured three mercantile stores, two assay offices, a brewery, six saloons, and two sawmills. Helena's post office was established Sept. 29, 1890.

Helena's residents spent the summer of 1887 digging tunnels and sorting rock. Ore assaying at less than twenty percent was thrown into the dump. In 1888, the richer ore was sewn into thirty inch bags, loaded onto seventeen mules and packed 100 miles to the nearest shipping point in Weiser. The route took them around the east side of Cuddy Mountain, across the Weiser River to Salubria (now a ghost town near Cambridge) before angling into Weiser.

The Kleinschmidts were encouraged with the results sent back from the Anaconda smelter in Montana. Assay tests revealed the ore contained up to seventy percent copper and each ton yielded fifty dollars in gold. The copper was sold at a premium in Europe, where it was used for flux in smelters.

Meanwhile, the American Mining Company was organized. Under the articles of incorporation, Albert Kleinschmidt owned a controlling 9/16 interest in the Peacock, White Monument, and Helena lodes. Also signing the documents were Carl Kleinschmidt and James Millisch, Albert's private secretary.

The operation had one major obstacle: transportation. A route change helped pick up the pace. Packstrings went as far as the present-day Bear guard station where they transferred their loads to freight wagons bound for the railhead in Weiser by way of Council.

The road to Council followed a slightly different path in those days. Construction began in 1885 and the road angled up and over the hill near the Bear cemetery, then shot directly to the site of the OX Ranch's Lick Creek barn.

A good rainstorm always caused a major mud bog to form near

Edward Lockwood, seated, and five fellow miners pause for a rest in Helena, the first boom town in the Seven Devils mining district. A post office was established there on September 29, 1890, but the population never exceeded 100. (Photo courtesy of the Idaho State Historical Society.)

the cemetery. In order to lighten their loads, freighters threw ore off their wagons. Stray piles of copper ore were an area landmark for years. Another reminder of the treacherous road lies underground: a thick layer of fence posts. A post under a bogged wagon wheel could provide excellent traction.

As mine production increased, the demand for freighters grew. Wages were attractive. Mine owners paid nine dollars per ton to have their ore shipped to the railroad, and hauling machinery and supplies into the district generated even more income.

The extra revenue was a boon to homesteaders beginning to drift into the area. Many farm wagons were reinforced to do double duty, and quite a few farm wives boosted their small children onto the wagon seat and started hauling cargo.

When mining in the district was at its peak, there were over eighty wagons on the road—all of them outfitted with bells, so

The city park is about the only recognizable feature in this 1897 photograph of Council. Residents gather under the flag for what may have been a Fourth of July celebration. (Photo courtesy of Dale Fisk.)

No mining-era photographs of freighters were located, however an outfit like this was typical. Ira Gilcrest and Jim Potter posed for this 1925 picture in Council. (Photo courtesy of the Bert Warner family.)

that oncoming traffic would take advantage of turnouts in the narrow road.

Even eighty wagons couldn't keep pace with mining production. Albert Kleinschmidt began to look for an alternative. His idea was announced to the public in the *Weiser Signal*'s October 4, 1889 edition:

> Some capitalists have been examining the Snake River from Huntington to the Seven Devils with the view of putting two steamers on the river to bring out the ore. Mr. Kleinschmidt is one of the proprietors of the Seven Devils district who was with the party.

The ore would reach the river on a road Kleinschmidt planned to construct from White Monument to Ballard's Landing.

The picks began to fly the summer of 1889. Small groups of men were scattered up and down the grade, most manning picks and shovels. Men in pairs ran two-handled scrapers pulled by a team of horses or mules. One man handled the team and the other guided the scraper. A few wielded large sledgehammers and pounded drill bits into the hard rock. Dynamite was placed in the resulting hole.

Two men apparently supervised the operation. Alec Houlahan, a highly educated Canadian, and Jim Ross, who officially announced the grade's completion.

The construction managers expected ten hours of peak performance from their men each day. The pace was steady and exhausting. The men swinging eight pound double jacks learned to snatch a short rest by keeping a broken drill bit in their pockets. When they needed a rest, they dropped the faulty bit into the hole and took their time fishing it out.

The pay scale ranged from fifty cents to two dollars per day, with workers under twenty-one receiving the lowest wages, grown men being paid one dollar and teamsters and drillers earning one dollar and fifty cents and two dollars respectively. Any employee who was more than five minutes late was docked a quarter day's pay.

Employment on the grade drew some settlers into the area,

John Eckles (second from left) and Archibald Richie (second from right) established this homestead cabin on the Snake River, at the mouth of Eckles Creek. Also pictured are (left to right) Charlie Walker, Henry Burt, and Andy Covert. Eckles provided miners and settlers with prize-winning fruit from his orchard. When winter weather made prospecting too rough, miners flocked to Eckles' cabin "like tomcats." (Photo courtesy of the Bert Warner family.)

including Amos Warner and his nine children. The Warners founded Bear, and three generations of the family still live there.

After two solid years of work, the Kleinschmidt Grade was completed on July 31, 1891. Stretching from the top of White Monument to the Snake River, it was twenty-two miles long. The road dropped about 5,800 feet and had a grade ranging from seven to nineteen percent. The final cost of the project was $30,000.

An *Idaho Daily Statesman* article reflected the enthusiasm and optimism of the time:

> Mr. Kleinschmidt and a party of Montana gentlemen passed through Weiser yesterday en route for the Seven Devils mine. They informed our

Ore carts clattered out of the Blue Jacket mine entrance, which is obscured by the steam engine, and dumped their cargo near sorting benches. (Photo courtesy of the Idaho State Historical Society.)

correspondent that twenty teams are on their way now from Montana that have contracted to haul 20,000 tons of ore from the mines to the new steamboat on the Snake River.

Experts say that $1,200,000 will be realized from the Peacock mine this summer, leaving 55,000 tons of ore still in sight.

This is Levi Allen's old mine and is doubtless the richest copper mine in the world. It is estimated that from 10,000 to 15,000 people will go to the mines of the Seven Devils District this summer.

The steamship mentioned in the article was named the *Norma* in honor of Albert Kleinschmidt's eldest daughter. The ship cost a reported $35,000 and she was built on the Idaho side of the Snake River, at Bridgeport.

Hoping to give the *Norma* an easier voyage, Johnny Rogers blasted rock out of Bay Horse Rapids.

The *Norma*'s maiden voyage on April 21, 1891 was a devastating anticlimax. Empty, the steamship barely negotiated the rocky rapids in Hells Canyon.

"At present owing to its many boulders in the channel the boat will not be able to run except during freshet (spring runoff) floods," reported the *Weiser Signal* on May 7. ". . . an

Burlap sacks full of high-grade ore surround these Blue Jacket mine workers at a sorting bench. Most ore mined in the Seven Devils district was low-grade, having a four to eight percent copper content. Shipping and smelting costs made it necessary to ship only high-grade ore, which generally assayed at thirty percent. (Photo courtesy of the Idaho State Historical Society.)

This view of the Blue Jacket mine shows the low-grade ore dump, an ore bin, the shipping platform, the blacksmith shop and the mine entrance. The mining operation continued all winter, with ore being sorted and sacked inside the bin. Freighters had a hectic schedule as soon as the snow melted. (Photo courtesy of the Idaho State Historical Society.)

appropriation by the government will be granted jointly to Oregon and Idaho and the river will be made navigable all the year round.''

The federal government did eventually spend close to $33,000 to remove boulders from a two and one-half mile stretch on the ''upper Snake River.'' The blasting took place from 1892 to 1895.

By that time it was too late for the *Norma.* Her captain, J.P. Miller, attempted the trip a second time, after the Kleinschmidt

Grade was completed. The October 1, 1891 *Signal* reported, "A rock was run into at Bay Horse Rapids some eight miles below Huntington. A big hole was punched in the boat's side and she was with difficulty getting back to the landing at the bridge."

The steamship which cost $35,000 to build was sold for $4,000 at a sheriff's sale. The $30,000 used to construct the Kleinschmidt Grade was also a wasted investment.

Adding to his troubles, Kleinschmidt jeopardized his control of the American Mining Company, Ltd. by selling his 9/16 interest in the Peacock, White Monument, and Helena lodes October 1, 1891. In exchange he received 16,000 shares in the company; each valued at ten dollars.

The move undermined Kleinschmidt's power, and the organization lacked a definitive leader. As a result, the company floundered for the next several years.

Meanwhile, mine operators were still hampered by sluggish transportation. Kleinschmidt built a road connecting the A.O. Huntley ranch with Bear. The road, which was completed in 1893, gave ore freighters a speedier route.

A grassy meadow above Huntley's cabin became a popular stopping place for freighters who wanted to rest or repair their rigs. Nels Swanson saw a business opportunity. He left Bear, where he had been assisting widow Amy Smith at the Bear Creek Store, and built a large log cabin in the middle of the meadow. After buying a wagon load of both dry goods and thirst quenchers, he was in the mercantile business.

Levi Allen built the next business in the area: a sawmill below the Huntley place. Allen's son, Charles, ran the mill. The market for the rough, unseasoned lumber increased as more miners and families drifted in.

When the Clark family arrived in October of 1897, there were six families living in the area plus a number of single men. They built a hotel which was popular with the bachelors for two reasons. First, Mrs. Clark made wonderful light bread, which she sometimes had to bake three times a day. The second drawing card was that the bread was served by Inez and Janie, Mrs. Clark's daughters.

Scarcely two months after the Clarks arrived, their settlement received a post office and an official identity. This was needed since newspaper stories randomly called the community Copper City or Copperopolis. Records show that Edward P. Hall was appointed postmaster on December, 1 1897. The town was called Cuprum, which is Latin for copper.

As the Kleinschmidts demonstrated, transporting copper ore to the smelter was a major stumbling block. Northwest Copper Company entrepreneurs attacked the problem from a different angle. They decided to bring the smelter to the mining district in 1897.

A company agent sent to oversee the smelter's installation caused some project delay. He became involved with under-the-table negotiations to locate the smelter at the foot of the Kleinschmidt Grade rather than in the heart of the district. The negotiators wanted to build a narrow gauge railroad down the Kleinschmidt, and they had devised a plan to transport the smelted minerals through Oregon, bypassing Idaho business interests. Plans fizzled when the New York investors refused to sign the contract.

After nearly a year's delay, the Cuprum smelter had its first trial run in the spring of 1898. The results were disappointing. Smelter production was forty percent lower than assay tests predicted. The trust company sold the smelter to the Iron Dyke mine, which was across the Snake River from Ballard's Landing.

Despite the smelter's failure, Cuprum experienced its most prosperous year in 1898. It was still the miners' central meeting place. A growing number of workers were producing record amounts of ore. The Blue Jacket mine employed thirty full-time miners that year who dynamited, shoveled, sorted, and sacked three railroad cars full of ore each week.

Cuprum's growth was boosted by an unrelated event. Construction was underway on a railroad heading north from Weiser. The railroad would miss Salubria and stop instead at Cambridge, a new town planned on the Weiser River. Many Salubria residents chose Cuprum's thriving business climate over Cambridge's growing pains.

The *Weiser Signal* helped lure Salubria residents with this description:

Cuprum has been the supply point for the mines for several years, and it has a population of enterprising people. There are two general stores, a drug store, a blacksmith shop, two livery stables, hotels, the 'Imperial' conducted by Mrs. E.M. Clark and daughters is in the center of town and considered first-class, a newspaper, the *Standard*, conducted by Edwin Elton and several wet goods establishments.

Three businesses offered alcoholic "wet goods," according to an account written by early resident Winifred Brown Lindsay. One, Leithstrom's, was located one-half mile from the center of Cuprum. The other two were located in town.

The only violent death during the mining era occurred at one of these establishments. Lindsay related this unsubstantiated version:

The sign reads, "Office, Blue Jacket Mines, F.J. French, Mgr." The Metropolitan Trust Company leased the mines from Albert Kleinschmidt in 1897. French was a New Yorker who became one of the most progressive thinkers in the district. He helped initiate plans to bring a smelter to Cuprum, and he provided manpower when the P.I.N. railroad grade to Landore was being built. The buildings were three years old when this picture was taken in 1900. (Photo courtesy of the Idaho State Historical Society.)

Blue Jacket miners fed in this cookhouse did not belong to I.W.W., the miners' union that had upset work in northern Idaho. Seven Devils miners claimed I. W. W. stood for "I Won't Work" and they called union supporters Wobblies. The Wobblies showed their resentment by burning down Cohen's tent store in Cuprum. They were promptly run out of town. (Photo courtesy of the Idaho State Historical Society.)

a relative newcomer to the area, a family man, entered the saloon to wet his whistle. At the end of the bar slouched a mean drunk who was shouting slurs at the newcomer. The drunk didn't get a reaction until he made loud speculations about the premarital occupation of the man's wife. The newcomer planted his fist in the drunk's face. The resulting fist fight ended when the drunk drew a knife. The newcomer was buried in his distant hometown. According to Lindsay, no arrests were made, and newspapers ignored the incident.

Cuprum's rosy future was changed when T.G. Jones rode into town the summer of 1898. He was quietly eating some of Mrs. Clark's flapjacks when Bill Ewan stepped into the hotel. Ewan shook his head in disbelief when he saw Jones, as he had last seen the man scalped and left for dead on one of Custer's battlefields. When the other restaurant patrons asked to see his scalped spot, Jones obligingly removed his hat.

Jones was looking for new business opportunities. He had managed the Homestake mine in the Black Hills for years, but when his wife left him for his brother, he was drawn to a new start in the Seven Devils.

Jones envisioned a new townsite. He filed on water and mining rights on Indian Creek, one and one-half miles up from its confluence with Garnet Creek. The site was named Landore (land of ore) in honor of his old home in Wales, where the world's largest smelter was supposedly located.

Landore's development was rapid. Jones focused all his attention on the fledgling town. Building a three percent grade from Landore to the Black Lake road insured his success.

Freighters immediately started using the new route to Bear, which was shorter and had an easier grade. As a result, Cuprum began to die.

Larger-scale transportation problems were still on developers' minds, and as a result, several plans to build railroads into the Seven Devils were in the offing. The most ambitious plan was backed by the Boston and Seven Devils Copper Company, which had Lewis A. Hall at the helm.

Hall, who was also president of the Pacific & Idaho Northern (PIN) railroad, was described by Winifred Lindsay as "young, enthusiastic, full of energy, ideas and showmanship, if not too much organization, and was backed by eastern capitalists, but mainly by his father's millions." His railroad and mining connections coupled with his financial backing spelled success.

The Boston and Seven Devils Company immediately began to purchase and lease claims. Among the claims purchased were the Decorah, Arkansas, and Kleinschmidt's interest in the Peacock. The December 21, 1899 *Weiser Signal* reported, "The Kleinschmidt interest in the Peacock has been one of the stumbling blocks in the development of the Seven Devils property. The sale was made on the basis of $1,000,000." Major properties leased included two other American Mining Company ventures: White Monument and Helena.

Downtown Landore featured ample packhorse parking and board sidewalks wide enough to accommodate children, sleeping dogs, and business patrons. In addition to dry goods, Dr. Brown's general store offered a telephone connection to the outside world. E.D. Edlin, pictured left, owned the town's weekly newspaper, The Seven Devils Standard. *Mr. and Mrs. Edlin hiked and skied a sixteen-mile radius to collect news for the paper, which was printed on a man-manipulated press. All but one issue of the* Standard *have been lost. (Photo courtesy of the Idaho State Historical Society.)*

While the mining interests were being secured, Lewis began concentrating on the PIN railroad's next destination: Landore. On May 27, 1899, Hall reported that thirteen miles of the grade were completed and 280 teams were working on the project. Twenty-three miles of the grade had been surveyed. Colorado Iron Works sold the group ninety-eight miles of rails, and a copper spike was ordered. Thomas Bates, a company official, was to drive it in with a sledgehammer during the completion ceremonies.

South Peacock mine owners devised a way to transport ore to the terminal point in Landore without using wagons. A three and

Posing with their winter mode of transportation are Dr. William Brown, Pete Miller, Frank Sullivan, Orson Smith, Lawrence Brown, Sam Stephens, and Bill Carrick. Snow depth averaged between seven and eight feet, making homemade tamarack skis the only travel option. The skis did have some minor problems: they were difficult to turn and impossible to stop. Incredible feats were performed on the skis. Men regularly used them to carry 120-pound packs of supplies and mail to stranded miners. (Photo courtesy of the Idaho State Historical Society.)

one-half mile long tramway was designed so that the full ore buckets would pull the empties back to the mine.

Mining projects and the railroad grade activity generated a steady stream of accident victims, increasing the need for medical services. Lewis convinced a young Salubria doctor, William M. Brown, to relocate in Cuprum. Brown's state pharmaceutical license made him especially useful.

Lewis built a hospital at the lower end of Cuprum, and the building, which was one of the largest in camp, had three rooms. The drugstore was in front. A narrow hallway led to the ward, which had several cots, and the kitchen was situated in the back. Mrs. Brown and the male cook served as nurses.

Activity in the hospital was short-lived because work on the railroad grade slackened, and then stopped completely in 1901. At first company officials claimed they would resume work after the winter snows. Rumors began circulating about Lewis forfeiting his interest in the American Mining Company, and the railroad's doom was sealed when the Boston and Seven Devils Company dissolved in 1901 for failure to pay taxes.

Courthouse records indicate Lewis also lost some personal property on Lick Creek. The site currently houses the OX Ranch bunkhouse, main corrals, and barn. In fact, it was probably Lewis who hired Charles Lynes to construct the Lick Creek barn. Foreclosure papers on this property were served on June 27, 1903.

Other investment groups attempted to build railroads, but few ventured beyond the planning stages. The most concrete evidence of their plans is filed away in county courthouses. Trees and brush have grown over the partially finished grades, but they are still visible today. OX cattle graze near what was the Boston and Seven Devils Company grade. The grade is easily spotted around Kinney Point, White Monument Mountain, and Camp Creek. Another abandoned grade is located at Railroad Saddle, two miles east of the Lick Creek lookout.

The railroad would have increased the district's daily output to 1,000 tons. In 1901, the freight wagons' capacity was only 100 tons per day.

Shipping constraints didn't seem to slow the work pace. The mines around Landore ran ten-hour shifts; one in the morning and one at night. The town never rolled up its sidewalks; saloons and hotels kept their doors open around the clock. The post office also kept evening hours, since the mail came in on Pete Kramer's midnight stage.

Winifred Lindsay, who was a child at the time, said the night life was rarely boisterous, although ''Payday, with its cards and refreshments, was usually more interesting.''

Day in and day out ore carts streamed out of the tunnels. Their contents were dumped into long chutes which led to the ore storage bins. The clattering racket echoed through the canyon.

Some modern problems accompanied the area's prosperity. The midnight traffic was a major nuisance. Landore founder T.G.

Jones had built a two-way bridge across Indian Creek which was one of the few flat surfaces in the area. Freighters liked to camp there for the night. This was fine until midnight, when Kramer's stage came flying through. Jones, who was mayor, decided to take official action. Signs reading, "No camping on this bridge," were posted and the problem was remedied.

Kramer's stage provided the fastest transportation into the Seven Devils. Stages left both Landore and Council at 1 p.m. every day except Sunday. Most passengers spent the night at Kramer's stage stop located at the halfway point. If passengers had extra fare and stamina, they could complete the eleven-hour trip in one hitch.

Kramer's stages brought more and more families to the area and the next civic project was building a school. After the trustees had purchased the two-seater desks, blackboards, primary charts, and the box stove which was surrounded by a large heating drum; they decided to forego buying a school bell. Twenty-five Blue Jacket miners thought a bell was necessary, so they pooled funds. An inscription on the bell read, "Presented by the employees of the Blue Jacket mine, March 1900." The first schoolteacher, Miss Cora Dale, organized a celebratory program to honor the miners.

For reasons that are unclear, a second, more modern school was constructed between Landore and its neighboring town, Decorah in 1901. The saloon tax, which was the largest source of school revenue, enabled the residents to build the finest rural schoolhouse in the county. The school was equipped with single desks, blackboards, wall maps, charts, abacuses, a globe, an unabridged dictionary, and a glass bookcase containing several books. The school building featured a large, covered porch, so that the children could jump rope and play games during stormy weather. Forty-two children, from five to eighteen years old, filled the school that September.

At this time, Decorah was having its heyday. C.W. Jones (no relation to Landore's mayor) founded the town in 1898 with a slightly different business angle. A stroll down the main street illustrated this difference. Three street lamps illuminated a saloon, one hotel, two stores, a barber shop, and three cat houses.

An opera house was built by Mrs. Clark, who had sold her

A quick visit and a drag on a cigar broke up the forty-mile journey between Landore and Council. The driver on the right is probably Pete Kramer, who operated a stage station at the halfway point. (Photo courtesy of the Idaho State Historical Society.)

hotel in Cuprum. This was reportedly the "best show house in Washington County." At that time, the county stretched from Weiser to New Meadows. Winifred Lindsay wrote that only one show was ever shown in the opera house. A young man rode forty miles in a stage to present "a flickering moving picture of a very fat lady (male acrobat) becoming entangled with a vegetable cart." Apparently there was no encore presentation.

The opera house did have a large, shiny dance floor. Children would gather momentum running, and then slide clear across the floor, so the building did provide some entertainment. Only a few dances were held there.

The Landore/Decorah schoolhouse operated eight years before the last teacher, Miss Lapp, closed the school in 1908. Enrollment had dropped from forty-two to four students. Pictured are students Edgar James, Mildred Brown, and Ida Cornett surrounding Miss Lapp. (Photo courtesy of the Idaho State Historical Society.)

Dr. William Brown became the owner of a general store in town when a customer signed over the deed to satisfy a debt. In addition to the drugstore merchandise he had sold in Cuprum (drugs, watches, perfumes, and candy), he now carried groceries, overalls, nails, frying pans, and horseshoes.

Decorah's main attraction was a saloon, owned by George Basset. He had previously owned a saloon in Council, which had become a wild and rowdy supply point for mines in the Salmon River, Warren, and Seven Devils regions. A man who had been robbed accused Basset of the deed. Basset promptly shot and killed his accuser, claiming it was self-defense. Although the jury acquitted him, he seemed eager to leave Council. Decorah beckoned and he built an extravagant saloon designed to entice the area's male population. Basset over-estimated the appeal of his business, and after running the saloon for a few months, he hired a caretaker and left the area.

As society dictated, women and children never ventured near the establishment, but they did have a burning curiosity. One day Keno, the caretaker, opened the saloon for a public tour. Most of the area's women and children accepted the invitation, including Winifred Lindsay, who wrote the following account:

> As one entered the barroom, the most conspicuous item was a gold framed picture which hung behind the long, highly polished bar. The women did not view the reclining, well-draped (by today's standards) female figure resting on one elbow on a red plush sofa because the picture had been turned to the wall. However, every youngster had a good peek when the tallest girl tipped the frame far enough out from the wall for all to see.
>
> From the bar, one entered the card room through swinging doors. This was a quite spacious room with a well-waxed floor because it was also the spot for dancing. Across the end was a balcony where the exceptionally fine violinist (an alcoholic) and his wife furnished the music. The balcony extended along one side of the room where four or five

Mine tailings and prospector's cabins surrounded the Decorah mine around the turn of the century. The nearby town of Decorah featured two big city attractions: street lamps and sporting houses. (Photo courtesy of the Idaho State Historical Society.)

curtained boxes provided a good viewpoint for spectators to watch the revelry below.

Behind the card room was the well-carpeted parlor with the red, plush furniture that fascinated all.

(In) the rear, accessible by a covered walk, were the rooms assigned to the fancy ladies who were never seen on the streets in daylight. There was a high-board fence around the clover lawn which extended to the rushing stream, and youngsters, from a vantage point on the hill across Indian

Landore was still in its heyday when this shot was taken, July 19, 1904. The boom town's population peaked at 1,000. The townsite is barely visible today. (Photo courtesy of the Idaho State Historical Society.)

Creek, sometimes caught a glimpse of these creatures as they sat in the lawn swing.

Decorah's life was brief but showy. Its post office closed August 30, 1902, scarcely a year and one-half after it opened. This was partially due to the PIN railroad failure. Miners and their backers were becoming increasingly pessimistic and mining activity reached an all-time low the winter of 1903.

A new idea caused a complete reversal in both attitude and mining activity. Another smelter was in the works. Ladd Metal Company of Portland leased mines owned by the American

Mining Company and purchased five acres of land from T.G. Jones. The move marked the beginning of Landore's most prosperous period.

W.H. Adams headed the project, which caused frenzied activity in Landore. While the smelting equipment and supplies were being moved from Homestead, Oregon, a crew of men were excavating the site, building the smelter's framework, and cutting cord wood to fuel the smelter. A new road was built so that ore-hauling freighters could drive over a wide platform covering several bins. Cargo could be unloaded in record time through openings in the platform.

Landore's population ballooned. Mayor Jones kept the most accurate population record in a ledger, where he recorded the names of home renters and buyers. He also noted family size. According to Jones' figures, Landore's population crept over the 1,000 mark at its height, but many of these people were transients.

Businesses grew with the population. Landore's streets made an H; the main street formed the cross-bar. Along those three streets, Charles H. Hill opened a banking department in his general store, three hotels housed transients and bachelors, and Lester P. Smith opened a law office. Additionally, there were two blacksmith shops, an assay office, a newspaper, two sawmills, and three saloons.

Walter James owned the butcher shop and supplied the surrounding area with beef. He refused to accept meat from area ranchers until it snowed on White Monument, a nearby mountain. That first snow indicated temperatures would remain cool enough to keep the meat until spring. The ranchers couldn't complete the delivery with a wagon, so they hauled the beef to the top of the saddle after it snowed. The meat was placed on cow hides, the hides were tied behind horses, and dragged to the butcher shop.

The smelter was ready for a trial run in September. The results were disappointing. Wood didn't generate enough heat to operate the smelter, so company officials decided to install coke-fueled furnaces.

The coke and iron flux necessary for the new smelting process

Long-time miners Gus Lapke and Flem Fife stand in the outskirts of Landore. The building on the left was a bunkhouse. The assay office and smelter are in the picture's center, and to the far right are the backs of the buildings lining Main Street. (Photo courtesy of the Idaho State Historical Society.)

were hauled in from Council, and investors watched their costs skyrocket. By the summer of 1905 copper ingots were being produced by the smelter, which was dumping shiny black slag into Indian Creek. Production was short-lived, though. Profits were eaten by transportation costs, so the Ladd Metal Company paid the bills and closed the operation.

Landore began to feel like a ghost town that winter. Buildings that once housed thriving businesses collapsed under the weight of the snow. A few residents refused to give up, however. Dr. William Brown and his family stayed, and they continued to operate the store. Dr. Brown's medical practice revolved around a slow but steady stream of accidents. Nobody seemed to get sick. His house calls required long, cold trips on homemade tamarack skis.

The James family also stayed, although only a few beef hung in their butcher shop. The family also owned a Landore Hotel which had previously been completely filled with miners paying forty dollars per month. Now, the occasional visitor was heartily welcomed.

An abandoned building on a hill served as a castle, an outlaw hideout, and a playhouse for the kids in town. Winifred Brown,

Dr. William Brown and his family almost single-handedly kept Landore from becoming a ghost town in the 1910s. Pictured are Mrs. Brown, Dr. Brown, Olive Euler, R. L. Euler, Inez Shaw, Winifred Brown (Lindsay), Mildred Brown, Della Shaw, Louis DeHaven Shaw (on hood), Mrs. C. R. Shaw, and George Jones. The old building served as the hospital in Cuprum, and was later moved to Landore, where it became a saloon. (Photo courtesy of the Idaho State Historical Society.)

Mildred Brown, Pearl James, and Anna James were among the children who used the building, which had previously been a cat house.

There was one mine unaffected by the smelter's closure. The gold miners at Black Lake still had steady paychecks. The mine's history, however, was full of frustrations and setbacks.

Two prospectors happened into the Black Lake area during the summer of 1880. George Wirtz and John Welch were discouraged with their findings on the Little Salmon, so they followed Rapid River to its source. They were completely unaware of mining activity in the area when they made their discovery: a ledge of gold-bearing quartz. The men gathered some samples and staked three claims: the Maid of Orin, the Gold Coin, and Black Lake.

Wirtz and Welch returned the next summer, having been grubstaked by men in Spokane. After building a small log cabin by Black Lake, they worked to uncover the quartz ledge for fifty dollars per month. Their monthly wages were low by standards of that day, but they stretched the fifty dollars to last the entire summer. When they returned to Spokane for the rest of their earnings, the backers refused to pay. Discouraged, the men didn't return to their claims until seven or eight years had passed. They had to file the claims again, since they had failed to complete the required yearly assessment work.

Wirtz and Welch realized they had a valuable set of claims. They also knew their holdings couldn't be developed without financial backing to build roads and buy machinery. Leery of fickle backers, they sold their claims to brothers Edwin and Simeon Ford. Washington County records show that the Maid of Orin claim sold for $11,000 on June 27, 1893.

The Fords owned a mercantile business in Cripple Creek, Colorado. They were attracted by the bustling business climate and the chance that the higher altitude there would improve Mrs. Edwin Ford's health. Her health continued to fail, however, and she disliked the town's atmosphere.

Ready for a move, the Fords' interest was sparked when they heard of the Seven Devils gold find. They showed some ore samples to D.C. Jackling, who had designed Cripple Creek's cyanide gold mill. Jackling's enthusiasm encouraged the Fords to move west.

Two years passed. The Fords were almost ready to purchase a cyanide mill when Wirtz and Welch's former Spokane partners demanded a half interest in the mine. The Fords refused on the grounds that the claims had been vacated when the backers failed to honor the partnership. The resulting lawsuit was in litigation for three years.

The Spokane partners won the first court decision by default, since Wirtz failed to appear and his testimony against his original partners was crucial.

Ford hired attorney William E. Borah and appealed. Borah reasoned there were two ways to win the case: either show fraud or faulty service of papers. He chose the first tactic. Borah argued that the first trial should have been held immediately after the Spokane partners filed suit. While waiting for the trial, the Fords had improved the property, making it more valuable. Borah suggested Wirtz had cooperated with his old partners, who hoped to receive a more valuable half interest. The case reached the United States Supreme Court. Borah won.

While the Black Lake issues were being settled, the Ford brothers explored other opportunities in the area. They leased and explored Placer Basin for two years, but the small pockets of gold ore discouraged future development.

Placer Basin's deposits did contain high grade ore, which prompted Charles Macy and John Ross to develop the property in later years. The camp had a post office by 1903. The settlement stretched one and one-fourth miles downstream from the sawmill and featured a boardinghouse, a large barn, a cook house, and several cabins. The Ford brothers had correctly assessed the claim. The site was abandoned for the first time by 1908, because ore deposits were too small and spotty to make the venture profitable.

In later years, Carl Swanstrom, who handled the OX Ranch's legal affairs, helped finance a mill at Placer Basin in the mid-Thirties. The depression-era operation provided much needed income to local residents, but mining activity was short-lived, ending in 1937.

The Fords also explored their claims along Indian Creek. They built a log cabin in 1897 that became the oldest building in Landore.

When the court decision was final, all attention was focused on Black Lake. Constructing a fourteen-mile road from Bear to Black Lake was the first priority. The road would have to accommodate the cyanide mill that had been ordered from Spokane.

The mill was located three-quarters of a mile below the mine on Lake Fork Creek. It took a creative engineer to design the ore

Black Lake's developments included an ore crusher (top) and ball mills (bottom) where the ore was mixed with cyanide, and rolled in canvas drums. The chemical eventually dissolved anything that wasn't gold. The camp was burned by the Forest Service during World War II, and the scrap metal was gathered and recycled for the war effort. (Photo courtesy of the Idaho State Historical Society.)

transportation system. The direct route between the mill and the mine, which was on the western side of Black Lake, crossed an incredible 1,500 feet of water without a span. An aerial tramway was designed and partially constructed.

Before it could be completed, a major obstacle, namely the High Dive on Smith Mountain, had to be overcome. Over 3,000 feet of uncut, heavy cable, had to be hauled to the tramway site over this steep, almost impassable stretch. George Russell was the project's teamster. His load was distributed in two wagons, each pulled by a long jerk-line of mules.

Anna Adams was a child living in Landore during this time. She remembered it took nearly a month before the cable was jacked up and over the High Dive. The project was a major source of family entertainment. Anna and her family piled into a wagon and drove over to watch Russell's progress. Their presence probably forced him to limit his vocabulary.

The cyanide mill was ready for delivery early in 1902, but exceptionally deep winter snows delayed its arrival. Men worked to clear the road by hand.

The mill produced its first gold in May of 1902. That summer, $5,000 in gold bullion was shipped to the Denver Mint. The mill burned down a short time later.

The fire started after a small change was made in the milling process. The ore arrived at the mill wet and it was sent through a dryer before being crushed by the rollers. When it was discovered that the ore could be crushed wet, the mill was closed to install a conveyor belt bypassing the dryer. They cranked up the mill again in late October.

The next morning at three, the entire mill was ablaze. The fire hydrants had been built just inside the mill's door to keep them from freezing, so they were useless. The Fords helplessly watched their investment burn. Only a few boxes of zinc were saved. Sim Ford believed the fire was caused by spontaneous combustion, although there were rumors of a jealous arsonist.

Since it was late in the season, operations were halted for the winter.

Another cyanide mill was ordered and the operation continued. Black Lake, with its steady population, earned a post office on September 18, 1903. Robert M. Barbour, who would later homestead part of the OX Ranch, was appointed postmaster.

Except for Black Lake, none of the mines in the Seven Devils district had direction after the Landore smelter closed. The situation attracted several promoters. Most had good intentions, but lacked the foresight and funds necessary for success. Others were downright dishonest.

Fred Smith was the first promoter. The ex-college professor leased the Arkansas mine shortly after the smelter shut down. He hired local men and a healthy amount of ore was being produced. There was one problem: Smith's account at Dr. Brown's store was growing longer and he kept postponing payday.

The miners, who needed their money, came up with a solution: a hanging. They stopped working and talk of hanging Smith became stronger. Somebody called the sheriff, but Dr. Brown and Sim Ford were able to reason with the miners before they found a tree with a stout limb. Smith left camp in a hurry and none of his debts were satisfied. His former employees and associates experienced a lean winter.

Edwards was the name of the next bell ringer. His wife and grown son accompanied him to the Blue Jacket mine and they moved into the superintendent's house. Winifred Lindsay said the condition of the house reflected the times. When Blue Jacket Superintendent Frank J. French lived there, the house was surrounded with a thick clover lawn. The house had grown shabby by the time the Edwards arrived.

After one summer, the family owed Dr. Brown $600 for both loans and merchandise, but the miners had been paid. Edwards had been told about Fred Smith's near miss several times. Mrs. Edwards and her son left for Arizona that fall.

Shortly after they left, Edwards entered the Browns' store with his hat in his hands. He asked to borrow $500. There were backers in Arizona, he claimed, who would pump enough money into the Blue Jacket to set off another boom. He needed to close the deal personally. Dr. Brown hedged and said he'd have to clear it with his wife.

"Absolutely not," was Mrs. Brown's answer. She explained the money would be needed to send their oldest daughter to boarding school. She left the men as they were heading toward the door. As Dr. Brown opened the door, Edwards grabbed his arm, and begged for the money. He left with a check and was never seen again.

Cliff Boran's tenure in Landore was short. He didn't pay his miners and, according to Anna James Adams, he carried his youngest child with him for protection. He figured nobody would kill him if he had a baby in his arms.

James also remembered a mining camp that ran out of food one winter. The miners hired the Carrick boys and Frank Laxon to pack supplies to them on snowshoes. The men were paid ten cents per pound and they packed up to 120 pounds on their backs. Speed and endurance contests between the three men became a major source of entertainment that winter.

The last of the ill-fated mine operators arrived in 1909. G.M. Boggs leased the Peacock. He paid his bills, but the locals doubted he could bring another boom into the Seven Devils . . . until his son came home from college.

Accompanying the Yalie were two young men whose wealth could make a difference. Harry Yale was a direct descendent of the university's founder, and Benjamin Thaw came from an entrepreneurial Pittsburgh family. Landore held its breath during their visit, but it seemed the young men chose prime fishing spots over making their fortunes in copper.

Boggs announced he was leaving to raise capital on the east coast, and he took Dr. Brown aside and asked him to handle the mine's checkbook. He explained he didn't want to leave the money with the mine foreman. Brown agreed to help. Sim Ford worried that Boggs would desert the property and, as a result, Brown would be held responsible for the mine's debts when the checking account emptied. Ford's fears were realized. Boggs never returned.

Newspaper accounts in 1913 stubbornly retained an optimistic angle. The February 21 issue of the *Council Leader* reported that the Seven Devils district would "hit full bore" and that F.H. Kleinschmidt of Helena had caused a trend by re-opening the Blue Jacket.

A May 22 article also raised hopes. Quoting Joe Reynolds of Cuprum, the paper predicted that interest in newer mines, like the Red Ledge and Azurite, would rekindle the dreams.

The Red Ledge mine development was fueled by Albert Kleinschmidt's funds. Union Pacific made plans to construct a railroad along the Snake from Homestead to Lewiston. When the railroad surveyed the area in 1911 and 1912, Kleinschmidt invested with gusto. He ordered air-powered mucking machines which filled ore buckets inside the mine. Diesel engines arrived in freight wagons drawn by ten horses; six horses pulled and four pushed from behind. The railroad never arrived, the 100-ton smelter which was to be built on Eagle Bar never materialized, and the mine was plagued by legal problems. The mine produced approximately $400,000 in copper, which barely covered twenty-five percent of the developing costs.

A *Council Leader* article published May 2, 1913 accurately hinted at the Seven Devils' future. It touted the area as a tourist haven and directed tourists to:

> . . . drive 20 miles to the Summit house at Kramer's. Should the trial of speed and distance possess you, 20 more miles will bring you to Landore.
>
> Landore is a 'quiescent' mining camp, having a store, post office, long distance telephone station, and a number of empty buildings. It affords the necessary conveniences for making a camping or tourist party comfortable. The semi-abandonment of the place gives to the stranger a feeling of freedom and relaxation.
>
> At Peacock, is the old town of Helena . . . looking desolate enough, but ready to accommodate the next operators of the Peacock mine.

Abandonment became the byword. One by one, the mines closed. Black Lake outlasted the others, but the Fords were forced to close the mill in 1914. Cyanide, which was crucial to the mill's operation, became impossible to obtain. The chemical came from Germany, which was engaged in World War I. After the mill closed, Ford continued to mine on a small scale.

The Browns were the last family to leave Landore. Dr. Brown sold his remaining merchandise to Bill Robertson, who operated the Bear Creek Store. Mrs. Brown resigned her postmaster commission, and John Thompson took her place on March 22, 1916. Thompson also agreed to caretake the general store building, which held winter provisions belinging to Sim Ford and Gus Lapke.

Late that summer, Thompson fell asleep while reading a book

Franz Kleinschmidt, right, continued to prospect in the area long after his father, Albert, faded from prominence. Hiking with the younger Kleinschmidt are Priscilla Rugg, Winifred Brown, Mildred Brown, and Kleinschmidt's wife, Mable. The photograph was taken on the abandoned Pacific and Northern Railroad grade, just above the Kleinschmidt Grade. (Photo courtesy of the Idaho State Historical Society.)

in bed. His reading light, a candle, started a fire in the general store. The flames awakened him and he escaped with only his life and the post office supplies. The fire also destroyed the buildings on either side of the general store.

Along with Ford's supplies, the fire devoured his hopes of continuing the operation at Black Lake. When the area's longest operating mine was closed, it was debt free. The mining equipment and supplies were left intact, since there was no legal owner. Property that wasn't sold for taxes disappeared over the years.

Tenacious individuals continued to mine in the area, but they produced more local color than copper. Albert Kleinschmidt's sons—Franz, Harry, Albert, and Harrison—fell into this category; it was said they were so smart they were crazy. The family had gained and lost tremendous fortunes in the mining industry and the sons struggled to make a living during the lean Twenties and Thirties.

Franz appeared at the Bear schoolhouse dances with his fiddle, and after playing quadrilles all night, he tucked the instrument under his arm and hiked home.

Harry and Al shared a cabin at the Blue Jacket. Bert Warner, a lifetime Bear resident, remembered that their cabin had no chairs and the brothers never had enough food. This was curious because they were supposedly receiving $1,000 each month for mining claims that had been sold.

The two brothers quarrelled one winter, and as a result, Harry and his dog batched in the cabin by themselves. The man suffered a heart attack and died, leaving the dog trapped in the cabin. Several weeks passed before some distant neighbors grew concerned, and when they opened Harry's cabin door, a relieved dog bounded out to greet them. He had survived by gnawing on his master.

Another persistent miner was Arthur "Frenchie" David, whose successful mining career had a senseless ending. He had a valuable mining claim located above the Bear Guard Station, and he put it on the market for $60,000 cash. An investor offered $40,000 cash and a note for the remaining $20,000, but Frenchie refused.

After the deal fell through, he became increasingly depressed and his health began to fail. Bert Warner remembers how

Frosty McConnell and Jess Smith pause in front of their dynamite-proof cabin. (Photo courtesy of Dick and Georgianna Parker.)

Frenchie began to hear voices while he piled a huge stack of cord wood outside his cabin. Whenever neighbors stopped to visit, he took them to the woodpile and made them promise to burn his body there, should he die. All conversations with Frenchie were punctuated with this morbid request, but his neighbors made an allowance for "local color," and didn't worry too much about his preoccupation.

Frenchie's young daughter, Lizzie, came to visit one summer. Her mother had been institutionalized for insanity when Lizzie was barely a year old, and her father made sure she would have a proper upbringing in boarding schools.

Lizzie was sent on an errand. When she came back, her father was dead. He had shot himself.

He had been planning his suicide for some time. Not wanting to leave Lizzie with a horribly gruesome spectacle, he decided to shoot himself in the side. Frenchie painstakingly carved a stick which enabled him to pull both triggers of his double-barreled shotgun. The stick was well-cured.

Frenchie's wish for cremation was delayed. His body was sent to Council and buried. A year later, Lizzie had the body exhumed and Frenchie's body was cremated in Boise. Locals believe his ashes were buried in the Bear cemetery.

Two other miners narrowly missed making a permanent visit to the cemetery. Frosty McConnell and Jesse (pronounced "Jess") Smith set up camp at Lockwood Saddle in the early Forties. The old guys lived off Frosty's meager pension from World War I, which he earned after a bullet shot off his right bicep, hit his helmet buckle, and grazed him under the chin.

The men worked at a leisurely pace, and they lingered over meals heated on the cook stove outside their tent. Their contentment was tarnished by one element: a renegade chipmunk was helping himself to the groceries.

Jesse, who was a crack shot, spotted the culprit, took aim, and fired. His shot hit both the chipmunk and their store of dynamite, which was stashed under a red fir windfall.

The explosion blew the windfall clear into camp. A lid flew off of the cook stove and winged Frosty on the head, knocking him off his chair. The dust cleared and the men dragged themselves off

Lizzie David had an unusual upbringing. When she was an infant, her mother was institutionalized. The August 21, 1891 Cambridge Citizen reported that Frenchie David brought his "now almost hopelessly insane" wife home. "If she does not recover her reason very soon he will send her to the asylum at Blackfoot," the paper noted with unusual candor. Frenchie refused to raise his daughter in the rough mining communities, so he sent her to expensive boarding schools. She broadened her cultural base by spending vacations with her father near Bear. (Photo courtesy of the Bert Warner family.)

the ground to survey the damage. Other than the gravel imbedded in their faces and the stove lid-shaped welt on Frosty's head, the men were miraculously uninjured. Their tent was shredded into six-inch strips and their groceries were completely scrambled.

They picked most of the gravel out of their faces, crawled into their Model A roadster, which now boasted a fringed convertible top, and drove into town to buy groceries . . . and more dynamite.

The miners built a cabin and continued their hard rock operation: driving steel with double jacks to drill holes, shooting the ore down, and hauling it out with a little ore cart. After two years of slow and steady work, they accumulated sixteen tons, or one railroad car full of ore. They shipped it to the smelter and eagerly awaited the payment, which would reimburse them for two years' labor. Tearing open the envelope they found a check for eighty-seven dollars.

Frosty blamed Jesse, who had been responsible for having the ore assayed during their partnership. He claimed that Jesse's skull housed nothing but a pile of bone shavings. And so ended one of the Seven Devils' last mining exploits.

Phebe Harding Warner had buried two of her eleven children by the time she and her husband, Amos, came to Bear in 1890. The community depended on her medical expertise, which came from a variety of home remedies and a well-thumbed copy of Dr. Gunn's Book. (Photo courtesy of the Bert Warner family.)

One

THE PIONEERS: 1878–1910

"We picked up a skull down there . . . across the creek there. Well, I guess it was Sam Warner that picked it up and hung it on a tree . . . and it hung there for ten years. I think it must have been (his) skull."

—Jesse Smith, 1971

Young Jesse Smith's eyes popped open, and he listened for the noise again to make sure he wasn't dreaming. The racket in the barnyard started up again, so the youngster kicked off the covers and raced to the door.

"What are you doing out here?" his father, Frank, hissed. "You go on back. Go on back to bed."

Jesse stayed where he was, watching the commotion erupt from the barn, which was on Bear Creek. Although it was dark, he could barely make out a figure leading the family's horses out through the corral. The thief's progress ended abruptly when a shot rang out and his body slumped to the ground. Jesse never knew who fired the shot—whether it was his father or Rattlesnake Jack, a notorious Indian fighter who was visiting at the time. To Jesse's horrified delight, the dead man was an Indian, one of the few left in the country.

Jesse remembered that his dad, "got the old bay mare, put the harness on her, tied him on her, and went out over the hill . . . down across the creek."

Then Jesse's dad heard rumors that there was a small encampment nearby, on what would become Jay and Lori Quilliam's place on the Wildhorse River. "They looked kinda wise around there for a few days, looking for Indians, but none showed up. Maybe they didn't know where they went to," said Jesse in a 1971 interview.

Very few American Indians remained when two-year-old Jesse's parents came to the Bear area; their covered wagon trundled through part of the present-day OX Ranch and stopped at Steves Creek. They accompanied his maternal grandfather, Amos Warner, his grandmother, and eight aunts and uncles, who ranged in age from three to twenty-three years old. Conflicting reports say their original destination was either Idaho's Clearwater region or the goldfields of Alaska.

Amos Warner thought they had stumbled upon a rancher's paradise. Bright green bunch grass and timothy carpeted the meadows and surrounding forests. Spring runoff filled the streams to their banks, and since Smith Mountain was still buried under snow, Amos figured there would be plenty of water year-round. The area had yet another appealing feature: the nearby mining activity was bound to create outside income opportunities.

After holding a family council, the Warners decided to remain in the area. They formalized the decision by chopping the date, June 12, 1890, into a pine tree.

Up until this point, Amos had led an adventurous life. A Mormon, he had been driven out of Illinois by religious persecutors. He sought refuge in Utah, where he participated in an unusual adoption procedure. His brother, Salmon, had traded a sheep and a sack of flour for the two-year-old son of a Shoshone chief. The boy's mother was killed during a massacre, and he stayed with an uncle before he was offered in trade. Salmon's wife wasn't pleased with the trade, so bachelor brother Amos brought the child home, after parting with a sheep, a goat, and a calf. Amos named the boy Frank S. Warner. A short time later Amos married Phebe Harding in Salt Lake City.

The couple had buried two of their eleven children before migrating to Steves Creek. Their adopted son, Frank, had already established his career as a Mormon missionary and schoolteacher before the family left Utah. He was the only family member who didn't join the homesteaders.

Amos Warner was a devout Mormon, but he apparently chose to ignore the church's stand against tobacco. His more pious descendants allegedly tried to hide his habit by making hazy prints of this photo, which shows him smoking a pipe. (Photo courtesy of the Bert Warner family.)

As soon as they decided to stay in Idaho, family members focused all their energy on winter preparations. Amos and his nineteen-year-old son, also named Amos, worked 10-hour days on the Kleinschmidt Grade. Their combined efforts added $1.50 to the family coffers each day. The rest of the family raced through chore lists trying to prepare for winter.

Eight-year-old Charley Warner paid close attention to adult conversations that fall. He had worked like a man all summer; helping build a cabin out of hand-hewn logs and shocking the native grass hay, which his older brothers and sisters cut with scythes.

Charley hoped his efforts would garner him an invitation to the fall hunting trip. The family's men would take a few days to ride through beautiful, rugged country, swap outrageous stories, and come home with enough deer meat to last the winter. Charley wanted to go in the worst way, but he was worried that his parents wouldn't let him.

When the hunting party left Bear Creek, Charley was among them. There were few deer in the immediate area, so they headed toward Salt Creek. Steve Robertson, the grizzled bachelor who lent his name to Steves Creek, offered to ride along, and Charley was fascinated by him.

Steve was a windy character who reportedly lied when the truth made a better story. He bragged about his phenomenal shooting skills all the way to hunting camp, and Charley absorbed every word.

The first evening Steve promised to shoot some grouse for supper, so he left camp, gun in hand. Four shots were heard, and then the mighty hunter returned with one grouse shot through the head. When asked why it had taken four shots to hit one grouse, Steve explained that the bird had been sitting in a wild cherry tree. In order to get a clear shot at its head, he'd had to shoot three cherries off the tree.

That first hunting trip launched a family tradition that is over 100 years old. Members of the third, fourth, and fifth generation still live and hunt in Bear.

The Warners' first winter was deceptively mild. All illusions were shattered during their second winter, which was one of the harshest in history. Five feet of snow buried what had been a "rancher's paradise" the spring before, and the temperature constantly hovered at thirty degrees below zero. The stack of hay shrank too rapidly. Before it was completely gone, most of the cattle and horses were dead, victims of what oldtimers called Mountain Fever.

After a financially and emotionally devastating winter, the Warner family regrouped and developed a new strategy. Amos and Phebe bought 160 acres from a homesteader on Wickiup Creek and built a cabin in front of the OX Ranch's present-day Seven Devils Lodge. Their new location was seven to ten degrees warmer in the winter.

The one-room cabin couldn't accommodate the entire clan, so the boys slept in the barn's hayloft during that second winter. The next year three rooms were added to the cabin.

Hoping to ease the strain on their livestock, the family planted four crops of alfalfa on a mining claim they held on Kinney Creek. The animals grazed there until the feed was gone, and then they were driven back to the homestead and fed all winter.

After a devastating winter on Bear Creek, the Amos Warners built this second log cabin on Wickiup Creek. Charley Warner constructed the frame house for his widowed mother in 1906. After it burned in the late 1940s, the Seven Devils Lodge was built on the site. (Photo courtesy of the Bert Warner family.)

A school was the next item on the priority list. A small log cabin was built on Lick Creek, and the Smiths and Warners pooled their funds to hire a teacher during the summer months. After losing their livestock, the families could afford to hire a teacher for only two months the first summer. As the families became more established, the schoolhouse was moved to Bear Creek, and sessions gradually increased to six months.

Walks to school became more entertaining when the Warner kids adopted a pet sandhill crane. While out exploring one spring, they found a nest with two crane eggs. They carefully carried the eggs home and slipped them under a hen to incubate. Both eggs hatched, but one bird killed the other. The survivor was a brassy addition to the family who never missed a chance to survey the supper table. If he saw a desirable snack, preferably a biscuit, he snatched it off the table before flying outside to eat.

The crane accompanied the children everywhere. He enjoyed

fishing trips, which were made possible after Joe and Charley Warner introduced trout to the area by packing several fish over a natural barrier, Bear Creek Falls.

The crane was particularly fond of sledding, choosing to ride up the hill perched on a convenient shoulder. Once the sledders pushed off, he was airborne and he raced the children to the bottom of the hill.

Another winter highlight became a 100-year tradition: the Bear dances. Amos and Phebe created a dance floor in their cabin by pushing the furniture aside. Dancing space was slightly tight, even though there were only five families in the area during the first gatherings.

The neighbors came in on bobsleds and horses. They shed their heavy coats, and the women crowded homemade apple pies and pound cakes on the kitchen table in preparation for a midnight supper.

The all-night dance started as soon as somebody picked up an instrument. Sam Warner played the violin, but the chief musician was his brother, Joe, who brought everyone to their feet with his guitar, mandolin, and banjo music. When his picking fingers got tired, he brought out a harmonica, accordion, or zither, and when more rhythm was needed, he twanged Jew's harp or rattled the bones. Joe also called the quadrilles, which are similar to square dances.

The entertainment ended when it was light enough to saddle or harness the horses. The guests traveled home just in time to start their morning chores.

One family, who had a place on Lick Creek, believed excess travel cut in on their visiting time. They remedied the problem by bringing their livestock with them. Bob and Mammy White tied their chickens' legs together and put them in the back of the wagon with their two boys. After a week's visit, their wagon was again loaded with chickens and boys, and they rolled toward the next neighbor's home, their milk cow bringing up the rear.

The Whites probably stopped to see Frank and Amy Smith after visiting Amy's parents, the Warners.

Amy and her identical twin sister, Ada, were the Warners' oldest daughters. They had already married brothers Frank and Cad Smith before coming to Bear Creek.

A favorite family story relates that Ada went on a shopping trip to Council. While in the store, she turned and was startled to see a reflection of herself in a full-length mirror. "Why Amy," she said, "I didn't think you were a comin' to town today."

Amy and her husband lived on Bear Creek, below the cemetery, which was an ideal stopping place for the ore freighters beginning to flow in and out of the Seven Devils mining district.

The Smiths recognized several business opportunities and slowly began expanding their operation. First, their home became an overnight stop for freighters and travelers.

Miners and ranchers created a demand for a supply point closer than Council, so the Smiths built a store and started a post office, which was recognized in 1892. Her father suggested they name the

Frank and Amy Smith's homestead was situated below the cemetery, on what is now Bear Creek Ranch. The industrious couple operated several businesses which flourished during the Seven Devils copper boom. These buildings housed a post office, a general store, a livery stable, and a freighting service. Weary travelers could also buy a meal and spend the night. (Photo courtesy of the Bert Warner family.)

community Bear, since there was a large population of black and grizzly bears in the area.

About the same time, Frank and his brother, Cad, formed a partnership, purchased a team, and started hauling freight to and from the mines. Profits from this venture were used to build a log barn and blacksmith shop where the general public could have teams shod and harnesses repaired.

The Smiths' prosperity was reversed by a freak accident one summer night. Their fifth child, a four-month-old girl named Charlotte, woke up screaming in the middle of the night. Half asleep, Frank stumbled out of bed to give her a bottle. On his way across the floor he stepped on a doll and shattered its bisque head. The shards of glass penetrated his bare heel. Three days later he was dead.

Frank had contracted blood poisoning and the only medical help available came from Phebe's home remedies and a well worn doctoring volume called *Dr. Gunn's Book*. Their desperate efforts failed, and on July 7, 1897, Frank became one of the first people buried in the Bear cemetery.

Frank's death saddled Amy with a tremendous amount of responsibility. She had five children and Jesse, her eldest son, was only ten years old. She was also left with a $250 debt, a homestead that needed proving up, ranching chores, a stage stop, and the post office. Her brothers helped with the haying and her parents looked after the children while she juggled all her tasks.

Amy's routine house chores alone would have exhausted most women. She cared for the cattle and chickens, made cheese and butter, raised a garden, and made soap. The well went dry that summer, and carrying heavy water buckets one-eighth of a mile was added to the daily tasks.

Canning fruit was another major undertaking, as it involved a fourteen mile pack trip to the Eckles Bar orchard on the Snake River. The trail, which passed the present-day Speropulos place, wound around Horse Mountain, and had an abundance of steep drop-offs where stock routinely lost their footing. They often died in a broken heap when they reached the bottom.

Amy made the return trip one day on a skittish mare. To complicate matters, her three-year-old son, Orson, rode behind

Frank and Amy Smith's home doubled as a post office. There is no positive identification for the people in this 1893 photograph, but Warner family members guess Amy Smith is on the far left and the others are Amos and Phebe Warner's younger children. (Photo courtesy of the Bert Warner family.)

her on the saddle, and Lois, her two-year-old, sat in front. The situation became more precarious when Amy saw a bear cross the trail ahead of them. Luckily, the mare was too preoccupied with the breathtaking view to notice the bear. The family and their fruit, which had been individually wrapped in leaves to protect it from bruising, arrived home intact.

About a decade before the Warners arrived, homesteaders drifted into Meadows Valley, approximately fifteen miles east of Bear. Caroline Osborn was a world-worn ten-year-old when she moved into Packer John's cabin with her family, including a new stepfather.

Caroline's German-born mother, Elizabeth Klein, migrated to America with her older sister in 1863. The young women sailed in a clipper ship around the horn of South America, and landed in San Francisco, California. After a year, they opted for a change of scenery. The women, then seventeen and nineteen years old, left

Bear area children attended school in this structure until the present-day school-house was built in 1911. Enjoying a muddy spring day are Isaac "Pug" Robertson, whose Rocky Comfort homestead is now part of the OX, Bud Robertson, Thelma Robertson, Edgar James, Vivian Robertson, Henry Haines, and Bergie Robertson. Astride the horse is Arthur Robertson, who was the first forest ranger in Bear. (Photo courtesy of the Bert Warner family.)

for Portland. Tales of western adventure prompted them to pack their belongings again in 1866. A boat took them down the Columbia River to Lewiston, where they put their bundles on pack animals and set out for Warren, Idaho, a mining camp.

Then, as now, rumors outdistanced the travelers. The miners were so eager to visit with the rare females, that they fell a large tree in the road. As a result, they enjoyed a leisurely conversation with the ladies. Their efforts to remove the obstacle were less than enthusiastic. Two years later, on October 23, 1868, Elizabeth married one of the conspirators, William Osborn.

William had come from an established whaling family in Martha's Vineyard, Massachusetts. Why he chose to live in the Idaho wilderness is still a family mystery.

When the gold at Warren played out in 1874, William moved his wife and four children to White Bird, Idaho. Elizabeth carried baby Annie on her saddle. Caroline, then four, made the 100-mile journey sitting in a box lashed to the side of a horse. Her two-year-old brother, Edward, occupied a similar box on the other side, and six-year-old Willie managed his own horse. The trail to White Bird was fraught with sheer drop-offs and other spots prone to packstring wrecks, but the family arrived safely.

The Osborns mined and farmed among their friendly Nez Perce neighbors for three years before the mood shifted, and the Indians became uneasy. Elizabeth wanted to move, but William claimed their healthy relationship with the tribe protected them from danger. He misjudged.

The Nez Perce were fed up with broken promises, and some renegades began drinking and looting. Word reached the Osborns, who immediately hid in a gulch with Elizabeth's brother-in-law, Harry Mason. The day stretched on and the children, aged three, five, seven, and nine, became cranky and hungry. Since everything was quiet, they decided to return to the cabin to gather provisions, and then escape by taking a boat downstream to Lewiston.

The renegades caught them just after they entered the cabin. They promised not to harm the Osborns if Mason, who was one of their antagonists, would surrender. It was rumored that Mason had horsewhipped a member of the tribe.

Mason stayed in the cabin, and Caroline and her younger

siblings watched the ensuing battle from under the bed. Before long, a bullet penetrated their father's chest and he died instantly. The marauders then set the cabin on fire. Caroline had only one thought on her mind, she later told her children: "I hope the fire burns us quickly, and it will all be over."

Chief Mox Mox, who was acquainted with the Osborns, promised Caroline's mother that her family would not be harmed if she took them to Slate Creek. After dragging the bodies of her husband and Harry Mason outside and covering them with blankets, she followed the chief's instructions.

The surviving Osborns huddled with about fifteen other refugees in a rock fort. The group, which had only one gun, apprehensively watched a nearby hillside for the next several days. Each day, Nez Perce warriors rode to the vantage point and peered down at the terrified settlers.

When the uprising was over, the widow brought her family back to Warren. Miners pitched in and provided the Osborns with housing and clothing. After the initial charity, Elizabeth insisted upon supporting the family herself by operating a laundry service. A minor scandal erupted when she agreed to wash for women who weren't so nobly employed. A number of upstanding citizens believed Elizabeth would be soiled by the reputations accompanying the garments. She ignored the rumblings.

Elizabeth's hours were long and her family's evening rest was interrupted by raucous gatherings in the Chinese saloon below their apartment. When she mentioned the inconvenience, the town fathers made the saloon owner close the business at 10:30 every evening.

After two years in Warren, Elizabeth agreed to marry Thomas Clay, who carried seventy-pound mail sacks 115 miles from Indian Valley to Warren on a weekly basis. The wedding date was set for February 15, 1879.

The day arrived, but the groom didn't. A severe winter storm halted activity in the area, and as the time crept by, the bride became increasingly apprehensive. She spent three days worrying that he'd been caught without shelter before she heard a familiar rap on the door on February 18. Wasting no time, they were married the same day.

Albert Campbell's mother, Caroline Osborn Campbell, saw her father killed by Nez Perce Indians as she hid under her parents' bed. She never overcame her fear. Years later, whenever Native Americans were in the vicinity, she grabbed her children and joined her husband in the fields. (Photo courtesy of Charlotte Campbell Armacost.)

Elizabeth didn't want her sons to become miners, so she convinced her husband to relocate the family in a ranching area. In 1880 the Clays became the fifth family to move into the Meadows Valley.

They moved into Packer John's cabin, which had been the site of Idaho Territory's first Democratic convention in 1863. During the winter the valley became deserted, and young Caroline passed long hours by running her fingers over the names convention delegates had carved in the cabin's walls.

Her stepfather, who still carried the Indian Valley/Warren mail route, saw his family only twice a week for the first few years, until the family could survive without his outside income.

The family had established a homestead by 1883 when a pack of wolves ravaged the valley. This account appeared in the *New Meadows Eagle*:

> One still, cold night, when Jack Frost was busy etching designs everywhere the wolves also came and began prowling for kitchen scraps. The (Clay) dog heard them and dashed out to chase the invaders away. Poor dog, it was his last act of valor. Ten hungry wolves pounced upon him and tore his body limb from limb. His blood and quivering muscles made a warm meal for them. They moved on seeking what else they might devour.
>
> Their depredations were so alarming that Lyman Smith, a beaver trapper who sold thousands of pelts to Canada's Hudson Bay Company, made a vow to break up the pack. His trusty Sharp's rifle plus cool nerve and keen marksmanship allowed him to pick off seven of the wolves that winter.

The Clays valued another bachelor neighbor, Charles Campbell, who eventually married their daughter, Caroline. Together they would build the Circle C ranch, which, for a time, would be the largest ranch in Idaho. And their son, Albert, would establish and build the OX Ranch.

In 1872, when Charles Campbell was nineteen, he decided the family farm in Jerseyville, Illinois, could not support all his brothers and sisters. He and his brother Bill decided to work their way west. Before he left, his father handed him a silver half-dollar dated 1824, the year of his father's birth. He was instructed to spend it only if he was hungry.

Charles later told his children that he had been hungry, but never that hungry. The silver piece has since passed through three generations with the same instructions. It has yet to be spent.

The brothers were headed for Virginia City, Nevada, but Charles stopped near Truckee where a rancher hired him. For four years he tried to quit his ranching job and join his mining brother. Whenever he gave notice, the rancher raised his wages and convinced him to stay.

During the summer of 1879, brother Bill had a new venture in mind. He suggested they homestead their own ranches in Idaho. Wearing a good suit of clothes, Charles drove his four-horse team straight through the Boise valley, which was still full of bandits.

On their journey north, the brothers crossed the Weiser River thirty-six times before Charles found a homestead site he liked. The brothers acquired squatter's rights on two adjoining 320-acre tracts. Although the brothers shared farm equipment, they maintained separate ranches. Bill knew his brother had an acquisitional mind, and was afraid Charles would bankrupt the operation by buying too much land. Bill was right on one count: Charles liked expansion. However, Bill underestimated his brother's business sense. Charles' ranch, the Circle C, became one of the largest ranches in Idaho.

When the Campbells arrived in Meadows Valley, only one family and three bachelors lived there.

Since the nearest railroad at the time was in Ogden, Utah, the brothers planned to sell their beef in mining camps, concentrating on Warren. While they waited for their seven head of mixed breed cattle herd to mature, they focused on producing butter from their dairy cattle. The butter was surrounded with brine and sealed in barrels so it would keep between the long trips into the mining camps.

"Dad was a worker," said Albert Campbell in a 1976 interview. "I don't think there was ever a man in the valley who could do any more work than he could. That first fall he cut hay with a scythe. They had a good easy winter."

The fair skinned, blue-eyed rancher met his future wife two years later. He described Caroline Osborn as a "barefooted little tot catching tadpoles." They married when she was eighteen and he was thirty-six.

All fifty members of the community were invited to attend the May 1, 1888 ceremony, which was held in the Clay home. The Justice of the Peace who performed the ceremony trudged from Council on snowshoes.

The *Meadows Eagle* belatedly reported the event's highlights. "After the ceremony, George Clark . . . got out his fiddle and dancing commenced and lasted until nearly morning. We had a big supper. In those days no supper was complete without oyster soup, canned of course, and pie. We had both, as well as cold meats, cakes, and coffee."

After a shivaree, Charles took his bride to a two-room cabin he'd built on the ranch.

Almost exactly a year later, on May 9, 1889, Albert William Campbell was born. He later claimed his initials stood for "A Wild Cowboy."

The Circle C Ranch and the Campbell household expanded simultaneously. Carrie was born three years later followed by Anna, Rollie, and Loyal. Albert boasted that he was the oldest and toughest of the five children, but not necessarily the brightest.

Albert was tough. When he was a toddler his mother put him down for a nap while she cooked for the haying crew. The heat was cranked up in the cookstove and the room became unbearably hot, so she pulled the glass out of the window and set it upright underneath the bed. Caroline heard her boy wail and raced over to find he had fallen on the glass and cut a large gash on his knee. Grandmother Elizabeth and her needle and thread were summoned. She stitched him back together.

Children had to be tough to survive, as was illustrated when the five youngest members of the Campbell clan came down with scarlet fever. The younger children were at the breakfast table when Albert entered the room. He appeared to be walking in his sleep, deliriously mumbling something about the house being on fire. Someone noticed the wall behind the cookstove was on fire, and the family forgot about the fever and jumped into action.

Charles A. Campbell was obsessive about punctuality. He repeatedly declared, "If I'm going to Hell, I'm going to get there on time." His son, Albert, founded the OX Ranch. (Photo courtesy of Charlotte Campbell Armacost.)

Charles was in Boise, so somebody needed to summon their Uncle Bill, who lived a mile and a half away. Carrie volunteered. Barefooted and wearing a coat over her nightgown, she crossed the frost-covered yard to the corral. They kept an old horse in the pasture who would gallop into the corral if he heard someone shake a can full of rocks. Carrie caught the old guy, crawled on his bare back, and raced to her uncle's house.

When they returned, it looked like the new frame house was a goner; smoke was boiling out of the roof. Carrie and Bill both grabbed full buckets, raced up the stairs, and poured water down the chimney. Meanwhile the younger children and their mother hurriedly dragged the beds out of the burning house. The house was saved, the beds moved back in and the children crawled under the covers and continued to convalesce. All of them survived the ordeal without aggravating their illness.

Albert liked to create his own ordeals, and his close friend and constant companion, Carrie, was frequently targeted. She was peeling apples one afternoon when Albert decided to agitate her. He started punching her bicep. She told him to stop. Albert ignored her order and continued pounding with the same rhythm and force. She kept shouting, "Don't do that," her voice's pitch rising each time. Finally, she'd had enough. Carrie slashed Albert's coat sleeve with a sweep of her paring knife. Finally their mother, Caroline, looked up. Her only comment: "Carrie, you could have hurt him. You'd better sew that up." Albert grinned like a cat, Carrie remembered.

Although Caroline never took an active role in the ranch's operation, she reigned over the household, somehow managing to maintain harmony among the volatile, highly independent family members. She was a valued neighbor and she rarely lost her composure. One of those rare moments came in full force when some Indians decided to bathe in the family's drinking water reservoir behind the house. Childhood memories overwhelmed her, and she was rattled for days after the unwelcome, but peaceful bathers left.

Caroline thoroughly enjoyed watching her children's interests develop. From the earliest times, Albert was fascinated by cattle and Carrie loved horses. When they weren't working, they were on their horses exploring the hills around the ranch.

Carrie started howling one morning, because Albert had left for his first day of school and she had to stay behind. The girl, who was barely four years old, cried for three solid days. Finally the teacher agreed to let Carrie visit school with the understanding she would leave when she became bored. Rather than tiring of the lessons, she became enthralled, and she was allowed to enroll in Albert's class.

The trips to and from school were a recreational outlet for the children. Anyone who tried to pass another's wagon was in an instant race, with the wagons' passengers screaming encouragement to their respective horse teams.

Rollie and Loyal Campbell developed their own contest in the winter. The boys shared a horse and took turns pulling each other on skis. The stakes were raised on the way home when the rider spurred the horse until it was at a dead run. It was the skier's challenge to keep his balance, for if he fell early, he had to cover the two and a half miles under his own power.

On winter weekends Albert and Rollie occasionally rode their horse, Pal, to Payette Lake for similar races. Driving the horse from behind, the boys slid across the lake on their shoe bottoms. The Campbell boys were almost stranded during a race when Pal's lines became entangled with those of another contestant. After the spectacular wreck, Pal decided he'd had enough recreation, and he left for home. Somebody headed him off before he stranded the boys.

As the children progressed through school, Albert became fidgety. Although he excelled in math, which was essential for any businessman, most of the lessons were providing little practical knowledge. Albert was convinced his time would be better spent on the ranch. His father was giving him more responsibility, which fueled his discontent. Carrie served as a buffer, talking him out of his frustration and encouraging him to continue his education.

At this time the ranch was continuing its steady growth, which was spurred by the Pacific and Idaho Northern (PIN) Railroad's anticipated arrival in New Meadows. Rather than trail their cattle to Warren or Boise, the Campbells gained direct access to several cattle markets when railroad construction was completed in 1911.

Growth for the Circle C Ranch was guaranteed when the Pacific, Idaho and Northern railroad arrived in New Meadows in 1911. Long cattle drives drifted into obsolescence as the railroad linked the ranch with previously impossible marketing opportunities. (Photo courtesy of the Idaho State Historical Society.)

Charles was grooming his children to take control of the operation. Albert was sent on his first cattle buying trip when he was ten. His dad asked him to look at some calves in Long Valley, near the town of Cascade, and instructed him to buy them for a good price if there were solid animals. The trip required Albert to find his way through about fifteen miles of wilderness, judge the cattle, make a fair deal, and then return home after spending the night. The ten-year-old returned victorious, having bought seven calves for ten dollars a piece. An eighty-year cattle buying career was offically launched.

With the help of his young children, Charles began to expand his operation. He showed them how to sow the feed grain by hand. Reaching into the seed sack hanging from his shoulder, he pulled out a handful of grain and began scattering it in a rhythmic, fluid motion while walking at a steady pace and stride. He stressed that consistency was important, otherwise the field would have bare spots in the spring.

During the first several seasons, the ripe grain was cut and fed like hay. Carrie and Rollie worked together shocking, or bunching together the freshly mowed grain.

Eventually the community bought a horse-drawn threshing machine. The neighbors formed a crew that traveled from farm to farm until the crop was harvested. The twenty to twenty-five man crews slept in barns and tents, and the frazzled farm wives worked to reward their appetites. The exhausting event was a community highlight which produced enough gossip to last the winter.

Charles was more attracted by the job's financial benefits. Caroline and the children ran the ranch while he earned one dollar per day and board by working with the crew.

This mercantile provided Meadows residents with everything from parasols to yard goods in 1910. Before the population of Meadows could support such businesses, the Campbells made a yearly pilgrimage to Boise for supplies. (Photo courtesy of the Idaho State Historical Society.)

The Circle C's dairy operation expanded, and butter was shipped as far away as Boise. Milk from the dairy herd was placed in large, flat pans each day. After the cream rose to the top, it was skimmed off and poured in a butter churn which was operated by a hand crank. After the mass thickened, it was placed on a wide board with sides and a roller was used to press excess milk from the butter. The butter was salted, packed in stone jars, and stored in a cold cellar.

The ranch's two- and three-year-old steers sold by the head, sometimes bringing as much as twenty dollars each. When a buyer offered Charles five cents a pound at the turn of the century, he knew prosperous days had arrived.

Then, as always, Charles was a thrifty planner. He budgeted $100 to buy the family's winter supplies and clothing. A portion of the income was used to expand the Campbell home, so that the first floor had five large rooms and the next two floors boasted eight large bedrooms. Hoping to prevent future catastrophes, he installed fire hoses in the house, which were supplied by a gravity-fed water system. That home and its system of fire hoses are still operable today.

In the general scheme of things, the house wasn't high on Charles' list of priorities. Most ranch revenues were filtered back into the operation. Cattle herds were improved, spring runoff was controlled by building a dam on Goose Creek, and a sawmill was constructed.

Settlers were flowing into the valley, and Charles knew a solid market for lumber was developing. He decided to build a water-powered sawmill and harvest timber off the ranch's land. He sold 1,000 board-feet of rough lumber for ten dollars, and the same amount of planed lumber cost sixteen dollars. Rollie helped him with the mill; his specialty was packing shingles. Eventually ranch demands on Charles' time forced him to sell the mill, but he kept the Pelton wheel, which converted running water into power.

The wheel was later used to power an electric generator. Around the turn of the century, the Circle C was the only place north of Weiser to have electric lights. Rollie recalled that the light in the barn burned twenty-four hours a day, since turning the power on and off would have shortened the bulb's life.

Albert critically examined and frequently imitated his father's business practices. Charles always had an eye toward expansion, and he was willing to borrow money to expedite the process; however, he wouldn't overextend himself. He refused to mortgage his land, machinery, or animals—a practice that his sons continued.

As the operation expanded, Charles become more dependent upon hired help. His management philosophy was simple: work them hard and feed them well. By and large, his hands stayed with him through the years. George Hurd had the longest tenure; he drew a Circle C paycheck for over sixty years.

Even though the ranch was one of the area's few employers, most of the cowboys respected the Campbells. Several admitted, however, that they became scarce on Sundays in order to have their day off.

Charles did have a few obsessions. He insisted that each family member maintain a good set of clothes, and repeatedly told about entering the valley with nothing but a team of horses and enough pride to wear a well-kept suit.

He was also a stickler for punctuality and keeping projects on schedule. "If I'm going to Hell," he'd declare, "I'm going to get there on time." In an interesting contrast, he never overloaded or rushed animals, particularly his horses.

It didn't take Albert long to combine his father's guiding principles with his own knack for the cattle business. The take charge personality that liked to needle people surfaced early.

When Rollie and Albert were still boys, they gathered a herd that included several of the neighbors' cattle. When the neighbors arrived to sort out their cattle, Charles asked Rollie and Albert to help. Albert immediately started giving orders and directing his elders, even though he was supposedly at an age to be seen and not heard. One of the men grumbled, "When did you start running things?"

Albert leaned forward in his saddle, looked him squarely in the eye and said, "While you're on my place, I'll be running things from here on." That was the rule for the next eight decades.

Albert found it increasingly difficult, however, to run the ranch from a two-seater desk in the back corner of the schoolhouse.

With Carrie's support he made it through the eighth grade but tensions mounted the next year.

The ninth grade curriculum included a course in Latin, which Albert considered a complete waste of time. "Couldn't figure out how I'd ever be able to talk Latin to a cow," he rationalized in later interviews. He informed the teacher he would not participate in the Latin lessons. She countered that he would study Latin or leave school. Albert thought her ultimatum was the ideal solution, and he left to confront the real world. He did leave knowing he was qualified for outside employment; the banker in Meadows had offered him a job.

Albert found his new work schedule far more agreeable. He fed cattle morning and night and kept the sawmill running. He also began a lifetime practice of "zooming from place to place," to quote Carrie, putting cattle deals together all over the country. By this time he could eye a cow and her calf, and guess their weights within a couple of pounds.

His pace was slackened about a year after he left school. After helping deliver a herd of 1,500 cattle on the Clearwater River, he decided to trade his horse for one that was half-broken. Rain made the trail home a little slick, and when Albert ducked to ride under a tree limb, his mare slipped, fell, and crushed his leg under her weight.

Albert's doctor set the leg without anesthetic, and the experience didn't leave Albert unscathed. From that day on, he grew faint at the sight of blood. To make matters worse, Albert's leg refused to heal and the doctor wanted to break and set the leg again.

He found another doctor who thought it would heal if wrapped tightly with a rubber band, but the doctor warned him the process would be painful. Sixteen-year-old Albert told the doctor, "That's all right. I can stand the hurting, but by God, you're not going to break it over."

He became restless while on the mend, so he took bookkeeping courses at Link's Business College in Boise. He learned quickly. After three and a half months he could complete ranch tax forms and balance the books.

Once Albert's leg was declared sound, he resumed his hectic

schedule. As he raced around the country buying cattle, completing ranch projects, and herding Circle C cattle to their new owners, he began to think about building a ranch of his own.

Slowly, he formulated the details. He wanted to retain his role at the Circle C, so the ranch would have to be within commuting distance. Yet it needed to be a separate entity with plenty of space to expand without retarding the Circle C's growth.

As he traveled on Circle C business, he began to scrutinize neighboring ranches. Would the owner sell for a good price? How could the ranch be stocked and managed? Would the investment pay?

Several places were considered and eliminated before he made his first offer. He was twenty-one. It was 1910.

Albert Campbell readies a Circle C heifer for branding in Round Valley, circa 1910. Although decked out in cowboy regalia, he never did wear cowboy boots. He preferred regular work boots. (Photo courtesy of Charlotte Campbell Armacost.)

Two

KNUCKLING DOWN: THE 1910s

"That country was steeper than a cow's face. It was tough to make a living there."

—*Toots Rogers*

Albert went to bed early that night, but he didn't let sleep interrupt his thinking. He put deals together and polished his negotiating skills even as he slept. His mind went into overdrive that particular night, because the next day he would make an offer on a ranch. His own ranch.

Several hours before daylight, he was wide awake and in the barn, saddling his horse. As his horse munched on a healthy ration of grain, Albert tightened the cinch, and then he reached for his rolled slicker, which concealed a branding iron. He was optimistic about the day's outcome.

Over twenty miles and a sunrise later, Albert and his horse climbed out of the Wildhorse River canyon, arriving at E.H. "Eef" Day's place in No Business Basin just in time for branding.

Day is still remembered for two distinctions. His long, flowing beard was not as unusual as his concept of safety. He worried about his daughters, Fay and Ruth, who had to cross the sometimes-treacherous Wildhorse River in order to reach the log schoolhouse. He dealt with the hazard by tying his girls' wrists to their saddle horns. Each morning the schoolmarm began her routine by untying the Day girls. The girls didn't fall into the river, and fortunately they never experienced a slipped saddle or a horse who decided to roll.

The girls were helping their mother prepare a huge noon meal for the branding crew when Albert rode in. After discussing the weather and the merits of Day's calf crop, Albert made his offer. Day accepted immediately and said, "You should have brought your own brand."

Albert grinned and untied the slicker from his saddle. As he unwrapped the "O" brand he explained, "I didn't want to be too conspicuous."

That afternoon Albert's herd was branded with three links, or a horizontal line of three touching O's.

In addition to the No Business place, Albert's 222-acre ranch included a parcel on the Wildhorse River. There is no record of the purchase price; however, Albert said in later interviews that his father loaned him $3,000 to begin his enterprise. According to Albert's brother, Rollie, a portion of that money was used to buy additional cattle, which Albert bought from a man in Council. The cows cost thirty dollars a head with their calves thrown in.

Albert's responsibilities on the Circle C made the day-to-day management of the Three Links Ranch difficult, so he soon formed a partnership with his cousin, Arthur Campbell. Arthur incorporated his Wildhorse homestead into the ranch, and agreed to handle daily operations.

Arthur's abilities complemented his cousin's. He enjoyed the endless stream of ranching projects, particularly those that were accomplished on horseback. The neighbors up and down Wildhorse agreed that he was a good hand with horses.

Albert, on the other hand, had the business sense that was crucial to the operation. He recognized opportunities in hay and cattle markets, and he had the financial backing to take advantage of them.

A chasm began to develop in the partnership when Arthur married. His wife, Abby, believed the work had been divided unfairly. Ill feelings grew to the point that the Campbells decided to dissolve the partnership.

Albert remembered that Abby initiated the discussion at the

breakfast table. "Art's doing all the work and you're doing all the gallivanting. I think we'd better just divide it up," she reportedly said.

The couple proposed a division and a few minor details were changed before Albert asked for a pen, a bottle of ink, and some paper. Four small pages of his confident scrawl dissolved the partnership, effective January 1, 1915.

Arthur and his wife retained their original homestead plus an additional piece of ground, three workhorses named Prince, Spud, and Bird, two saddle horses called Shortie and Kid, their pick of four cows, and a small variety of farm implements and tools. They kept the Forest Service permit adjoining their land.

Albert kept the remainder of the Day place, the cattle, twenty tons of hay, and he agreed to assume the debt. The document stated that his cattle would be branded OX on the left hip. The OX Ranch was launched.

As always, Albert kept an eye toward expansion and the next place he acquired belonged to Arthur MacPherson, a Scottish national who listed his occupation as engineer in the 1900 census. His place, which has now been almost completely flooded by the Oxbow Dam, was on the Snake River at the mouth of Salt Creek. It boasted a natural hot spring and a fruit orchard, which had provided many homesteaders in the upper country with their canning stock.

No specific details of the purchase have survived except that when the two Scotsmen began to negotiate, the sparks flew.

There were several ranches Albert wanted to eventually add to his holdings, but their tenacious owners weren't likely to sell without a little outside encouragement. One such operation belonged to Friend and Carmeta Moore, who owned Starveout Ranch. Their place was due west of No Business Basin.

One afternoon Albert rode over the grassy ridge separating the two ranches. As he approached the log house, Carmeta explained that her husband was away on business, but she would be happy to boil some coffee. Albert accepted the invitation, pulled a chair up to the round oak table and began to discuss cattle prices, range conditions, and news from the neighborhood.

The Moore's small, blond-headed daughter, Helena, probably opted to play with her cats during the visit.

Albert, who had previously offered to buy the place, came to the reason for his visit just before he left. He started speculating about the future, predicting the seventeen families who lived along the Wildhorse River would soon be unable to make a living. Once they began to leave the country, he said, the schoolhouse would close its doors and the area's mail service would stop.

Carmeta was stunned by his grim outlook, and repeated it later to her husband. The couple dismissed Albert's thoughts as a ploy to own Starveout.

The story has a double irony, as Albert's prophecy was correct, even though it came to pass much later than he originally thought. The school closed in 1946 and the mail stage stopped its twice weekly run shortly thereafter. However, civilization's retreat didn't daunt Starveout's owners. Still a rancher, Helena Moore Schmidt occupies the house her father built. She shares her home with a few grey cats and a cow dog aptly named Rough.

Helena's ranch predates the OX by a few months, as the Moores came into the area in April of 1910.

Friend, who signed his name F.A., was in the vicinity even earlier. He joined his brother, Al, and a partner, William Wallace Irwin, in a ranching venture in No Business Basin. Occasionally the socially starved bachelors headed for Cambridge to raise a little havoc. On one such excursion, Friend met his future bride, Carmeta Cole.

The couple was married in 1907. Friend dissolved his partnership in the Basin, even though Carmeta protested. He declared that the wilderness was no place for a lady.

The couple moved to Tacoma, Washington, where Friend worked as a carpenter and a millwright. He helped build a paper mill, and just as it was completed, it burned down. By the time the mill was rebuilt, three years had passed. The couple was expecting a baby and homesick, so they decided to move back to Idaho.

Helena was born in Weiser March 26, 1910. Ten days later, as soon as Carmeta was able to travel, the new family was rolling toward Starveout in a wagon. They had purchased a homestead from Big Foot John Gerbidge whose feet were so large he had to make his own shoes out of animal hides.

Posed in front of the Emery's first home in Wildhorse are Emma Bailey, Claud, Mary, Billy, and Archie Emery. The older woman is Mary Emery's mother. The photograph was taken in 1899. Third and fourth generation Emerys currently own and operate the ranch. (Photo courtesy of the Arnold Emery family.)

Gerbidge wasn't responsible for his homestead's unusual name. That was bestowed by the first two families who settled in Wildhorse: the Emerys and the Meyers. When the group arrived in 1892, they had to depend on wild bunch grass to feed their cattle in the winter. The Emerys agreed to feed the hand-cut hay, if the Meyers would bring them groceries. As the winter progressed, food supplies dwindled, and the Meyers never brought the family supplies. Finally the Emerys were forced to move, leaving an empty pantry and a landmark named Starveout.

Moving, almost two decades later, must have been a stressful

A traveling photographer captured the Emerys in front of their second Wildhorse home in 1910. Pictured are Ed, Mary, Charlie, Archie, and Billy Emery. Arnold and Ruth Emery still occupy the home. (Photo courtesy of the Arnold Emery family.)

Sig and Ella Meyers, left, were among the first settlers in Wildhorse. Son Frank, son-in-law Aus Groseclose, and daughters Anna and Amy gathered for this 1910 portrait. Apples are still being harvested from Sig's abandoned orchard, which he expanded by planting cuttings from his mature trees. (Photo courtesy of the Arnold Emery family.)

"U-Haul—an adventure in moving" had a slightly different interpretation in 1910. Friend and Carmeta Moore depended upon these packhorses to transport their haying equipment and household goods to their Starveout ranch. Belle, the mare on the left, didn't survive the adventure. (Photo courtesy of Helena Moore Schmidt.)

undertaking for the Moores. The wagon road ended four miles below the homestead site, and everything had to be carried up the precariously steep trail on pack animals. Smaller items such as dishes and groceries were handled easily, but securing haying equipment and bulky furniture on the back of a mule was a tricky job.

The move was made with only one fatality. The disassembled hay rake was carefully secured to a black mare's back. The mare, Belle, was a cinch binder—she didn't like a tight cinch, but her load and the steep trail made it necessary. She was steadily climbing the trail when she decided she couldn't handle the cinch anymore. She reared back to free herself of the load, and ended up falling backwards over the edge of the trail. The horse and haying equipment alternately crushed each other as they tumbled down the hill. Friend raced down the hill to discover she had died instantly of a broken neck.

Tension mounted as the mangled hay rake was tied to another horse, but it completed the trip without incident.

The new family moved into a tent, and work began on a cabin. Friend used two saddle ponies to drag logs from the wooded area about a mile above the house. The cabin walls were built using a rolling hitch with a chain. The horses pulled the logs up wooden skids, and then Friend positioned and secured them. Carmeta's job was to drive the horses, although she later joked she was just holding the lines up out of the dirt. At the time, she didn't know much about driving a team.

The Moores used little lumber in their home, as it was expensive and difficult to transport. Boards too long to be packed had to be dragged behind the horses.

Well before winter, the two-room house was weather tight with hand-split shakes covering the roof. The house had a dirt floor, and flour sacks covered the windows until money for glass and flooring could be saved.

Carmeta kept the food in an old clothing wardrobe which had been converted into a pantry, and the milk was kept outside in

Young Helena Moore accompanies her mother, right, and her aunt on a shopping trip to Brownlee. The older women rode in split skirts that scandalized the general population, even though they featured fabric panels that buttoned discreetly over the split. (Photo courtesy of Helena Moore Schmidt.)

Helena always chose shadowing her dad over more lady-like, domestic pursuits. Here she helps her father rake hay. (Photo courtesy of Helena Moore Schmidt.)

the spring. The family couldn't afford cast iron pans, so they settled for tin and enamelware.

Grocery shopping was a major event, even though the Brownlee store was barely two miles away on the Jim Summers Trail. The store carried staples including flour, sugar, salt, and axe handles.

Brownlee dances were known for their colorful fights, and Friend bought a relic from one of those fights, an axe handle covered with dried blood, at the Brownlee store. Months later his mother came to visit from Everett, Washington. When she asked about it, she was told the truth, and the woman couldn't understand what had induced her son to live in such an uncivilized place.

Even if the location was remote, Carmeta was determined that Helena would be raised a lady. Helena wore dresses nearly all the time, and before she had her picture taken, Carmeta hurriedly tied a large, white bow in her hair.

Helena tolerated the dresses and bows, but she was happiest when she was either trailing her dad or riding a horse.

Helena wears a bow, and her best friend, Roxy, wears a fancy bridle for the camera. Roxy was a retired racehorse the Moores purchased from Jack Kramer. Her colts also became Helena's charges, and they were loved and petted from the time they first stood on their wobbly legs. She never had to "break" her horses. (Photo courtesy of Helena Moore Schmidt.)

Ice cream socials were a much-anticipated event in Wildhorse. Even though they had to brave miles of dusty trail, the ladies refused to wear anything but their best white dresses. (Photo courtesy of Helena Moore Schmidt.)

Friend Moore and a sister-in-law gather snow for freezing the ice cream. (Photo courtesy of Helena Moore Schmidt.)

This shot was taken above the Moore's home place on Starveout. Helena broke her arm when her saddle slipped and she threw out an arm to break the fall. The trip to the nearest doctor in Cambridge was a painful thirty miles long. The doctor confirmed the arm was broken by grating the bone ends back and forth. He gave Helena ether before setting the break. (Photo courtesy of Helena Moore Schmidt.)

Eventually, schooling had to be crowded into her busy schedule. Her first four years of lessons took place at the kitchen table. Carmeta obtained books from the Brownlee school district, and she taught Helena for a few hours each morning and afternoon.

When Helena reached the fourth grade level, her parents decided it was time she enrolled in the public school system. Friend had to renew his batching skills during the week, while his wife and daughter lived in a cabin closer to the Wildhorse schoolhouse.

On her first day of school in 1918, eight-year-old Helena became increasingly apprehensive as she walked the two miles to her destination. It was all so new. She inched her way across the fallen cottonwood that bridged the Wildhorse River and cautiously peered in the doorway of the log schoolhouse. A woodstove surrounded by desks stood in the center of the room. Opposite the door, a woman in her early twenties sat behind the teacher's desk. She assigned Helena a desk, and showed her where to put her lunch pail, her new tablet, and bottle of ink. Helena relaxed when she recognized most of her seven classmates, including Charlie Emery.

Helena idolized her teacher and generally enjoyed school, although she did take an unexpected bath one morning. Water occasionally splashed and froze on the log footbridge by the schoolhouse. Helena was halfway across the log when she slipped and tumbled into the river. She retrieved her lunch bucket, which came floating down to her, and continued on to school. That morning she took her lessons while standing in front of the woodstove.

The dangerous crossing caused Wildhorse residents to seek funding for a new schoolhouse on the other side of the river. Frank Fanning, the only carpenter in the area besides Friend Moore, constructed the one-room building out of lumber.

Fanning occasionally worked for Albert Campbell, but he is remembered for surviving a terrible sawmill accident. Somehow his head was caught under the blade, which sawed through the skull, putting out an eye. Council's Dr. Alvin Thurston picked most of the sawdust off his brain before sewing it up. Miraculously, Fanning suffered no brain damage.

Helena Moore entered the fourth grade in this original Wildhorse schoolhouse, before the building was abandoned for a new site across the river. After the Wildhorse school closed its doors in 1946, the newer schoolhouse was used to store hay. (Photo courtesy of Helena Moore Schmidt.)

Like Fanning and several other area homesteaders, Friend Moore earned extra cash by helping Albert Campbell during haying season. In fact, study of the only surviving OX Ranch bookkeeping records, dating from 1917 to 1924, reveals that Albert employed, purchased stallion services, or bought hay and cattle from many of the neighbors he eventually bought out.

The books also indicate Albert's independent venture maintained ties to Circle C resources. Until Albert established a line of credit at the First Bank of Council, his father loaned him money at current interest rates. Even after Albert established a working relationship with the Council bank, the Circle C continued to be a source of working capital and livestock. The transactions between the two ranches were mutually beneficial, family members emphasize, since Albert was simultaneously buying and selling cattle for both ranches.

ASSETS

January 1, 1918

Wildhorse Ranch, 222 acres	$8,000.00
MacPherson Ranch, 74 acres	1,000.00
580 cattle @ $40	23,200.00
20 horses	1,200.00
207 tons of hay @ $10	2,070.00
Implements	325.00
Bills Receivable	4,750.00
First Bank of Council	143.96
Automobile	800.00
Total	$41,488.96

January 1, 1919

Ranch	$ 9,000.00
935 Cattle @ 45	42,075.00
Horses	1,220.00
Implements	525.00
First Bank of Council	1,414.03
Weiser Loan and Trust, Co.	67.71
Automobile	800.00
Bills Receivable	6,750.00
Arthur Campbell, on acct.	289.57
E. H. Day, on acct.	150.00
Liberty Bonds	500.00
Total	$62,791.31

Albert Campbell (left) and Bill Peters (right) stop for a visit with Mark Winkler. The Winkler family was among the first settlers in Council. Mark's brother, Bill, became the county sheriff. (Photo courtesy of Charlotte Campbell Armacost.)

Albert's faded accounting entries indicate he bought mostly Circle C cattle to build his herd. In 1917 his dad carried the note for 253 cattle at nine percent interest. The average cost was forty-eight dollars per head.

For two years, 1917 and 1918, Albert listed his assets at the year's end. The figures show an ambitious thirty-three percent growth rate:

These accounting figures underscore Albert's business philosophy, which was influenced by his father's vision of the future. Charles Campbell believed that as the nation's population grew, the demand for land would increase. He foresaw a time when soaring real estate prices would stifle ranch expansion. When that time came, he reasoned, money could be spent on ranch improvements and equipment. In the meantime, everything except building the herd and expanding the ranch ran on a shoestring budget.

Albert's help occasionally found this philosophy frustrating, but a sense of humor helped them muddle through. Such was the case when Albert finally agreed to purchase a truck for the ranch in the 1930s. It didn't take much capital outlay to buy the bright blue, rickety mail stage that had developed chronic rattles after years of jolting down the Wildhorse road. The rig was past retirement age and often more of a hindrance than a help. The cowboys dubbed it the Blue Ox, and one of them found a cartoon which was permanently displayed on the dashboard.

The drawing depicted two grizzled cowboys standing in front of some rundown outbuildings. One remarked to the other, "Just when he has enough money to dress like a cowboy, he buys another ranch."

What was arguably Albert's greatest asset didn't appear on his balance sheet: his hired hands. He looked toward the Circle C for help in this area as well.

The books indicate Pat Farrel was the OX foreman in 1917, earning fifty dollars a month plus room and board. The big, friendly Irishman was a bachelor from New Meadows who had worked on the Circle C. Even though he played a major role on the OX, which included drafting checks from Albert's account, he continued to spend a couple of months each year working for the Circle C.

Bill Clark was another steady hand who first worked at the Circle C. Raised on the Salmon River, he was a hard worker who was drawing top wages in 1918. He earned eighty-five dollars a month.

While he was working in the Basin, Clark befriended an elderly neighbor, No Business Smith, who refused to sell to Albert. Clark visited the old man frequently, bringing him groceries and taking the edge off his loneliness by listening to stories about the good old days. When Smith died, he left his place to Clark, who honored the old man's wishes by never selling the place to the OX Ranch.

Claude Childers exchanged his cowboy boots for a soldier's uniform when he was twenty-two. After serving in World War I, he returned to the OX Ranch. He was to stay for another fifty years. (Photo courtesy of the Council Museum.)

In a separate incident, Clark was getting ready for haying when he noticed Tuffy, a neighbor's dog, had wandered into the Basin. The dog had never strayed in the past, which led him to believe his neighbors were in trouble. Dropping his work, he saddled a horse and followed the steep trail to the mouth of Wildhorse, where he swam his horse across the Snake to the Gordon's ranch. Mabel Gordon Ray and her sister, Phyllis Gordon Cranor, were girls when a soaked Bill Clark appeared with their equally wet dog. He was relieved to hear there was no emergency. The girls' father had left to hay with the Nixons on Dukes Creek, and they suspected the dog was searching for him.

Around 1917, another young man rode into the Basin. He was stringbean thin and quiet, and he would play a major role in the OX's daily operation for the next fifty years. His name was Claude Childers. His first hitch with the OX didn't last long however, because the twenty-two-year-old was called into the service. The United States had entered The Great War, known now as World War I.

The war had its impact on the Campbell family as well: both Albert and Rollie were drafted. A letter from Harry C. Shellworth, perhaps the family attorney, was fired off to the Selective Service Board on August 21, 1917.

Shellworth attempted to gain exemptions for Albert and Rollie; asserting that the men had been directly responsible for 2,500 head of cattle since their father retired in 1911.

The letter argued,

> . . . if said Albert W. Campbell and Rollie L. Campbell are permitted to continue in said cattle business, they will be able to, and will increase the available supply of beef for the market and that neither of them can be taken from said business without direct substantial national loss to the meat producing ability of the country.

The letter achieved only half of the desired results. Albert was granted permission to remain on the ranch, while Rollie was assigned to the Veterinary Corps, where he stayed stateside for the duration of the war.

The Wildhorse community sent another young man to World War I. Archie Emery's first stop was the Harder place at the mouth of Wildhorse. Mrs. Harder, who was a nurse, gave him the required physical examination. It's likely that Archie's visit concluded with a pastry out of Mrs. Harder's glass showcase. She was an excellent cook, and nearly seventy years later, former guests can still describe her desserts in mouth-watering detail.

The Harders operated a sizable orchard on what is now McCormick Park and the OX Wildhorse Headquarters. Until 1992 part of the herd wintered and calved there, but the site bore little resemblance to its orchard days. The property shrunk and landmarks were flooded when the Oxbow dam was put into operation.

The Harders' fruit-growing business had a major obstacle: transportation. A train had been running to Copperfield, Oregon, since 1909, which gave the Harders ready access to outside markets, but they still had to transport their fragile, perishable produce across the Snake River.

The problem was remedied by stringing a cable across the river to save rowing. They converted the basement of their two-story house, which was located on the south side of the Wildhorse River, into a fruit-packing shed. There, Mr. Harder constructed fruit boxes out of lumber that he ferried across the river. Boxed apples, peaches, apricots, grapes, and almonds were kept in the cool basement until the train's next scheduled arrival.

Like their immediate neighbors, the Harders' meat staple was pork. The Snake River canyon was too hot to keep beef, so they slaughtered one or two hogs each year, curing the meat by parboiling it until it was salty enough to keep. Even so, they were constantly waging battle against hungry, hard-shelled meat bugs.

The presence of meat bugs and primitive transportation aside, the edges of civilization were beginning to appear, particularly around Bear. The *Council Leader*, predecessor to the *Adams County Leader*, chronicled the change.

The most ambitious attempt to bring sophistication into the community was spawned by the Bear Creek Literary Society. An ambitious schoolteacher, Professor W.H. Grant, led the effort. The society's charter membership gathered in October of 1911 to hear Grant lecture on imagination. Future debate topics included Indian suffering versus Negro suffering, should women be given the right to vote, and whether country living was more conducive to happiness than life in the city.

Society members also gathered several Sundays to hear Professor Grant preach.

When a group of socialists scheduled a meeting in Bear, the enthusiasm waned. "Everyone was so busy in the fields," the June 6, 1912 *Leader* explained.

Not to be upstaged, Wildhorse also formed an organization, the *Leader* reported. Archie Bardmas, whose land would become part of the OX, was appointed chairman. The short-lived club started a modest library in a member's home, and for ten cents they ordered 100 copies of a pamphlet titled, "Who the Hell is the Devil?" Apparently the publication wasn't a runaway best seller, because after a few weeks there was no report of the group's activities.

Scandal rocked the community when this item appeared in the

paper: "It is rumored that Collis Lynes and Miss Ida Cornett went huckleberrying Sunday, but forgot to take their buckets." Lynes Saddle was named for this bucketless young man. His father, Charles, built the OX's Lick Creek barn in 1902.

News filtered in from Bachelor's Flat, which is now known as the OX's Barbour Flat. Bobby Barbour, who was famous for packing a quarter of beef into Black Lake on his back, was delivering pork to Bear and up the line.

His brother, Anthony, harvested some "fine onions grown from seed," and he ventured into Council to attend a dance and watch a moving picture show featuring the Keystone Cops. He topped off the visit by renewing his *Council Leader* subscription and buying a "fine stallion." It's not known whether he was tempted by the Stetson hat sale. The four dollar hats were going for three dollars and twenty-five cents.

The Barbour's nearest neighbor, Archie Bardmas, lived on Buckshot Bench. The paper reported he was "hauling lumber from the Clement sawmill to his place in Bachelor's Town, with which to build him a house." His December project came to a standstill when he lost all his nails in Bear. Readers were asked to keep an eye open for them.

Also in the news were the Mackey families, who owned land on Rocky Comfort and the site of the present-day OX Ranch manager's house. This staid account of their wild buggy ride was published in 1911:

> Last Friday, while returning home from the school building, Edward Mackey's team failed to utilize the public highway and as a consequence, the driver was thrown from the vehicle when rocks were encountered.
>
> The team became speedy, leaving its driver to meander the shady forest alone. With this speed, the team soon separated themselves from the hack when a forest stump offered satisfactory obstruction.
>
> The inmates, which numbered four, moved unpleasantly over the dashboard. However, no

particular harm resulted; but the hack had to be hauled in for a number of repairs.

The hack driver's niece, Ruth Mackey, was honored at a party the next month. A fortune-telling cake highlighted the event. Baked inside were a coin, a baby doll, and a button. The hostess explained that whoever got the coin would be rich in the coming year. The baby doll meant marriage and the button indicated continued bachelorhood.

Charley Warner was probably at the party, as he was sparking Ruth. If the cake was accurate, Charley's piece had the button.

He was still pursuing Ruth two years later, after her family moved to Long Beach, California. His prolonged visit to California was fruitless, and the thirty-one-year-old bachelor returned to his ranch.

By this time, Charley's holdings had grown appreciably from the 160-acre homestead located immediately west of the Seven Devils Lodge. The acreage had already been homesteaded when the Warners arrived. They offered to trade a milk cow for homesteader's rights, and the owner agreed. Charley had his start.

His parents were both dead by 1914, and each child was willed twenty-three acres, except for the twins, Amy and Ada, who each received ten acres. Charley eventually bought his parents' ranch from his brothers and sisters, although his sister Jane and her husband, Earl Shelton, ranched their parcel for two years.

Their home, which sat between the Seven Devils airstrip and the pond, was slightly over a mile from the main road. The loneliness of the place finally caused them to move in 1916.

To the west of the Sheltons, across Wickiup Creek, lived an old bachelor named Dorsett. With his help, Charley and Arthur Robertson shoveled the network of irrigation ditches by hand.

The Seven Devils mining district provided the beef market which put Charley's ranch on a paying basis. On at least one occasion, he drove a herd to a boardinghouse in Landore, where he was paid on delivery.

When Charley was nearing retirement, a teen-aged Dick Parker helped him with his cowboying. He told Dick that a contract with Black Lake had saved his hide. Dates are hazy, but the beef was selling for two cents a pound in Portland at the time, and that price wouldn't cover freight from Council to Portland. Charley's deal with Black Lake yielded a much more encouraging eight cents a pound. Every other day he picked a fat steer out of the herd, shot it, and hefted the gutted carcass into a wagon. The trips took most of the day, but they put his ranch in the black.

He acquired a passenger on one of the return trips. Charley charged the man an outrageous two dollars for the ride into Bear, and he decided to give the passenger his money's worth. He whipped up the horses and sent them careening down the perilous road. Much to Charley's satisfaction, a glassy-eyed, wobbly-kneed individual stumbled off the wagon in Bear.

Charley was engaged in more tedious work on Kinney Creek when he noticed a young boy across the river. The boy was skidding logs with a horse, and Charley watched his progress with interest. The boy felt his stare, turned, and waved.

Not much time passed before Charley met the boy's father, John Hendrix. He told Hendrix he had a waving acquaintance with his son.

"That's no boy," Hendrix grumbled, "that's my daughter, Lena."

Charley had left an indelible impression on his future father-in-law.

It seems the Warners' honeymoon was over before they finished saying their wedding vows. Lena became withdrawn and despondent.

Her daily routine focused on a wavy-maned horse Charley had given her for a wedding present. Each morning, she dressed, went outside, and saddled her horse, which she named Socks. She was inactive the rest of the day until just before sunset, when she unsaddled the animal.

Lena followed the pattern day after day, only pausing to give birth to her two sons. Roy James, or Toby, was born in 1914. His brother, listed as "Boy Warner" on the birth certificate, arrived eighteen months later. Nobody named the newest addition to the family; they just called him Baby.

When Baby was still in diapers, Lena met Bill Hogg, who was working for A.O. Huntley on Indian Creek. Hogg was a rodeo rider from Pendleton, Oregon.

Glen Saling (right) helps Charley Warner and his sons with a farming project. Charley didn't believe in naming things. Toby was named by his mother, but the younger boy, Lawrence, had to name himself. (Photo courtesy of the Bert Warner family.)

Lena and her young family began to rendezvous with Hogg. Baby rode in front of her on the saddle, and Toby held on from behind. The activity was cut short when Charley caught the foursome riding together.

The old shoe top, which served as a scabbard for his automatic pistol, slowed his reaction time. He fired a warning shot for his sons' sake, and Hogg spurred his horse into a dead run through the trees. He knew Charley was a deadshot; he never wasted ammunition.

Charley later told Dick Parker that he followed Hogg to Mary Smith's house, which was located on the Bear turnoff road. A sawmill currently occupies the site. Hogg's sweating horse stood in front of the house, its reins touching the ground. Brandishing his pistol, Charley entered the house, confronted Smith and demanded, "Where's Hogg?"

She said Hogg had jumped off his horse and run into the woods. Charley, who was ready to shoot, gave her house a thorough search before trying to track him outside.

When Charley was out of sight, she went into her kitchen and lifted the hidden floor panel that covered the potato bin. Hogg escaped, and a rash of local speculation began. The neighbors agreed that had Charley found Hogg, Smith would have eaten plenty of mashed potatoes that winter.

Lena left that day, taking her horse, her clothes, and $150. The divorce was finalized on April, 16, 1922. The newspaper reported that Lena failed to appear at the trial.

Years later the Warner boys were riding along the Snake when their cousin, Jesse Smith, told them to wait. "See that woman?" he said, pointing across the river, "That's your mother." By that time, she had married Bill Hogg.

When the boys became reacquainted with their mother, she explained she'd felt isolated and stifled in Bear. She left her boys because she knew their father could provide for them.

Charley seemed indifferent to the estrangement. When Tim Lydston, a cattle buyer, dropped by for a meal, he asked about Lena. He was told matter-of-factly, "The Hoggs got her."

The summer following the separation was a rough one for Charley. Care for the two small boys was added to his workload,

Earl Shelton married Charley Warner's sister, Jane. The couple lived in a cabin below the present-day Seven Devils airstrip between 1914 and 1916. (Photo courtesy of the Bert Warner family.)

and when his projects were at a peak, he broke his leg while running a ditcher.

Landore's Dr. Brown set it that evening. When Charley woke up the next morning, his leg was lying askew, so Dr. Brown set it again. The break, which was in the middle of his shin, never healed properly. The mismatched bone ends were held together by gristle. As a result, he could barely walk and he spent the rest of his life working out of an old form-fitter saddle.

The strange bend in his leg earned him a new nickname: Crookshank. He liked it.

Years later, Council's Dr. Alvin Thurston recommended an operation in Portland. He explained a sheep's shin would be grafted to his leg, and that the procedure would be similar to fixing a piece of woodwork. Charley said there was no way he'd have anything to do with a sheep or its bones. He added that he'd rather lie out under a pine tree and die. End of discussion.

Charley couldn't run both the ranch and the household, so he hired Edith Shelton and some of the Whitlow girls to help. When Baby was three, the girls decided it was time he had a name. Charley didn't have a preference; he never even named his dogs and horses. The girls decided Baby should choose his own name, so one of them pulled down a bulky, old dictionary, opened it to the section on names, and began reading aloud. The little boy liked the name Lawrence.

The Whitlow girls were as efficient with household chores as they were with naming children. One day, after a particularly large feed, Charley volunteered to help with the dishes, and he issued a challenge: he bet he could wash enough dishes to keep all three or four girls drying. The race was on. Charley dunked dishes in and out of the soapy water without bothering to clean them. One of the girls complained. With a twinkle in his eye he growled, "It's an awfully poor dish dryer who can't get what the washer misses." The dishes continued to leave the soapy water at a lightening pace, and the Whitlow girls sharpened their drying skills.

Charley's routine was uninterrupted by World War I. After the war ended, cattle prices plummeted, and stock growers faced some grim years. Charley kept his business alive, even though his previous mainstay, the Black Lake market, had long since crumbled.

The depressed market caused other ranches to fold, including the area's largest operator, A.O. Huntley. When his place went under foreclosure, his assets included over 600 head of show-quality Hereford cattle, the old Eckels place on the Snake River, a three-story Victorian mansion, and a colossal barn located on Indian Creek.

Huntley's rise and fall from prominence is one of the area's most colorful stories. Outlandish tales about the man and his family still circulate.

Huntley, who was born in Wisconsin, was lured west by the Coeur d'Alene gold strike in 1883. He first worked in a twelve by sixteen foot cabin which slept forty men. The twenty-three-year-old earned fifteen dollars a week by cooking three meals a day. The menu rarely varied: beans, bacon, bread, and coffee with an occasional taste of canned fruit. Before long, the strike fizzled, and Huntley criss-crossed the territory, holding a variety of jobs before he chanced into the Seven Devils country.

In a 1934 *Idaho Statesman* article, Huntley wrote that he had come into the area with two partners and 100 head of cattle. The partnership was probably short-lived, as there was no other reference to these unnamed partners.

Huntley homesteaded in 1890, and he later recalled that low cattle prices made for a long struggle. However, Seven Devils mining activity provided the rancher with two windfalls. First, Albert Kleinschmidt financed a road linking Huntley's homestead on Indian Creek to the outside world. Second, the area's growth attracted two brothers, Lou and Ben Caswell.

The Caswell brothers were placer miners who spent more than four years establishing semi-permanent camps in the Seven Devils and around Thunder Mountain. A daily diary kept by Lou Caswell chronicles the men's activities as they mined, built cabins, and made clothing out of deer hides. The routine was broken by an occasional visit to Huntley's cabin, their unofficial head-quarters, where they swapped stories, helped finish projects, and made a lucrative business proposition.

In 1895, late in the season, the brothers struck pay dirt, but

Each winter takes its toll on the old Huntley barn. Prohibitive costs have prevented restoration efforts. An earlier photo (above) shows some of the barn's original structure. The bottom photo was taken in 1987. (Photos courtesy of Corky and Pat Gossi and Doug McKinney.)

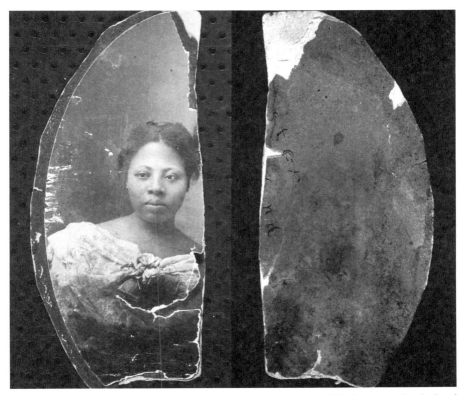

Not much is known about "Brother Jim" Bramlett, the black man who helped Huntley build the barn. Jim refused to talk about his background and family, which caused much local speculation. Decades after his homestead cabin was abandoned, the new owners' son, Joe Richards, was poking around inside. He found this photograph under a loose floorboard. Who was she? And who was the person cut out of the photograph? Scissors snipped the only clue. Four letters survived the cropping: s-t-e-r. Was it sister? Ester? We'll probably never know. (Photo courtesy of David and Debra Richards Tate.)

they were running out of provisions and winter was approaching. They were only able to extract $200 worth of gold dust before they were forced to leave.

Back at Huntley's cabin, they made a proposition. If Huntley would grubstake them for fifty dollars, they would locate him in the claims. He agreed.

The return on his investment was phenomenal. Different sources claimed he realized between $60,000 and $90,000 from his one-third interest in the the claims. In his *Statesman* article,

Wanda Richards pauses in the doorway of Jim's cabin for this 1967 photo. The cabin's roof has long since disintegrated. (Photo courtesy of David and Debra Richards Tate.)

Huntley recalled the brothers mined the claim for the next five years, taking a total of $20,000 in dust. In 1901 the principal claims were sold for $100,000. The resulting gold rush enabled them to sell their reserve claim the next spring for $125,000.

Huntley immediately funneled his fortune into the ranch. The most flamboyant improvement was a barn, constructed between 1905 and 1910. "Brother Jim" reportedly built the structure. He was a reclusive man, rumored to be an ex-slave, who lived about two miles southwest of Huntley.

When it was finished, the barn was touted as a modern marvel. It featured an overhanging roof, so that workers would be in the shade while using a Jackson fork to stack hay in the loft. Hay chutes with tip boards sped up the feeding process. Railroad tracks ran through the center of the barn, making manure disposal

A.O. Huntley built this home on Indian Creek, hoping he'd share it with his bride one day. Newspapers dubbed it "The Palace of Hells Canyon." (Photo courtesy of Tina Warner.)

efficient. The water troughs filled automatically, and the barn was the first structure in the country with electricity.

The electricity became a bone of contention among his hands, who had to work doubly hard for their twenty dollar monthly paychecks. After a particularly exhausting day, his help plodded into the yard only to find floodlights had been installed in the corral. Huntley wanted to work cattle at night. The men balked at the idea, which was reluctantly abandoned.

Huntley himself was a workaholic; his contemporaries agreed he regularly did the work of two men. He relentlessly pursued his goals, as illustrated one winter when he was riding for stock on Allison Creek.

The trails along the Snake River breaks are precarious during the best weather conditions. Ice turns them into a deathtrap. Undaunted, Huntley headed for the lower country on a nasty day. He had dismounted and was leading his horse over a particularly dangerous stretch, when the animal lost its footing and tumbled down the sheer incline to its death. Without hesitating, he pulled the saddle off the dead animal and marched back to the barn, where he saddled another horse and resumed his journey—this time successfully.

He was nearing his forties when he became obsessed with another goal: he wanted a bride. Since there were no local prospects, he concentrated on building the mystery woman a home. His sawmill, which was powered by Indian Creek, began producing an awesome stack of lumber.

Although it was never completely finished, he created a showplace. Rooms in the lower level could be opened to create a large ballroom, the site of several local functions. A steady stream of freighters brought the finest oak furniture and brass beds available from Marshall Fields of Chicago. Soon the house was equipped with everything except a bride.

He found her during a particularly discouraging trip to La Grande, Oregon. He had taken cattle there, hoping to get a better price. He was forced to sell them for fifteen dollars a head, or one and a half cents a pound.

The woman who caught his eye was a schoolteacher from Cove, Oregon. Pearl was close to forty years old when she became Mrs. Huntley.

This circa 1912 photo shows the Huntley home being wired for electricity. (Photo courtesy of the Idaho State Historical Society.)

Subtle clues indicate the local population didn't warm to the couple, and jealousy was probably a factor. The Huntleys' standard of living contrasted sharply with that of their neighbors, who squeaked out a living on their 160-acre homesteads. When their neighbors on Windy Ridge earned $300 in a year, they celebrated their good fortune. Life with electricity, ballrooms, and automatic watering troughs was almost beyond their comprehension. The chasm widened when Huntley's wife and daughter, Marion, began to spend most of their time in Oregon.

The rumor mill was fueled and some wild stories spilled out. For example, there was much speculation about Huntley's glass eye. The most plausible story said he'd lost his eye while riding in brush, although vague rumors about a shooting circulated. Another version said that Mrs. Huntley found her husband's mismatched eyes unattractive, so she nagged him until he had a working eye removed. She was reportedly satisfied when he received his color-coordinated glass eye.

Huntley's cattle operation was also under fierce scrutiny. He rejected the locally accepted practice of running mixed-breed stock, and instead chose show quality, horned Herefords.

It was rumored his weaning practices were off kilter. Huntley allegedly weaned the calves when they were one or two months old, six or seven months earlier than normal. According to the story, he then stuck them in the barn's basement to "quicken" their growth. Since the room lacked any form of ventilation, there was no way for the manure to dry, and as a result, all his calves reportedly became diseased and died.

Huntley didn't market his cattle in a conventional manner. His herd was advertised in a catalog based out of the Midwest. Interested buyers submitted bids through the mail.

Curious about the blue-blooded Herefords, Albert Campbell bought three or four cows from Huntley during World War I, before prices plummeted. They were herded to No Business Basin, and they arrived sore-footed. When the cattle recovered, they were turned out on the steep hillsides where one of them promptly fell to her death.

Albert was almost pleased when the expensive, high-bred cattle proved to be inferior to his own. Years later he would point out the purebreds' daughters and granddaughters saying, "See her? She's not worth a damn. She's going down the road (to slaughter)."

It was probably market conditions, not ranching practices, that eventually put Huntley out of business. After World War I, plunging cattle prices caused his select market to evaporate.

The events leading to the ranch's foreclosure are hazy. Huntley offered this ambiguous explanation: "Our fortunes ebbed . . . complications multiplied, involving disastrous obligations.

"So we closed out the old home and moved to southern Oregon and acquired a little place to call our own in a milder clime and with less necessity for the super-strenuous life."

The "milder clime" was in Myrtle Creek, Oregon, where the Huntleys grew vegetables on a small truck farm.

The Indian Creek ranch, including the house and most of its furnishings, was sold in quick succession to a cattleman named Gossi, a sheep owner named Voekel and, finally, in 1929, to George Speropulos, an ambitious Greek whose sheep bands grazed the acreage for years.

Whether Huntley felt a cattleman's natural indignation over the ranch's new wooly inhabitants is unknown. However, a trace of melancholy can be detected in a 1927 letter addressed to "Friend Campbell:" "The wife and I are quite comfortable with no hired help to look after or bother with and plenty of good things to eat and a very neighborly community, so I guess we ought not to kick."

Huntley's decline contrasted with the magnificent business opportunity Congress created for his neighbors. Prohibition was enacted on January 16, 1920, and bootleg liquor became the area's number one cash crop.

George Degitz homesteaded on
Windy Ridge, and frequently
locked horns with Albert and his
cowboys. Albert ended up with
his place and Degitz moved to
Homestead, Oregon, where he
had bartended for years. (Photo
courtesy of Chuck Degitz.)

Three

LOCAL COLOR: The 1920s

"Those homesteaders on Windy Ridge wouldn't have had any cash flow if the government hadn't stepped in with a new program. They called it Prohibition."
                    —Ken Pecora, 5-K Ranch owner

As the black Model A lurched down Windy Ridge road, Sheriff Bill Winkler contemplated the farmsteads perched on the barren, steep hillsides. People who scratched out a living here were survivors, and that didn't make the task at hand any easier. He was going to arrest a moonshiner.

Winkler didn't drive. Automobiles came into use after he was well into adulthood, and Winkler delayed his driving lessons for years. County Prosecutor Carl Swanstrom, who often handled illegal liquor cases single-handedly, agreed to pilot the Ford. Swanstrom was also Albert Campbell's attorney.

Unlike some of their contemporaries, who thought chasing moonshiners spiced their daily routine, Winkler and Swanstrom usually gave these remote lawbreakers low priority. By the time they drove to the Bear/Windy Ridge area, made the arrest, and broke up the still, the whole day was shot. Occasionally news on the grapevine traveled faster than the revenuers could, and they would find the alleged bootlegger with a painfully innocent look on his face, which was sweaty from exertion. In this situation, there was a complete lack of incriminating evidence around the suspect's home.

Council's main street had grown significantly by the 1920s. After a devastating fire in 1914, a town ordinance required

Although Winkler and Swanstrom rarely apprehended area moonshiners on their own initiative, a formal complaint changed things considerably. Such was the case here.

The moonshiner in question, Mrs. Rome, was fiercely independent. When she was widowed in Austria, she decided to give her young family a new start in the United States. After selling the household goods and scraping the family's meager savings together, Mrs. Rome found she could only buy passage for herself and three of her four children. Anna, who was in her early teens, was left in Austria. Her mother promised to send for her as soon as the family saved enough cash.

Somehow the family came to homestead on Windy Ridge. They had chosen a subsistence lifestyle that might yield enough cash to buy flour and sugar. Earning enough money to pay for Anna's passage was a pipe dream.

An alternate plan began to form in her mind. They had a

masonry construction. The small city park saplings (right) have grown into stately trees. (Photo courtesy of Dale Fisk.)

neighbor, George Degitz, who nearly always had cash. Although he proved up on a homestead, it's rumored that he found gambling to be far more lucrative and interesting.

Even though Degitz (pronounced Daggit) was in his forties, Mrs. Rome thought he would make a suitable husband for her sixteen-year-old Anna. Their marriage would give Anna a comfortable lifestyle, and most important, the family would be together again.

The marriage rapidly evolved into a master/slave arrangement, according to neighbors. Degitz slept all day, while Anna tended the crops and livestock. Before dusk, Degitz emerged, saddled his white horse, gave Anna a new set of orders, and headed over the hill to his bartending job. Some say he liked to gamble, but his son hotly denies the story.

Anna spent many lonesome evenings crocheting curtains and socks by the light of a kerosene lamp.

She didn't even get a break when she bore children. When each of her four sons was born, she spent the night in bed. The next morning she was out pitching hay and following her husband's directives.

"Anna, the water bucket is empty," became a tongue-in-cheek saying in neighboring households.

The marriage dissolved after the fourth son was born, and it cemented Mrs. Rome's determination to become financially independent. Prohibition provided the opportunity and the miners in Homestead, Oregon, welcomed her whiskey.

When Sheriff Winkler and County Prosecutor Swanstrom drove into the yard, Mrs. Rome was a stout woman in her early sixties. She listened calmly as Winkler arrested her, and told her she would be riding back to Council with them. She said she needed to gather some things in her bedroom first, so the men waited outside, giving her a few private moments.

All of a sudden she appeared in her doorway. Stark naked. "If you're going to take me in, you'll take me as I am," she announced in broken English.

What happened next is disputed by the local population. The most popular version claims that Winkler, a bachelor, turned beet red and quickly left without his nude prisoner. A few people contend Swanstrom helped Winkler wrap the woman in a blanket, and they hefted her into the car. After the still was destroyed, the threesome drove to Council. There was no conviction, apparently.

By this time the Rome children had grown and scattered. Their mother soon decided to sell the homestead to Albert Campbell.

Albert also eventually bought land belonging to the region's most persistent bootlegger, Bobby Barbour.

Barbour's original ambitions and the date of his arrival are unknown, but long-time resident Anna Adams remembered that he co-owned a store in Cuprum before the turn of the century. When Cuprum declined, he dissolved his partnership and opened a new store in Decorah.

He was Black Lake's postmaster in 1903, according to post office records. Different stories claim the small man could pack between eighty and 123 pounds on his back while cross-country skiing.

The 1910 census indicates he was born in Missouri in 1871. His brother, Anthony, was four years older and listed as the household's head, which is ironic, because Bobby always ran the show.

Anthony kept to himself and he stayed busy with household chores. One local story said he had been kicked in the head, and doctors repaired the hole with a silver plate.

Unlike most of his neighbors, Bobby had a few dollars when he homesteaded. It was most likely money he had earned during the Seven Devils boom. As a result, he was able to stock his ranch from the start.

The brothers started with hogs, which had the run of Barbour Flat and Sheep Peak. He sold pork to his neighbors, and once a year he sponsored a hog drive. Neighbors helped him herd the often uncooperative animals to the railroad in Council.

The hogs saved him from a possible prison term. Early in his ranching career, Bobby discovered that moonshine, at five dollars a gallon, was more profitable than livestock.

He built carefully hidden stills at the head of Salt Creek and on Sheep Peak. He made the mash out of grain (usually barley or corn), sugar, yeast, and water. After allowing it to ferment in a wooden barrel, it was distilled by an elaborate array of copper coils and a copper pot heated by a wood fire.

Someone warned Bobby that the revenuers were coming and he flew into action, eliminating every piece of evidence. He fed the fermenting mash to his hogs, who gulped it down. Carl Swanstrom drove onto the Flat just after the last lump of mash was swallowed. His search failed to reveal a still, but, curiously enough, his path was often blocked by a hog that was staggering drunkenly. Knowing that a hog with a hangover wouldn't incriminate Barbour, Swanstrom headed for town empty-handed.

The local population later joked that Swanstrom should have arrested the hogs for public intoxication.

The close call didn't dampen Bobby's enthusiasm for the business. Connoisseurs claimed his whiskey was top of the line, and he kept his customers satisfied, especially at area dances.

Prior to a dance, Bobby stashed bottles of whiskey in the schoolhouse vicinity. After a customer placed his order, Bobby disappeared for several minutes, returning with the potent liquid.

Bobby Barbour lived in this house, above Lafferty Camp, after serving a State Penitentiary term for bootlegging. The revenuers didn't appreciate Bobby's creative sense of humor. He had evaded arrest earlier by feeding the evidence to his hogs. (Photo courtesy of Dick and Georgianna Parker.)

After a few such trips, the fight was on. Drinking was allowed, but discouraged inside the schoolhouse. They didn't want fights to interrupt the dancing. Even so, unruly party-goers occasionally left through a closed schoolhouse window.

Although moonshine was his chief moneymaker, Bobby spent considerable time helping his neighbors, and he continued to raise livestock.

He had three or four cows, and decided he wanted to increase his herd. When Albert Campbell came riding by his place, he flagged him down and asked if he could use an OX bull to service his cows. Albert said that would be fine, if Bobby would drive it in. When he was finished with the bull, Bobby drove him back into the OX pasture. The bull had other ideas. He repeatedly walked through Bobby's fence to graze the greener pasture. Finally Bobby lost his patience and grabbed his gun. What happened next has been disputed. Some say he killed the bull. Others say he shot off one of the bull's horns, and the semi-polled animal quickly decided to graze elsewhere. Whatever happened, the OX strain in Bobby's herd was probably limited to that one year.

Bobby was an ambitious character and almost everything he did generated colorful stories. Those stories don't always illustrate the gentle, helpful side of his personality. Those who remember him were children or teenagers when he was at his peak. They remember an energetic little man who began every sentence with, "My goodness." Margaret Robertson Lindgren, who grew up on Rocky Comfort, described him as, ". . . a good little fellow. Such a good neighbor to everybody."

As a result, the community was surprised and saddened to hear that the revenuers finally caught him. Bobby built a still on Flat Creek, and the smoke from his wood fire caught their attention. They were investigating because someone, most likely one of Bobby's out-of-town cousins, filed a complaint. After arresting Bobby, they broke the still and scattered the mash.

The dust had barely settled in their tire tracks, when Ord Geist hurried to the still and began scooping mash off the ground. He was determined to make and sell a batch, so that Bobby could make bail.

The judge sentenced Bobby to a six-month term in the penitentiary. Bobby asked his neighbors to look after Anthony, who was having mental problems, and he left for Boise. When he arrived someone asked, "What are you in for?"

"Bootlegging," he replied.

"Well, you'll have plenty of company," the man assured him.

The sentence couldn't have come at a worse time. With the advice of a Council banker, Bobby had sold all his hogs and purchased sheep. They would be much easier to drive, explained the banker. Not knowing much about sheep, Bobby purchased a flock of gummer ewes. Without teeth they couldn't eat, and the whole herd died.

The penitentiary put a damper on his second source of income, so he lost his place and emerged from jail owing $2,600 to his creditors.

Another tragedy struck while Bobby was behind bars. Anthony began having horrible hallucinations that bugs were attacking him. Neighbors put him on a bed of hay, and hauled him into town. Anthony never returned.

Rather than dwell on his misfortunes, Bobby immediately went to work after his release. He moved to a place above Lafferty Camp and set up a whole new system of stills. This time he used kerosene burners, which eliminated the tattletale smoke. Through moonshine sales, he gradually paid his $2,600 debt, and he bought a '27 or '28 Chevrolet pick-up to make deliveries. Steady sales enabled him to purchase a sportier delivery vehicle, and he chose a blue and black Chevy roadster with a rumble seat.

Bobby continued to bootleg even after Prohibition was repealed in 1933. He was close to eighty and he could barely see when Bert Warner, his brother, Clarence Warner, and Dick Parker logged around his place. He took Bert aside, told him where the still was, and asked him to be careful. Bert never could find it.

When Bert was fourteen he started riding with his Uncle Charley Warner. Whenever possible, they stopped at a neighbor's house for their mid-day break. As a result, Bert became acquainted with several Windy Ridge moonshiners.

They liked to eat at Frank Wall's cabin by the Azurite mine. Albert eventually bought his place, which came with a grazing permit.

Frank Wall was most famous for his ability to aggravate people. He once invited a late-arriving guest to use his pasture. He neglected to mention, however, that his "pasture" was unfenced. The unlucky soul spent most of the day scrambling over seemingly endless stretches of steep ground before he found his horse. Wall and his horses are standing in Cuprum. (Photo courtesy of Becky Dunnington Hall.)

Wall's kitchen wasn't too clean, but he served a good meal. Conversation usually flowed to his favorite topic: aggravating people.

He loved to tell about a man who rode by his cabin one evening. When Wall invited him to stay the night, the man accepted gratefully. He crawled off his horse, unsaddled it, and asked where he could pasture it. Wall answered casually, "Just turn him loose here."

The man slipped off the bridle, looked around, and a worried look crossed his face. "How big is this pasture?" he asked.

"Oh," Wall said, "The Snake River is on one side and Charley Warner's on the other."

The man probably had the opportunity to see plenty of territory before he found his horse.

Wall loved to needle Sam Rolphin, who owned the store at Homestead, Oregon. If pressed far enough, Rolphin reacted with absurd, but explosive threats.

Waiting until the store was jammed with people, Wall sidled in and started his attack. Picking up a random item he shouted, "Why, this price is too damned high! I can send away to the Safeway in Weiser and get it for fifty cents less."

His next target was the cheese. "Look at this mold," he broadcast, "Safeway would never sell moldy cheese."

Rolphin, who struggled to keep his cool, invariably exploded after a few well placed comments. His patience snapped instantly, however, when Wall offered in-store comparison shopping.

Once he ordered a ham from Safeway, picked it up at Homestead's railroad station, and brought it directly to Rolphin's crowded store. The customers grouped around him when he unwrapped the ham and described how good it tasted. "You'll never find a ham like this in Rolphin's store. Better send to Safeway."

At this, Rolphin blew up. He threatened to shoot Wall, and when the threats reached a level of mad desperation, the agitator and his ham left.

Wall's greatest fame came from his habitual thievery. He packed enormous loads of tools and machinery from mines, both active and abandoned. If he found a neighbor's still, he'd cart it off. Most of his hoard was stashed in and around his cabin, making it look like the nest of a very large pack rat.

Wall had a flock of chickens, and he decided he would feed them with the neighbor's grain. He traveled down the Indian Creek side of Windy Ridge until he came to the place, walked in the barn, and left with a 100 pound sack of wheat on his shoulder.

"The guys, they started shooting at me," he told Charley and Bert in his syncopated accent. "I just run like a son of a bitch up that hill with the wheat on my shoulder."

Tales of Wall's thievery reached Paul Bunyan proportions. One story tells of a blacksmith shop that was abandoned after the Kleinschmidt Grade was completed. A passerby was startled when he saw the building shake and move. "It's nothing," his companion reassured him. "That's just Wall packing it off."

Wall carried his brew to the Cuprum dances. He poured the potent stuff into quart mason jars, bundled them in a sack, and he was off to the party.

If he still felt enterprising on the return trip, he might scout out the homestead above his, which belonged to Frank McCann. On a lucky night, he would locate McCann's still, dismantle it, and cram his sack with copper coils and other bootlegging paraphernalia. There was nobody he loved to aggravate more than this neighbor.

McCann did his part to fuel the feud. He was also a practiced still thief, and he could hurl insults with enough sting to penetrate Wall's thick hide.

The two men only stopped squabbling during major holidays, and it was a grudging truce. The men were nearly always invited to the same family celebration, and while they were most cordial to their hosts, they carefully maintained an icy, but silent hostility toward each other.

McCann was another Windy Ridge neighbor Charley and Bert liked to visit while they were riding for cattle, although it was best to avoid him at lunchtime. Dirt didn't bother him, so he didn't bother dirt.

The Warners rode by one afternoon and the old bachelor was so eager for company, that they stopped. He insisted upon making a snack, and young Bert was fascinated as he watched McCann knead and shape the biscuits. The only clean spots on his body were his hands, where the sticky biscuits peeled off the grime.

He offered his guests some cider, which he kept in a tin bucket. They drank sparingly, but even so they later became deathly sick. The cider's acid dissolved the tin, which is a fatal poison.

McCann had a crippled hand which he hid behind his back, except when he played his fiddle at the Bear Creek dances. He played beautifully when he wasn't peddling a little whiskey. He was friendly, but he refused to talk about himself.

Albert Campbell's focus during the Prohibition era sharply contrasted with that of his neighbors. He used the time to quietly build a foundation for his ranch. During the early Twenties he curtailed expansion, focusing on building the herd, and improving his relationship with the fledgling Forest Service instead.

All OX Ranch ground, past and present, fell within the Weiser National Forest which was established in 1910. Several years passed before the Forest Service formulated a workable set of objectives and created grazing allotments.

Homesteaders who were used to unlimited, unrestricted grazing on the open range resented the governing body. Charley Warner's feelings on the subject were echoed by most area ranchers. He hated the Forest Service and didn't try to mask his feelings. He wasn't about to let an ignorant, college-educated government employee tell him how to run his cattle. Whenever possible, he ignored Forest Service directives, and stubbornly retained full control of his herd size and grazing schedule.

Charley's actions were largely applauded by his peers. Even so, fighting the system cost him. As the years passed, the Forest Service whittled away sizable chunks of his grazing permit.

Albert, who was a fiercely independent Republican, didn't want his business run by the government either, but he was foresighted enough to realize two things. First, the range was being overgrazed in the old system, and if the practice was allowed to continue, the range would be ruined for future use. Second, he realized obstinacy wouldn't make the Forest Service go away. If he wanted to maintain control of his ranch, he would need to cultivate a mutually helpful working relationship with the agency.

Albert summarized the Forest Service's progress in a "statement of range conditions," which was found among his personal papers:

> I figure the hardest times we have ever had to run stock was from about 1900 until the creation of the national forests. Sheep were taking the country, coming right down to the ranch. Since the forests were created, much has been done in the way of management of stock on the range, and the protection to the communities.
>
> It's true that the forests are not carrying the number of stock that they did when the national forests were created, but I feel that this is not due to deterioration of the range, but the cause has been the controlling of fires, which has allowed large areas of young timber to take the place of the grass, and, after all, the principal reason for creating the national forests was to grow timber and protect the watersheds.

> While the operation costs on the national forests
> have materially increased, I feel that enough has
> been accomplished to more than offset the increase.
> I feel that one of the greatest accomplishments that
> has been made is the allotting of range. As it used
> to be before the forests were created everybody was
> endeavoring to get there first, and much damage
> was done by this method of handling.

Although Albert fundamentally agreed with the agency's goals,
his association with the Forest Service had its strained moments
through the decades. No specific stories emerged out of either the
surviving OX or Forest Service correspondence, but letters from
several different eras contained tight-lipped passages indicating
the two locked horns over the years.

The Forest Service was still in its developmental stages in the
Twenties, and the rangers undoubtedly found Albert's unique
spirit of cooperation refreshing. His attitude was rewarded. He
entered the 1920s with 590 cattle running on an exclusive use
permit that included a Bear/Indian Creek allotment, Rocky
Comfort, and a Wildhorse/Crooked River allotment.

By 1928 he had increased his herd by over a third, and the
Forest Service obligingly expanded his permit and issued a
distribution/salting plan. Starting on the Snake River, the 805
cattle grazed Azurite Gulch, Windy Ridge, Indian Creek, Elk
Creek, and Sheep Rock, entering each area as soon as the forage
was ready. After June 16, the herd was divided and placed on the
following summer ranges: 100 head on Steves Creek; 300 on Lick,
Deer, Cow, and Fawn Creeks and Gladhart Gulch; 100 in Summit
Gulch; and 300 on Bear Creek. In time, Albert acquired land in
and around that impressively widespread permit.

Albert never let expansion ideas drift far from his thoughts, and
with the future in mind, he asked his youngest brother, Loyal, to
homestead a 640-acre tract at the mouth of Salt Creek. It
adjoined the MacPherson ranch Albert had purchased a few years
before.

Loyal was close to twenty-two years old when he filed on the
homestead, and the first order of business was building a one-

Dressed to the nines, Campbell brothers Albert, Rollie, and Loyal meet the celebration head-on. (Photo courtesy of Charlotte Campbell Armacost.)

room, fourteen by sixteen foot cabin. He helped build the single board walls from lumber salvaged from an old house down river.

Once the house was constructed, Loyal set up his bedstead on the porch. Most river dwellers practiced this custom, hoping to catch any breeze straying through the sweltering canyon. The bed filled the porch completely, creating an obstacle course for anyone trying to enter the house.

During the winter the bed was squeezed into a space between the stove and other furnishings. He constantly stoked the cook-stove with thorn bushes and willows, but the thin-walled cabin let much of the heat seep outside.

Drinking and wash water had to be carried from Salt Creek, and a luxurious bath in the hot spring saved lots of time and effort.

Loyal wasn't much of a cook, so when the fruit trees in the old MacPherson orchard started to bear, he came close to foundering on apples, peaches, pears, and cherries. Occasionally his friend and neighbor, Jim Wright, took pity on him and stirred together a large batch of gift chili. More often than not, Loyal would happen by Wright's house just about suppertime.

His cooking woes were over when he brought his bride, Mary Levengood Campbell, to the house in 1923. She cheerfully relieved Loyal of all his domestic burdens, although whenever possible she saddled her horse and helped with the riding.

Grocery shopping was one of her more unconventional tasks. Once a month she made a list and gave it to the baggage man, Mike Malone, who saw that her order was filled. The train came into Copperfield, Oregon, twice a week and provided the local population with a much appreciated link to Weiser.

Mary and Loyal usually scheduled their trips to Homestead on train days. If they timed it right, they could flag down the locomotive, and ride the four miles between the town and their rowboat landing on the Oregon side.

The tracks passed through a mile-long tunnel, which is now submerged by water from the Oxbow dam. Since the train schedule was irregular, the Campbells always tried to detect its arrival by putting an ear to the track. The method wasn't always accurate. On more than one occasion they had to press themselves against the tunnel's rock wall while the train thundered past.

The couple worked indirectly for the OX Ranch. The ranch's books don't clarify the working relationship, but their efforts strengthened the link between the Wildhorse and Salt Creek ranches.

The MacPherson ranch was the first to be hayed, and the two became part of the haying crew. The place had a one-room house with a sizable cellar, which Mary transformed into a productive kitchen.

During the winter Albert divided his herd into as many as three groups. He never adopted a set pattern for winter feeding; the yearly plan changed according to hay supplies and characteristics of the herd. As a general rule, he wintered most of the cattle in No Business Basin, and the overflow was driven to the

MacPherson place. If there wasn't enough feed there, they were herded across the Snake River into Pine Valley where Albert contracted for their feed and care.

Loyal helped distribute and feed the cattle, and one spring he had to shovel a path before they could reach upper country grazing. Heavy snowfall characterized that particular winter, and the trails were blocked with snowdrifts.

The couple's roles as Snake River homesteaders lasted only a couple of years. As soon as they fulfilled the homestead requirements and became the property's legal owners, they transferred ownership to Albert. In trade, they received a ranch in New Meadows.

Throughout his life Albert funneled all his energy and thoughts into one entity: the cattle business. He never pursued any hobbies, nor did he enjoy diversions. "He went to a dance once in a while, when he couldn't get out of it," his sister Carrie remembered. "He liked girls and children, but didn't seem to have the time for them."

It was highly improbable, but the thirty-three-year-old who was happily set in his ways found one diversion. Her name was Grace Lufkin. She was Council's new schoolteacher, and she boarded in a brick hotel.

The hotel was completely full one evening when Albert asked to rent a room. Albert was a valued customer, so the innkeeper bustled upstairs to see about shuttling boarders. Grace agreed to share a room with another teacher, so she quickly gathered her night things and vacated the room. Sometime during the exchange Albert and Grace were introduced.

She was an attractive woman, but Albert wasn't particularly interested in conformation. He was more taken by her intelligence and independence. During their brief conversation, he sensed she had uncommon emotional and moral strength.

The next morning Grace found a box of candy on her dresser. An invitation to the weekend dance followed, but she had to decline. Dances frequently turned into drunken brawls and the school board, fearing guilt by association, forbade its teachers to attend.

As a compromise measure, Albert took Grace to dinner in the

restaurant below the hotel. She wasn't feeling well, so she ordered corn flakes. Her date gallantly insisted on buying her dinner—all ten cents' worth. Grace later claimed Albert courted her because he thought he'd found a bargain.

As they became more acquainted, Albert learned his school-teacher was almost ten years his junior. She and an older sister were raised in a small, progressive Nebraska town, where her father was a merchant.

By the time Grace was sixteen, both parents were dead. Her aunt, Cora Lufkin, invited her to finish high school in Long Beach, California. She spent her vacations in Walla Walla, Washington, where her paternal grandparents lived.

Her parents had left a small inheritance; there was just enough for a college education. Grace opted to attend the University of Nebraska, where she excelled. She became a member of the Alpha Chi Omega sorority, and was elected to the Phi Beta Kappa honorary.

As graduation approached, Grace faced some tough decisions. Most graduates, especially the women, chose jobs located close to their network of family and friends. This option didn't suit Grace. While traveling between Nebraska, California, and Washington, she had become fascinated with life "out west." After researching job opportunities, she found a teaching vacancy in Council, Idaho—a town full of western flavor. She didn't know a soul in Council; the move would put her hundreds of miles from all of her friends and family. She jumped at it.

"Several people said that Mom was ahead of her time. She was a business woman and she wasn't afraid to travel," said her daughter, Charlotte Campbell Armacost.

Her career and her courtship had at least one thing in common: they presented a challenge.

The courtship had its exuberant, care-free moments when Albert tied the family's Swedish sleigh bells to the cutter, and showed Grace his favorite spots. It's probable he also told her crucial facts about those places: the number of cattle they would support and if the area's predominant grass made good forage.

"Mother had other men interested in her, but Dad fascinated her," said their daughter, Charlotte.

Albert and Grace emerge from their wedding on August 24, 1924. They were married in Walla Walla, Washington in the home of Grace's grandparents. (Photo courtesy of Charlotte Campbell Armacost.)

There were also stressful moments. Grace leased a horse at the livery stable, but she never rode. She liked to bring the animal treats and talk to it while she rubbed its neck. Someone told Albert his girl was leasing a horse, and suggested he bring down one of the ranch horses. Albert surprised her with a new mount, and suggested they go for a ride. No sooner was she in the saddle, when the horse took off at a dead run. Even after Albert caught up to her and stopped the horse, she maintained a death grip on the horn and a wide-eyed, terrified expression. Albert started laughing and he continued to laugh about the incident throughout their fifty-five-year marriage. She refused to ride again.

The couple had a major obstacle to navigate before their relationship could progress: Grace had to win approval from Albert's sister. By that time, Carrie had married Dr. Robert Whiteman and was living in Cambridge. Grace passed Carrie's penetrating scrutiny, so the couple eventually became engaged.

The wedding took place August 24, 1924 at her grandparents' home in Walla Walla.

From the start, their relationship was based on mutual respect and admiration rather than hearts and flowers. This was evident even during the honeymoon. Religion was a fundamental part of Grace's life, whereas Albert wasn't a church-goer. It took masterful negotiation, but the Albert Campbells attended church together the first Sunday they were married. Grace, in turn, spent most of the following day at a bull sale.

When they returned to New Meadows, Albert resumed his non-stop schedule. When his cowboys, or boys, as he called them, slapped him on the back in congratulations he grinned as he down-played the occasion. "The trip to Walla Walla wasn't a complete waste of time," he said repeatedly, "I picked up some good bulls at the sale."

Albert moved his bride into the family home in New Meadows. His father had built the big ranch and a big house to match. He reasoned his children and their spouses would stay, making one big happy family. It didn't quite work that way.

When Grace moved in, Albert's mother was still lady of the house, and Rollie's wife, Marguerite, was very definitely second in command. Having no place in the pecking order grew old quickly, and Grace asked Albert for a separate house.

She was persistent in her request, and Albert agreed with her logic, but never did anything about it. When she tried to pin him to a time line, he became vague.

The situation became intolerable after their daughter, Alberta, was born in 1925. Grace and the baby moved into a tent pitched outside the house, but the move failed to spur Albert into action. The next tactic took a lot of spunk: she rented a room at the Meadows Valley Hotel.

Albert became concerned when he came home from a business trip, and couldn't find his family. His father revealed their wherabouts and admonished, "You had better get that woman under control."

Grace had finally made her point. It was then that Albert bought their life-long home on Heigho Avenue in New Meadows.

He later told her that he admired her determination and resourcefulness during the ordeal.

Although Grace had no particular interest in the "hands-on" aspects of the cattle business, she proved to be an invaluable help to Albert throughout their marriage. Albert taught her how to keep books for both the OX and the Circle C, and her attention to detail provided an anchor for Albert, whose mind was always racing ahead to the next project. And since he was managing both ranches, there were an overwhelming number of projects to consider.

Wanting to promote the beef industry on a higher level, he became president of the Idaho Cattleman's Association (ICA) in 1924, a position he held until 1937. He also presided over the Idaho Wool Growers Association and Idaho Cattle and Horse Growers Association from 1927–1929. These groups, particularly ICA, became politically influential, and much of the credit goes to Grace, who made sure Albert saw important messages and sent immediate replies.

The surviving business files from this period are filled with yellowed, duplicate correspondence. Albert usually used a pencil to draft the rough copy. A carbon of Grace's typewritten version, which omits occasional spelling errors, is efficiently clipped to the draft.

While Grace juggled the files, Albert ran the ranch, and his

Grace Campbell and her infant daughter, Alberta, set up housekeeping in the Meadows Valley Hotel. Grace refused to move until Albert agreed to buy a separate residence. The hotel has since burned. (Photo courtesy of the Idaho State Historical Society.)

plans were progressing splendidly. He shared the good fortune with his help. His top hand, Bill Clark, was paid $100 monthly, and Claude Childers' wages skyrocketed from forty dollars in 1920 to seventy dollars in 1923.

Albert was particular about his help; he wanted them to possess the same qualities he looked for in a friend: judgment, ambition, honesty, and trustworthiness. He couldn't tolerate people who were "not too heavy," his expression for someone who wouldn't work. He hired people who were sharp enough to manage things for extended periods, as they were essential to Albert's roving style of management.

A young man who met Albert's standards rode into the Basin one spring afternoon in the mid-Twenties. He hadn't finished eighth grade, and he needed a pair of boots, but he had a one-eyed grey mare, and he was ready to work. His name was Dick Armacost.

When Dick was six, his father died. His mother moved the family to Cambridge, where she struggled to provide her children with a solid home and education. Dick grew weary of the education part; he longed to be working outside. When his mother remarried, his feelings intensified.

This worried his mother, and when a financially sound relative from Salt Lake City invited Dick to finish his schooling there, she didn't hesitate.

Excited about the challenge, Dick's uncle immediately began efforts to citify his young charge. A shopping trip yielded a new suit of clothes, which Dick sold at the first opportunity to obtain passage home.

Determined to pursue his ambition, he crawled on his old, gift horse, and set off to find work. He thought he'd seek out his brother, Bailey, who worked on the OX Ranch. He'd been told the ranch was "up Wildhorse," so not knowing about any trails, he reined his horse into the riverbed and experienced the ride of his life.

The river was boiling with spring runoff, and wave after wave washed over the boy and his mount. How the horse maintained its footing is a mystery.

When the pair arrived in the Basin, both were drenched and the horse had thrown three shoes. Claude Childers' brother, Shorty, said he would have never believed it if he hadn't seen it with his own eyes. The ride made Dick somewhat of a celebrity.

Albert liked what he saw in the boy, but he respected Mrs. Armacost's regard for education. Dick was hired under one condition: he had to finish the eighth grade. After a year in the Brownlee schoolhouse, he focused on becoming Albert's top hand.

The ranch had received another boost when Fitz Mink rode into the Basin in 1921, asking for part-time work. He was also helping his grandfather and uncle run their place on Hornet Creek.

Fitz's knack with horses and uncanny roping skills quickly earned him a permanent position on the Campbell ranches. Albert shuttled him between the OX and Circle C for years, and the tradition continued with his son, Herb, and his grandson, Myron.

After a stint with the Circle C, Fitz returned to the OX in 1928. This time his wife and year-old son accompanied him.

Albert asked him to train an uncooperative, but promising bay gelding. The horse liked to leap sideways just as the rider was mounting. Those who weren't familiar with the bay's trick found themselves standing in the air. Fitz put his left foot in the stirrup and, anticipating the leap, threw his weight to the right. The strategy didn't work. He found himself on the ground. When he looked up, he saw Albert with a large grin on his face and a sharp stick in his hand. He had poked the horse, making it leap to the left.

After Fitz had ridden the gelding for awhile, he wasn't too eager to give it up. Albert came by Salt Creek one day and asked for his horse. Albert was gone for just an hour and a half when he rode back into camp and pulled off his saddle. Fitz added the horse to his string, and it became a favorite.

Fitz's wife taught school at Bear Creek two years. One of her former students said she was "kind of cranky, but a good teacher." Then he got a glint in his eye and offered some insights into her crankiness. While under her supervision, students learned that stuffing the stove pipe with wet gunny sacks insured a shortened school day. Students and smoke billowed out of the door at the same time.

The Minks' young son, Herb, learned some of life's fundamental lessons on the OX. He was quickly potty trained when his mother made a practice of dunking his wet bottom in the cold spring at Lick Creek.

He also received a spanking from Albert. The crime? He was playing with a live rattlesnake on Barbour Flat. He made a game of dragging the snake by its tail.

Rattlesnakes were rarely befriended in No Business Basin, which almost became a Childers family operation in the Twenties. Claude's brothers, J.B. "Shorty," and Roy "Boo" joined the ranks. Shorty's wife, Ruth, cooked fine meals for the haying crew.

In the middle part of the decade, Claude brought a bride into the Basin, which made the Wildhorse grapevine buzz for years. Dora was an attractive redhead from Buhl, Idaho, who brought a new element into the Wildhorse community: high fashion.

The rugged, modest lifestyle in Wildhorse put limits on female vanity. Ladies contented themselves with a white dress for ice cream socials and perhaps a bauble or two. Every day was Sunday to Dora. She even wore a corset, a ridiculous vanity for a rancher's wife who might be needed to buck bales or milk cows.

Years after Dora left the ladies were still shaking their heads. Darline Whiteley, who was a small child when she moved into the Basin in the mid-Thirties, remembered the conversations: "She cinched herself up like a darn horse," was one of the more descriptive comments.

Dora eventually became disenchanted with the Basin, and she urged Claude to find work in Council. He reluctantly obliged, and found work in the hardware store, but the marriage dissolved.

The community was shocked again when they heard Tom Clark drowned in the Snake River while swimming. Tom, who was Bill Clark's brother, occasionally hired on with the OX during busy times.

Someone discovered his clothes on the Oregon side, but there was no trace of the body. Bert Vaughn, who then owned the ranch at the mouth of Wildhorse, proposed they try to raise the body with underwater dynamite charges. Since he had experience with the explosives, he volunteered his services.

Vaughn, who was in one of the two dynamite laden rowboats, was directing the operation when the caps under his seat somehow caught fire. The man in the second boat had the presence of mind to throw his caps overboard, before Vaughns' boat blew. Vaughn miraculously survived the explosion, but he lost his eyes and nearly lost his legs.

The tragedy compounded when diabetes forced doctors to remove Mrs. Vaughn's legs a short while later. The family had no alternative but to sell the ranch, and move to Halfway, Oregon. Neighbors later saw the couple at a fair. They had learned to merge their strengths. He was pushing her wheelchair, and she told him how to avoid obstacles.

Months after the accident Nina Nixon, the Vaughn's former neighbor, walked into the Weiser post office. As she stepped up to the window, she experienced a terrible shock. Tom Clark was staring back at her.

Clark, it was later explained, had left his wife for another woman. Wanting to avoid confrontation, he staged his own drowning. He left his clothes on the Oregon side, and swam across the river where his girlfriend was waiting with a change of clothes and a horse.

The community was incensed, and for weeks there were rumblings about lynching Clark. Eventually the clamor died down.

Heitho Speropulos knew few English words when this photograph was taken. Her daughter, Mary, was born shortly after the family moved to their ranch near Cuprum. Heitho was a bit leery of her remote surroundings, especially when a Greek-speaking sheepherder jokingly told her that mountain lions would snatch her baby away. (Photo courtesy of Heitho Speropulos.)

Four

HANGING TIGHT: THE 1930s

"My boy, Nick, should marry your daughter, Alberta. Then, for as far as you could see, it would be Speropulos and Campbell. Then old man Campbell would die, and as far as you could see, it would all be Speropulos."

—*George Speropulos to Albert Campbell*

The Greek bride swayed gently as she gazed out the train's window. For two days her eyes had searched the unfolding western landscape, but they had failed to find the land of opportunity described so vividly at home, in Greece. She had heard all Americans were rich people. Why, then, did all the houses look like shacks? "What have I gotten myself into?" she wondered as she glanced over at her brand-new husband.

Twenty-one-year-old Heitho had met George Speropulos a few weeks before. "He's a good man," her uncle assured her before their first meeting, "He always sends his parents money from the United States."

Speropulos, who was in his early thirties, had immigrated to the United States when he was fifteen. Landing first in Portland, Oregon, his business skills were honed as he held a variety of jobs, including a one-year stint at a paper mill.

A cousin, who had also immigrated from Greece, encouraged him to become a partner in a sheep venture. The partnership purchased 15,000 head of sheep, but poor management caused the investors to lose everything. Although Speropulos' monetary loss was small when compared to his later holdings, the event shaped the course of his life in two ways. First, he would never again enter a business partnership. Second, he'd found his niche: he wanted sheep of his own.

As the years passed, he accumulated experience and savings. He wanted to marry a woman who shared both his values and his Greek Orthodox religion before he started his own enterprise. He traveled to Greece to find her in 1928.

Heitho quickly accepted his proposal, relying solely on her uncle's endorsement and impressions gathered during their speedy courtship. There was barely time for a trousseau to be sewn before the wedding.

By the end of the arduous train journey, Heitho still didn't understand why her husband chose to herd sheep in Idaho, clear across the United States. Why not settle for one of the more convenient eastern states? Her puzzlement continued as he prepared to launch the business by purchasing a band of 3,500 sheep.

When he showed her the ranch he wanted to buy, she thought he had truly brought her to the end of the world. There was no school, no church, and no town, unless you counted the 100 renegade miners who lived in and around Cuprum. She cried when she saw the place.

At least the house was suitable; newspaper reporters called it "the palace of Hells Canyon." When she walked inside, she was surprised to see the house was still partly furnished. On the lower floor, the two bedroom suites had brass beds. The living room featured a huge fireplace, a massive rolltop desk, and a book collection. She thumbed through a few volumes, but the English words were meaningless. Judging from the few illustrations, most of them were history books.

French doors separated the living room from the dining room, and exploration of the kitchen revealed a pantry and a door that opened into a sizable woodshed.

Heitho ran her hand along the finely crafted wooden bannister as she stepped up to the second story. A long hallway bisected the floor, ending at a veranda. Six bedrooms and two baths opened onto it.

The third floor featured another kitchen and three more verandas. She walked back through the house, counting sixteen rooms, including the basement. "Everything is quality," she thought, drinking in previously unnoticed details. "This is how homes should be."

The couple owned the sheep free and clear, but buying the old Huntley place required financing. Ever since the stock market crashed on October 24, 1929, loans had become non-existent, and Speropulos tackled the problem in his usual shrewd manner. He marched into the Weiser bank, and presented an impressive business plan to the bank president. Speropulos estimated that

When the family's home burned, Heitho only had time to grab her children and a couple of treasured photographs. Seated are Mary, Heitho, George, and Nick Speropulos. George's brother, John, is standing. (Photo courtesy of Heitho Speropulos.)

between 2,500 and 3,000 lambs would be harvested from his flock in the fall. Livestock market activity indicated he would realize a healthy profit. Speropulos was persuasive, and the bank finally agreed to loan him $13,000.

While many ranchers were barely hanging on to their places, Speropulos steadily whittled away at the debt. The note was stamped "paid in full" in 1939.

The ranch was listed for $20,000, but the Speropulos' $14,000 offer was readily accepted. The deal had closed by January, 1930. When the couple moved into the house, their firstborn, Mary, was forty days old. Caring for the little girl and setting up the household kept Heitho busy, but she had her lonely moments.

The couple went to a few Bear schoolhouse dances, but it was impossible to become acquainted when she didn't speak the language.

She could visit with the sheepherders who came from the old country, but those conversations weren't always comforting. One ornery herder told her the area was full of rattlesnakes and cougars. The cougars, he warned her, were likely to snatch the baby out of her arms. Terrified, she questioned her husband at the first opportunity. "That's silly," he said. Before she could feel relieved he added, "The cougars would kill you first."

Despite the dire warnings, Heitho ventured outside to plant her garden that spring. Friends had given her seeds before she left Greece, so the vegetables and sweet basil reminded her of home.

It's likely she also planted a lovely purple and white flower, which blossoms like a sweet pea. Livestock won't eat the non-native plant, which has spread to hillsides miles from the Speropulos garden.

Its Latin name is *Salvia sclarea*, and since it has no common name, most locals call it Greek weed. The most descriptive name came from OX Cow Boss Frank Anderson, who, after sniffing the plants' delicate blossoms, decided Indian armpit was the most appropriate name.

Its vile, permeating odor has been used to make social statements. Amos Camp, a some-time OX cowboy and full-time character, once gathered a huge bouquet which he presented to a female foe in Cuprum.

A free spirit, Amos Camp reportedly told people, "I worked a year for the OX one summer." (Photo courtesy of the Bert Warner family.)

Like Heitho's garden, Speropulos' sheep venture flourished from the very start. The first crop of lambs sold for fifteen dollars a head, which made the Weiser bankers grin and the local, die-hard cattlemen clinch their teeth.

Speropulos was never quiet about his profits, particularly when a little crowing would raise some hackles. The crowning joy of any spectacular deal came when he told Charley Warner about it. Charley thought sheep were meadow maggots and the people who owned them were one step lower. Speropulos' victory trips developed a pattern: first Charley hotly denied that anyone could make that much money, and then he got mad. Speropulos wisely took his leave just as Charley's temper came to a rolling boil.

The famed profits were seriously dented one time when a herder lost 300 sheep to coyotes. The man was American, which prompted Speropulos to hire Greeks almost exclusively, until immigration quotas barred their entry.

His standard crew included two herders, who ran separate

bands, and a camp tender who ran a packstring between the camps, keeping them well supplied with food and medicine. This routine was followed while the grass lasted, usually from April 15 through most of November. In the fall, the old ewes were sold and replaced with yearlings, which lambed more efficiently.

During the early years they also hired a man to irrigate and harvest hay. He stayed in the barn, where the hay was stored.

Speropulos headed to Council every two weeks for groceries. Shopping list regulars included a case of eggs and a carton of oranges, both of which were divided among the herders. He also bought ham and other meat that would keep without refrigeration. A milk cow and a steady supply of fresh lamb kept the home place well supplied.

Sometime during their second summer on Indian Creek, Speropulos decided it was time for his wife to have a driving lesson. He ushered Heitho and the car into the middle of a pasture, explained the fundamentals, and left. Heitho spent hours lurching through the field by herself until she got the hang of it.

She tackled the language barrier with the same resoluteness. After their second child, Nick, was born, Heitho became even more determined to master English. Very little English was spoken in her isolated situation, so whenever they had a local dinner guest she struggled to make sense of the words. Consequently, the first phrase she timidly tried was, "Please pass the corn." Years of eavesdropping and a Greek/English dictionary gave her mastery of the language, although she never conquered its quirky spelling rules. "What does a 'K' have to do with the word 'knife?'" she asked.

Her children learned both languages and observed customs from both countries. Every year Heitho baked *kourbgedes*, a traditional Easter cookie. Greek Independence Day, March 25, was observed as well as the Fourth of July, although part of the American celebration shocked her. The neighbors who came for the lamb barbecue drank so much homemade beer, that they eventually passed out on the lawn.

Albert Campbell's visits were always anticipated. He loved to spar with Speropulos, giving him grief about his good-for-nothing flock, while eating every bite of his lamb supper. He would finish and ask how a no-account sheepman had ever won a woman like Heitho.

Die-hard cattle ranchers couldn't believe that he'd stoop to eating lamb. "I'm just helping reduce the sheep population," Albert reportedly explained.

Albert respected Speropulos' shrewdness. The sheepman believed that if you watched the pennies, the dollars would take care of themselves. Consequently, he never paid cash on the barrel. When he received a bill for, say, fourteen dollars and sixty-five cents, he paid it with a fourteen dollar check. Most of his creditors called the accounts even, figuring it wasn't worth the hassle to collect the spare change.

He used a similar principal when trailing his sheep over Albert's Windy Ridge Forest Service allotment. He allowed the flock to meander through the range for a few days, rather than bringing them directly to his allotment. Albert's cattle frequently and repeatedly visited the neighbors' pastures, but Albert refused to play host to Speropulos. His protests didn't remedy the situation, so the two men agreed to meet with Forest Service officials in Copperfield, Oregon.

Before the meeting started, Albert walked up to the bar, plunked down a twenty dollar bill, and ordered a round of drinks. Speropulos conspicuously palmed the bill, and slipped it in his pocket. When the bartender asked for payment, Albert reached for his billfold and pulled out another twenty. A young forest official asked, "Didn't you see Speropulos take that bill?"

"Speropulos has been stealing from me for years. I'm used to it."

Albert's point settled the debate. From then on, the sheep kept to the Kleinschmidt Grade.

In 1935, relatives from the old country announced they were coming for a visit. Hammers pounded, wallpaper was hung, and new dishes were chosen in an intense effort to revitalize the house. One evening, after a particularly exhausting day, a pile of wallpaper was thrown into the fireplace. The chimney caught fire and the couple barely had time to grab their children and a few family heirlooms on the way out.

The fire burned hot, and only a smoldering foundation

remained of their home the next morning. They unceremoniously moved into the adjacent garage and started again.

Speropulos pulled a carpenter, who had seven children, out of a bread line, and the family stayed through the winter, building the small house that still stands today.

Even though the ranch was on a little-traveled road, a steady stream of people who were hard-hit by the Depression knocked on the door, hoping to work in exchange for food. The experience shocked Heitho. Greece had its poverty class, but at least everyone had food.

Bear neighbors gather for a major undertaking: threshing. From left: Hershel Robsertson, Archie Bardmas, Bud Robertson, Harry S. Gum, Aus Grosclose, and Arthur Robertson. Albert Campbell bought many of their homesteads. (Photo courtesy of the Bert Warner family.)

She took pity on an older man with a sales approach. He promised to teach her conversational English and American cooking in exchange for his meals. He mostly ate and napped in his tent, but he did show her how to make banana cream pie with a lard and water crust. Under his supervision she also mastered macaroni and baked chicken.

Up the road a few miles, transients also tried to exchange work for board at the Herschel Robertsons, who lived on Rocky Comfort; but unless they happened by during spring planting or haying, they were out of luck.

Herschel was born in Alpine, Idaho, and raised in Bear, where his relations were pillars of the community. His dad, Arthur, operated a sawmill north of the schoolhouse, near Bert and Tina Warner's present-day home. He also provided the community with dental care—his most vital tool being a wicked-looking pair of forceps that extracted even the most firmly rooted teeth.

The dentist's cousin, William T. Robertson, ran the store and the post office. Bear's anonymous correspondent to the *Adams County Leader*, who proclaimed Robertson mayor, had a hot item in his news column in 1933. It seems His Honor found half of his prize chickens gone one morning, and he was convinced a Democrat had stolen them. A Republican, he reasoned to the reporter, would have taken all of them.

Herschel's bride, Hazel, came from the Cheyenne, Wyoming area, so she was familiar with a windy, treeless, and dry existence on the Rocky Comfort homestead.

The original 160-acre homestead had only ten acres of farmable ground. The rest was strewn with chunks of pock-marked igneous rock, evidence of the region's earlier volcanic activity. A twenty-head grazing permit from the Forest Service and a camouflaged still, somewhere on the breaks of Crooked River, provided the family with a living.

Eventually Robertson bought out three other homesteaders including Pug Robertson (his brother), August "Gus" Shirmer, and Frank Rippleman.

Pug, whose homestead was on the breaks of Crooked River, occasionally cowboyed for the OX.

Shirmer's place was on the west side of the road. He built a small barn and a granary, and batched—somewhat discontentedly—in a little shack.

The Robertsons' only child, Margaret, was fascinated when Shirmer took delivery on a fancy new Ford. It was one of the first automobiles she had ever seen, and the curtained windows and built-in flower vases awed the little girl.

When Shirmer wearied of his bachelor existence, and brought a mail order bride from Germany, young Margaret became an English tutor. Mrs. Shirmer was a tireless student, and the two spent hours over their makeshift textbook: a Montgomery Ward catalog.

Margaret remembers two elements dominated life on Rocky Comfort: hard work and loneliness. She was her dad's top hand, and her duties included maintaining their thirty to forty head of cattle and haying.

Haying was a community effort. Margaret spent the season racing between her duties in the field and in the kitchen, where she prepared meals for the ravenous crew.

She also helped care for their dryland garden, which boasted some of the world's best tasting potatoes. There was no way to irrigate the garden, so it produced just enough to feed the family.

Washing was taken to the well on the old Shirmer place, where they kept the boiler. Margaret got bored once when her mother and grandmother were doing the laundry, so she clambered up a tree by the well. She was reaching for another limb when she found herself face to face with a pair of beady, angry eyes. Margaret shinnied down the tree in record time, and the weasel rummaged in the bird's nest for another egg to suck.

Water was a major concern on Rocky Comfort. The wells were usually dry by July, which meant it was time to load barrels into the back of the wagon. They were then filled with stream water, bucket by bucket.

The most tedious and lonesome time of year was winter. An almost constant wind rattled the house and blew falling snow, until Margaret couldn't see her hand in front of her face at chore time. At night the coyotes howled, and the Robertson cow dogs answered. It was next to impossible to sleep during the canine chorus.

Visitors were rare, and the family spent winter evenings reading to themselves using coal oil lamps for light. Margaret's mother, Hazel, occasionally picked up a crochet hook or mended a tattered shirt.

Margaret's best friend was Bob, a shepherd/collie mix with a bobbed tail. He was a wonderful listener who kept secrets, and he loved to trail his mistress, whether she was doing chores or exploring the country on horseback.

She also had a pet magpie who could talk. The female bird loved to harass a frequent visitor, Harry Gum, a seasoned bachelor who lived on Flat Creek, near Barbour Flat. Agitation increased to an unbearable degree when Gum sold his place to Charley Warner, and made the Robertson household his base of operations. After that he had a constant, unwelcome companion. The magpie loved to sit on Harry's shoulder and pull on his beard, because nothing infuriated him more. He swatted and kicked her away, but it never seemed to daunt her. Just when he thought the coast was clear, he would glance down and find her untying his shoes.

One afternoon, he couldn't find his glasses. The more he searched, the angrier he became. Finally he burst out, "That magpie packed off my glasses."

When someone said, "But Harry, they're on top of your head," he was mad at the magpie for making him look foolish.

School provided Margaret with the only opportunity to be around other children. Her dad thought the five-mile horseback ride between the homestead and the Bear schoolhouse was too much for a little girl, so Margaret boarded with an aunt and uncle who lived at Brownlee, Oregon, until she was about ten.

It didn't take long for Margaret to conclude that watching her father spar with Albert Campbell was far more educational than school.

To Albert's business-oriented mind, the Depression created opportunity of unimaginable proportions. Both the OX and Circle C ranches experienced their most dramatic growth during this period, because the Campbells had cash reserves when most people were barely scraping by.

During the Depression, homesteaders' survival depended on one thing: cash money. In years past, they depended on moonshine and selling a cow or two for money enough to buy staple groceries and pay taxes.

Cattle sales failed to produce much revenue, since cattle prices plunged to the point that Union Pacific required cattle shippers to guarantee freight. Too often the cattle receipts didn't even cover shipping costs.

Moonshine profit grew spotty for two reasons. First, Prohibition's repeal in 1933 opened the market to large-scale entrepreneurs who made competition tough for those who operated out of the back of a Model T. Second, hardly anybody had money. A homesteader might swap a few chickens for a quart jar of shine, just as he paid doctor's bills with a deer's hind quarter, or offset his grocer's bill by trading sacks full of potatoes or parsnips.

The county, however, would not accept deer meat or produce. They demanded cash on the barrel, and if taxes were delinquent for three years, the property was auctioned on the courthouse steps, often for less than a dollar an acre.

Subsistence ranchers couldn't circumvent foreclosure with a bank loan. The already shaky institutions only granted loans to their most solid customers.

During the Thirties, the *Adams County Leader* featured page after page of delinquent tax notices, which Albert studied religiously. A series of successful bids stretched OX boundaries to include most of Windy Ridge and Barbour Flat, plus holdings in the Lick Creek drainage.

Some of the parcels were abandoned homesteads. Their owners assessed the situation as hopeless, and moved to take advantage of public assistance programs established by President Franklin D. Roosevelt in 1932.

Other landowners held on with every ounce of strength they could muster. For most, it was a losing battle, and they saw Albert Campbell as a vulture hovering overhead, waiting and hoping for their ranch to fail.

To be fair, Albert offered several ranchers their only choice besides foreclosure when he bought them out. Adams County records don't reveal the purchase prices, but Bert Warner remembers prices were shrewdly negotiated, but reasonable. As a child, Warner heard countless discussions about Albert's acquisitions in the area.

Other ranchers, like Herschel Robertson, saw no compassion in

Albert's actions and believed that he would one day be herding cattle in hell. Although it was probably unreasonable to think Albert would use his cash to keep his neighbors afloat, they thought it was unthinkable that he would scheme to push them over the edge.

Stories to that effect began to circulate through the region, and it is difficult to separate fact from fiction.

Almost everybody whose range adjoined Albert's reported he liked to crowd things a little bit. OX cattle tended to wander into other forest permits and they had an uncanny ability to "find" holes in neighbors' fences.

The crowding was used as an ultimatum at least once. Albert was riding across Barbour Flat with one of his hands when he stopped his horse in front of Bill Reynolds' one-room cabin.

Reynolds had weathered many seasons on the Flat and had told the *Adams County Leader* that, "Idaho has the world cheated for scenic beauty and summer climate, but it's hell in the winter." Even with the hard winters, Reynolds wanted to spend his remaining days on his place.

Albert and the hand ducked as they passed through Reynolds' low doorway and joined the old man for a cup of coffee. After general discussion about the weather and cattle prices, Albert focused on the visit's purpose. He raised his voice so the near-deaf Reynolds could understand his offer to buy the place.

Albert had made similar offers in the past, but Reynolds, who was a friendly sort, always turned him down. He explained that the Flat was his home. He admitted he couldn't get around as well as he used to, but he'd accumulated enough cattle and provisions to last until he died. He was rather looking forward to his semi-retirement years, he said.

Albert said that sounded fine, except most of the OX herd would be spending the summer on the Flat, and darned if he wasn't short-handed. He was sorry, but he strongly doubted his boys would be able to keep the fences up.

The conversation didn't last much longer. When Albert pushed away from the table, the OX Ranch was 160 acres larger. And an old man had so many tears streaming down his face that he couldn't see.

Marco Bernardi owned this typical Windy Ridge homestead. Although it had a majestic view, there was little relief from sweltering temperatures. (Photo courtesy of U.S. Forest Service.)

The hand felt so bad, he wanted to crawl through a crack in the floor. "If this is what it takes to get rich," he thought, "then I'll never be rich."

Then there was Joe Smith. His real name was Marco Bernardi, but the Austrian thought the other name was easier to pronounce. He ran a few head of cattle, and raised his own hay for winter feeding.

Albert reportedly stopped by one day with a proposal. Jotting a few figures on paper, he showed Smith it would be more profitable to sell his herd and concentrate on a hay crop. Albert, who was the major hay buyer in the area, said he could use the extra hay.

Bernardi sold his herd, quickly spent the cash, and lived quite happily for a couple of years. He was forced to sell his place when Albert didn't need his hay one year.

Albert never acknowledged these transactions in any correspondence or subsequent interviews; however, a situation along the same vein indicates a more rational approach. Albert wrote the following letter to Frank Husak, who owned a homestead on Windy Ridge:

> While I was at Salt Creek a few days ago, the boys told me that your fence was pretty badly down. In fact, someone has taken the wire off from some of it. Consequently, my cattle fed it off partly while they were on the Rome place, before we put them on the forest the third of April.
>
> I am enclosing a check for fifty dollars for rental for the entire season of 1934, and if you care to accept it, I shall try to use the rest of the grass this fall when the cattle come off the forest.
>
> Please endorse the check under the notation on the back and it will do for a lease. If for any reason you do not want to let me have the place, you may return the check.

Albert tested most of the area ranchers, and they earned his respect when they matched wits with him.

Herschel Robertson was no exception. He wouldn't stand for Albert's shenanigans, but he loved a chance to reciprocate. It was difficult to get under Albert's hide, but Herschel did it with just three words: Black Angus bull. He casually mentioned that he had decided to crossbreed his cattle, and Albert came unglued.

Albert was a devout Hereford man who could think of nothing more horrifying than a bunch of black calves with white faces. And since Forest Service permits had no fences, that's exactly what he would have.

Albert casually explained why an Angus bull would be the ruination of Herschel's herd, but his arguments were dismissed. Sputtering, he tried to make a stronger argument. Finally, he begged Herschel not to introduce the black bull, and he promised free use of his bulls, which always had top blood lines. Herschel had won a round with Albert, and he got to improve his herd. That was a day worth remembering.

Shortly after that, Margaret Robertson married Raymond Lindgren and left the ranch. Her dad suffered complications from a ruptured appendix, and died a few years later. Hazel was eager to leave Rocky Comfort, but she refused to sell to Albert. Leasing the place to Deb Shaw seemed a good temporary plan, until a buyer could be located.

Mention Deb's name to any of his old acquaintances, and without fail they shake their heads and roll their eyes. He gave new meaning to the term "local color."

Deb was born on Hornet Creek, and he held a variety of jobs in the area. Early in his career he was a hard rock miner, working with his father in the Seven Devils. Once they set off a dynamite charge, waited, and nothing happened. When Deb went up to investigate, the explosives blew, filling one of his eye sockets with loose rock.

Having one eye didn't handicap him during his short tenure as an OX cowboy. Dick Armacost was always amused by his morning routine. Before he crawled out of his bedroll, he stuck his hat on his head, struck a match across the bottom of his bare foot, and lit a cigarette.

He loved to agitate Albert, and the perfect opportunity surfaced in Council. Albert had parked his car and left the keys in the ignition, which was standard procedure. Deb crawled in, started the car, and parked it in front of the fire hydrant. He then combed the town until he found the sheriff. Deb indignantly told him about Albert's "infraction" and watched as the sheriff wrote out the ticket. Before the ink was dry, Deb parked the car back in its original place.

Another time, Albert came into town with three of his crew. Albert was not a drinker, so he hit the sack while the others imbibed. They were short of cash and decided Albert could be persuaded to finance the rest of their party. Deb led the way to Albert's room, and while the men held him down, he cut a sash cord and tickled Albert on his feet and up his nose until he agreed to write a fifty dollar check. Deb had a knack for finding vulnerable spots.

Deb took a bride in 1936; the woman had been teaching in Bear. The newlyweds lived in a cabin on Indian Creek that needed

Deb Shaw captures a "delicacy" which will soon be bound for an eastern restaurant. Deb and his rattlesnakes mesmerized theatre-goers for a time; a documentary revealed his techniques. (Photo courtesy of Mike Bledsoe.)

to be winterized by chinking the cracks with mud. When it looked like they were finished, Deb asked his wife to go inside and check for any holes they might have missed. She found a sizable hole in one corner and called, "I see some daylight over here."

"Where?" asked Deb.

She moved closer, "Over here, in the corner."

"Where?" he asked.

"Right here," she shouted, putting her face right up to the crack. Before she could shut her mouth, a handful of mud came sailing through the hole. At that moment, the honeymoon was probably over.

When the couple moved to Rocky Comfort, Deb was able to pursue a favorite and lucrative occupation: rattlesnake hunting. After milking the live snake for venom, he tossed it into a fifty-gallon barrel. When the barrel was full of snakes, he shipped them back east, where exclusive restaurants served the delicacy.

Members of the Warner family and a few neighbors found a sunny spot to stage this winter group portrait. Back row: Lawrence Warner, a Pyser boy, Mavis Warner, Eva Shelton Warner, Toby Warner, Charley Warner, and Clarence Warner. Front row: another Pyser boy, Bert Warner, Joe Warner, and John Sprowls. (Photo courtesy of the Bert Warner family.)

Someone made a film about Deb and his snake operation, which was shown at the Council movie theater before the feature presentations. The audience followed Deb as he crept into a cave and calmly gathered a sack full of rattlers. The movie impressed and sometimes horrified theater-goers, especially when he admitted he had been bitten, but knew how to squeeze the poison out.

His wife didn't share his enthusiasm for the creatures, and he liked to toy with her fear. He once filled a gunny sack with three or four snakes and set it outside the kitchen screen door. After backing off a few paces, he shouted for her to come outside. She hit the door at a run, and when the swinging door jarred the snakes, the rattling sounded like instant death. She was so petrified, she couldn't move.

While he was on the Rocky Comfort place, he ran hogs in the National Forest, which was strictly prohibited. Albert finally complained to the authorities, and Deb was ordered to remove the hogs. He became vengeful. A few days later, Albert's dog decided to tour Rocky Comfort. Deb demonstrated his feelings about trespassing animals by grabbing the dog, forcing its mouth open, and pinching off its fang teeth. He allowed the dog to stagger home and deliver the message.

Albert rarely seemed to have tangles with the Warner clan. He had an unusual respect for them; perhaps he identified with their strong family ties. When some homesteaders, who were relative latecomers, asked him why he crowded everyone except the Warners, he reportedly answered, "They were here before I was, and that gives them certain privileges."

He offered to buy out the Warners, and he particularly wanted a forty-acre parcel on Windy Ridge that was completely surrounded by OX Depression acquisitions. He never got that or any other Warner property.

Charley Warner's Forest Service permit ran from the top of Smith Mountain to Bear Creek. When it was at its largest, the permit also included Deep Creek, Red Ledge, Lime Point, and a piece of ground that ran from the Snake River to the top of Horse Mountain.

Calving usually occurred on the home place, in the large pasture in front of the house. The area was carefully fenced, and all the pine trees sporting low boughs were trimmed, since cows abort their calves if they eat green pine needles.

Having the cattle winter on the main hayfield had two advantages. First, the field was naturally fertilized. Second, the hay could be cut and stacked right in the field, with stout fences surrounding the haystacks, keeping the animals from devouring their winter feed.

Charley occasionally wintered his cattle along the Snake River at Big Bar, which was also a productive hay field. The location's mild winters and early springs appealed to the cattleman, plus the location created a natural grazing pattern. When the bunch grass surrounding Big Bar grew to about four inches high, the cattle were turned out. By the time the early grass was eaten, a new patch at a higher elevation was ready for grazing. In this manner the cattle worked their way to the top of Charley's range, climbing over 6,300 feet. Spring didn't come to the range's high point, 8,005-foot Smith Mountain, until July; so when Charley used Big Bar, his cattle grew fat on four month's worth of spring and early summer forage.

Only one thing marred the high country grazing: larkspur. The plant has a lovely purple flower, but it spells death for cattle. Years of grubbing larkspur plants have helped curb the problem, but it still causes an occasional fatality. All that's left of last summer's victim is a red and white hide and a pile of bones.

It was bones of a different sort that made haying at Big Bar interesting. The spot had been a favorite wintering ground for American Indians as far back as 4,500 BC, according to Forest Service archeological reports. The most recent inhabitants were Sheepeaters, a branch of the Shoshone tribe. The Warner haying crew was always turning up American Indian artifacts, including human bones. Charley's oldest son, Toby, once found a human arm bone that was honeycombed in the middle. After lengthy discussion, the crew decided that the arm had been broken and had grown back together in this unusual way.

Haying was a major family and neighborhood affair, and the Depression created more than the usual amount of haying help at Charley's place. Among the people looking for work were Joe and Averill Edwards, whom Charley hired in 1933.

Joe had broken horses for the Pacific Livestock Company before moving his family to a mining claim on the Snake River. When the Edwards family ran out of money, they came to Charley for work. He immediately hired them for the haying crew, and the family of four moved into his homestead cabin, which was located west of the Seven Devils Lodge. A fishing pond currently occupies the site.

Exploring the log cabin was a quick task for the Edwards girls, Tina (pronounced TINE-a) and Helen. A kitchen and living room were situated on the bottom floor and there were two bedrooms upstairs.

The girls were much more interested in Charley, who told fantastic yarns. He swore his ranch had a special money rock. Throw a nickel under the rock, he instructed, and a dollar would magically take its place. Most children who heard his claim were shrewd for their age. They realized that high yield investments

Bert Warner feeds a colt at his dad's homestead, just below the Bear Guard Station. Some of the homestead buildings are still standing. Bert's father, Joe, was Charley Warner's older brother. (Photo courtesy of the Bert Warner family.)

carry an equally high risk. The sparkle in Charley's eyes was probably another tip-off.

Seven-year-old Helen became Charley's shadow, especially during the evening milking. When she saw Charley heading toward the barn with his milking pail, she grabbed her blue tin cup from the house and chased after him. While he was milking, she sat back on her haunches and waited for him to fill her cup straight from the udder. Tina didn't share her sister's enthusiasm for warm milk; her day's highlight usually took place in the Bear schoolhouse. The nine-year-old loved school and read everything she could get her hands on.

Reading didn't occupy all of Tina's attention; the schoolhouse offered another diversion that was equally engrossing, but far more exasperating. His name was Bert Warner. He was Charley's 10-year-old nephew.

Bert's imagination caused several teachers to consider early retirement. If the student sitting in front of him happened to be a little girl with pigtails, she was likely to leave school with two-tone hair, since Bert devised an alternate use for his inkwell.

Whenever he pulled a stunt like that, the teacher made him run outside to find and cut a willow switch. Students had a standard procedure for this task. They looked for the scrawniest specimen available, hoping the licks would be less painful. The teacher always rejected switches that were unable to make a statement, and the child was sent out to find another one. Thinking about the sting each prospective willow branch would create was probably more painful than the punishment itself.

Bert wasn't alone in his capers or in his whippings. His friend, Bobby Dunnington, was always game for a prank, and the two boys pruned the willow bushes regularly.

Bert and Bobby grew tired of the lickings, and they agreed something needed to be done about the teacher's hot temper. They reasoned that an abrupt plunge into icy Bear Creek was the perfect prescription. The teacher crossed the creek every morning on the way to school, and the boys decided to sabotage the footbridge, so that it would collapse as she crossed.

The men are living today, which indicates the plan backfired. The teacher took an alternate route to school that morning, so she missed the trap. The unsuspecting victim was Frank Wall, who had given up his career as a moonshiner/scavenger for a "peaceful" retirement in Bear.

The duo teamed up for another noteworthy event the winter before Tina and her family came to the area. The boys decided to build the ultimate, fast-gliding sled. They spent hours rubbing pitch and wax onto its runners. The finished product, they speculated, would shatter all previous speed records on the sledding hill across from the schoolhouse.

Their hunch was correct, but they picked the wrong person for a test run: their teacher. Miss Davis was fresh out of normal school, which provided post-high school training for teachers at

Showing his famous mechanical abilities, Lawrence Warner (right) and an unknown helper cut ice blocks out of a pond. The blocks were transported to a well-insulated shed and covered with sawdust. This method of refrigeration often lasted well into the summer. (Photo courtesy of the Bert Warner family.)

that time. The eighteen- or nineteen-year-old teacher had drawn an exhausting first year teaching assignment, but when she found herself on top of the sledding hill, perched on a supersonic sled, her other taxing experiences paled in comparison.

As soon as the sled was launched, Miss Davis's screeches reverberated up and down Bear Creek. Trees, rocks, and fence posts flew by at an alarming rate, and the terrified woman desperately tried to slow her progress by dragging a foot. When the sled finally coasted to a stop, Miss Davis took inventory. She was alive, but not unscathed—her leg was broken.

The January 27, 1933 *Adams County Leader* reported that she was unable to teach right after the accident. Mavis Warner, a ninth grade student and Bert's older sister, became the substitute teacher.

The *Leader* did not report the fate of the sled or its creators. School board member W.W. Whitlow, who was Bobby's grandfather, saw that the sled was burned. The punishment stung worse than any switch.

During recess a few months later, Bert was taking his turn on a bicycle. He was peddling around the schoolyard at a good clip, when a small, but insistent Tina Edwards informed him it was her turn. "I ran out to protest," she remembered, "and wham, over the top of me he went."

Bert's hit-and-run victim eventually became his bride, but the unconventional courtship was interrupted when Tina's family left Bear in 1934.

Charley was sorry to see his help go, but by this time his boys had grown to be full-fledged ranch hands. The industrious teenagers had another distinction: they redefined the term "personality conflict."

The younger brother, Lawrence, was an outgoing soul who didn't share his father's passion for the cattle business. Instead, he was interested in anything mechanical—be it haying equipment or sawmills.

Toby was born a cowboy. He loved horses, cattle, and the rugged terrain where they grazed. He was quiet and a little bit bashful, but he commanded respect.

Both boys called their dad "Charley," but beyond that they had no common ground. Nobody understood the reason for their rift, and the boys made no effort to disguise it. They refused to pass food to each other at the dinner table, and they were prone to more violent displays.

A neighbor needing to borrow a tool rode into the yard, and thought he heard someone target practicing in the barn. He guessed right, to a certain extent. Toby and Lawrence were both shooting—using each other as targets.

Toby didn't come home one winter evening, and as the hours passed Charley began to worry. He had a feeling Toby had been hurt, but he wasn't sure his bum leg could handle a rescue mission.

Charley regularly rode horses through places people were afraid to walk, but deep snow eliminated that strategy. Toby was

Toby Warner had ready-made camps stashed all over the country. As a result, his extended trips took little planning. A gigantic ponderosa pine with a cat face, or fire scar, made an ideal place to stash supplies. Toby Warner and Faye Adams enjoy the shade. (Photo courtesy of the Lawrence Warner family.)

George Degitz and Toby Warner were avowed enemies. (Photo courtesy of Chuck Degitz.)

probably somewhere between the house and his own homestead cabin on Indian Creek, which was about ten miles away. It was an impossible distance for Charley, but after a while he dug out the snowshoes.

Lawrence wouldn't let his dad go. He volunteered to search for his brother.

Charley had two hopes as he watched his youngest son stride over the hill. He wanted Toby to be all right, and he wondered if the unusual situation would somehow bring his sons together.

Several hours later Lawrence returned. Alone. As he stomped

Chuck Degitz helped his older brother, George, retrieve Toby Warner's body from the Snake River. (Photo courtesy of Chuck Degitz.)

the snow off his boots, he related that Toby was safely inside the Indian Creek cabin with a broken leg.

Relieved, Charley asked, "How did it happen?"

"I don't know," replied Lawrence, "I just peeked in the window."

Toby was an independent spirit who had no use for automobiles. His dad bought the family's first car, a Model T, in the late 1920s. He was trying to learn how to drive the contraption when he took Toby for a ride—right up the trunk of a tree. His son vowed never to ride in a car again.

He much preferred horses, and before he was too old he had camp gear stashed all over the country. When he caught and saddled a horse it was anybody's bet whether he would be gone for the afternoon or a couple of weeks. On his longer forays he might track and kill cougars, and occasionally he became a self-appointed marshall. The isolated rustling incidents which took place around Dukes Creek never crept north while Toby was keeping vigil.

Toby often liked to put a little challenge into his solitary expeditions. Charley repeatedly saw his son rope an unbroken horse, slip a saddle on its back, and ride it in the corral until the bucking stopped. At that point, he would motion for someone to open the gate. After a week or so, he would return with a well-started horse and very few stories to share.

He even liked to put a little challenge in his courtship. One girl he wanted to visit lived near Pittsburgh Landing, and he decided to ride along the Snake River. Few people had gone that route, for reasons which quickly became apparent. Sheer canyon walls abruptly interrupted trails on either side of the river; so Toby and his horse had to swim the river seventeen times to get to their destination. He circled through the Seven Devils Mountains on the return trip.

Toby was not a pacifist, which he proved whenever he caught the Degitz brothers on his side of the river. The boys' grandmother was Mrs. Rome, the notorious moonshiner on Windy Ridge. Toby once made them cross the river and throw their boots in the water. He watched as they gingerly stepped over sharp rocks during the humiliating trip home to Homestead, Oregon.

The Degitz brothers planned their share of revenge episodes, the most vivid taking place at a party in Homestead. Toby was beaten until he was unconscious, and then a woman wearing spike heels marched over his neck and chest, leaving him riddled with puncture wounds. His attackers knew they had gone too far, and left him in a woodshed to die. That wasn't Toby's plan. When he regained consciousness, he came barreling out of the door swinging an axe handle. When he was finished, several people were seriously injured.

W.W. Whitlow (left) and an unidentified hunter bring supper home. A pious man, Whitlow led the prayers at Toby Warner's funeral. (Photo courtesy of Becky Dunnington Hall.)

Shortly after the Homestead free-for-all, Toby was riding a snaky appaloosa mare across the Snake River on the Brownlee bridge. The mare bucked, throwing him on his head. As a result, he was plagued by agonizing headaches, but he refused to let them interfere with his work.

A couple of weeks later Toby and his dog, Bob, came off the mountain to get groceries in Homestead. When he reached the banks of the Snake River, he waved at Joe McCarthy, who was sitting on his porch reading a newspaper. McCarthy watched as Toby untied his rowboat and began rowing to the other side.

A few minutes later McCarthy happened to look up. Toby's boat was in the middle of the river. It was empty.

Toby's body failed to resurface, and Charley desperately offered a $1,000 reward. George Degitz and his youngest brother, Chuck,

Mary Whitlow made the best cookies on Bear Creek, according to Bert Warner. She was also a religious person. Even the family's pet parrot realized the consequences of saying dirty words. (Photo courtesy of Becky Dunnington Hall.)

joined the search, and eventually found Toby's badly decomposed body two weeks after he disappeared.

A heart-broken Charley Warner offered George Degitz the promised reward. "Toby and I have been enemies all our lives," Degitz said. "I won't take the money."

Nobody ever knew for sure what happened to Toby; his body offered no clues. He probably fell overboard as a result of his head injury, but foul play was always a nagging possibility.

Charley adopted Toby's dog, and for years he'd stoop down, scratch the animal behind the ears, and mutter, "Sure wish you could talk, old Bob."

Toby was buried in the Bear cemetery on a sparkling May day. He was twenty-three.

There were seven Whitlow girls and one boy, Austin. Pictured from left are Lois, Wilma, Ester, Ada, Zoe, Janey, and Susan. (Photo courtesy of Becky Dunnington Hall.)

Charley broke down as W.W. Whitlow led the final prayer.

Mr. Whitlow usually officiated at funerals, and this one was particularly tough. Since Toby shied away from social functions and spent most of his life exploring the country, he was mostly known by reputation. He had, however, ridden a few colts for the Whitlows, and they felt a personal loss.

The Whitlows came into the country on October 12, 1916, after their home in Midvale, Idaho, burned. The fire started when a visiting cousin absent-mindedly left a burning cigarette on a window sill. The curtains caught fire, and a September breeze fanned the flames into a roaring blaze. The family of ten barely had time to escape.

The summer before, Mr. Whitlow had purchased a homestead on Lick Creek from two bachelors. He intended to use the acreage as summer range, but the fire made it necessary to move the family into its crude fourteen by sixteen foot cabin.

W.W. Whitlow hailed from Kansas. His first initial stood for William, and he added the second initial for effect. Most people, including Albert Campbell, called him Mr. Whitlow.

His bride was the former Mary "Maude" Stewart, whose family migrated from Missouri to Midvale. Tom Mackey, an early Bear-area resident, was her uncle.

The fire was a big blow to the family; they lost all their household possessions as well as their home. The couple came to Lick Creek with a hodgepodge of furniture donated by friends, six of their eight children, and an uncle, Dan Couch, who lived with the family.

With quarters so cramped, getting the children off to school became a major production. It took an hour and a half to cover the five-mile trip to the Bear schoolhouse, so preparations began early. Mrs. Whitlow fixed their lunches and served breakfast, while her husband harnessed the mules and readied the sled.

Winter days were short. The students never saw their home in the daylight during school days. They left in the dark, and by the time they pulled into the barn, the kerosene lamps were lit.

Zoe, the oldest daughter still at home, usually drove the team. Sometimes they encountered neighbors hauling hay with a six-horse team. The one-track road made passing impossible, so the men would hop off the sled and shovel a turnout for the children.

Scanning the snow banks for secret messages made the chilly trips less monotonous. Clyde Mackey, an older cousin, started the correspondence when he was hauling hay out of Steves Creek. When they found his note, the girls piled off the sled and carefully etched a reply.

Eighteen students attended the Bear school after the five Whitlow girls enrolled, and each year brought a new teacher. Bear's primitive conditions discouraged most teachers, so the school board often hired people who were either fresh out of normal school, well past retirement age, or had spotty credentials. One of their teachers was unable to work arithmetic problems.

W. W. WHITLOW

BEAR, IDAHO

Ranchman — Stockgrower

Resident of Idaho for 39 years
of Adams County 22 years

Democratic Candidate For

STATE REPRESENTATIVE

Your Vote Solicited

W.W. Whitlow ran successfully for several public offices. Although a usually unflappable man, he was devastated when he lost one election . . . to a woman. (Photo courtesy of Becky Dunnington Hall.)

The best part of the school year was Christmas. After the children participated in an elaborate program, Santa Claus trundled into the schoolhouse and distributed treats purchased by the district. Santa had a remarkable resemblance to Mr. Whitlow one year. The North Pole resident never stayed for the square dance and roast chicken dinner, which concluded the celebration.

Christmas was a major highlight in the Whitlow household, because the two oldest girls came home. Everyone pitched in to prepare a turkey and venison feast, which was often shared with Charley Warner's brother, Joe, his wife, Eva, and their three children: Clarence, Mavis, and Bert.

The younger Warners, especially Bert, thought Mrs. Whitlow was wonderful. Unlike most mothers, she was unafraid of small, sticky fingers, and she frequently hosted taffy pulls during the winter. They usually made the candy from honey harvested from the Whitlow hives.

Taffy pulls and other social events were treasured, as they weren't held frequently. The Whitlows, like other area families, spent little time socializing.

Winter evenings were spent poring over the *Adams County*

Two Whitlow girls enjoy an afternoon outing. (Photo courtesy of Becky Dunnington Hall.)

Leader or *Ladies' Home Journal.* Books were always given as Christmas and birthday gifts, and they were passed around the family. Those who weren't reading played a few hands of rummy or solitaire, and the whole crew often munched on a giant bowl of popcorn.

The evening activities concluded when Mr. Whitlow opened the family Bible and started to read. Family ethics and philosophies were taken from the Bible; they never worked on Sundays and there was never any smoking or drinking, except on one memorable occasion.

Mr. Whitlow was elected to various county and state offices during the Twenties, Thirties, and Forties. One November he lost his bid for state senator—to a woman. A bottle of liquor helped numb the humiliation.

Humiliation was normally a foreign emotion to Mr. Whitlow, as his work ethic testifies. He worked incessantly and he expected things to be run his way; people who worked for him said there was a right way, a wrong way, and a Whitlow way of doing things.

He ran cattle and sheep, which he sheared himself. He had no use for modern machinery, so all haying was done with horse-drawn equipment, which could be dangerous.

His only son, Austin, was raking hay when the team spooked

Carrie Parker was a stylish young woman from Maine. Her family settled near Weiser, and the local newspaper reported she was a charter member of the Women's Relief Society. Her future husband, Ferdinand Desoto McFadden, or "Sote," had a homestead on Mann Creek, a few miles north of Weiser. (Photo courtesy of Clarence and Marie McFadden.)

Survival was a daily struggle for the McFadden family. Carrie didn't make it. She died shortly after this photo was taken. She had been ailing for some time, but a doctor was never called. As a result, the cause of her death is unknown. (Photo courtesy of Clarence and Marie McFadden.)

Mabel McFadden tours the country on a pet steer. The steer disappeared one fall. Albert Campbell sent them a check for fifty dollars and a note explaining that the steer had been accidentally taken to the stockyards in Baker, Oregon. (Photo courtesy of Clarence and Marie McFadden.)

and started to run. He lost his balance and fell underneath the rake, its tines repeatedly spearing his back as it rolled over his body. Landore's Dr. William Brown dressed the wounds. Austin recovered completely, although he carried the nasty-looking scars for the rest of his life.

When the pressing chores were finished, Mr. Whitlow had three seemingly endless pet projects: eradicating thistles, burning stumps, and digging irrigation ditches.

Canadian thistles flourish during the late summer, when most other plant life seems defeated by heat and lack of water. Animals won't feed on the prickly plant, which eagerly invades freshly disturbed ground.

Grubbing the noxious weed was a thankless job, and Mr. Whitlow's help spent hours verifying that opinion. Whacking the thistles off at the base didn't daunt them; their chopped stalks immediately sprouted eager, new shoots. There were no herbicides, so Whitlow and his help dug around each plant's taproot and pulled the prickly plant out with heavily gloved hands. After all that effort, the thistle yankers were usually rewarded with a frustrating sight—a forgotten plant happily releasing its downy seeds in the wind; insuring another year of grubbing.

Stump burning was more gratifying work, since the results were permanent. In the days before bulldozers, present-day Bear resident Bud McGahey helped the Whitlows clear several hayfields. The task involved cutting timber with a cross-cut saw and chopping underbrush away by hand. The flammable scrub was piled around the stumps, set on fire, and the stumps burned flush to the ground.

Mr. Whitlow's youngest hired hand, Clarence McFadden, helped with his third pet project: irrigation ditches. During his two-year tenure with the family, he spent a considerable number of hours on the working end of a shovel.

Clarence was supporting himself by the time he was eight years old; his family suffered more than its share of hardships during the Depression.

His mother was Bobby Barbour's grandniece, and the family relationship plus homesteading opportunities induced them to leave Weiser and set up housekeeping on Barbour Flat. The

Clarence McFadden shows off his fairly reliable school transportation. When Pete Kramer offered a screaming deal on the horse, Clarence's father bought it. The horse had one idiosyncrasy: he bucked off the day's first rider. After the requisite bucking, there were no further problems . . . until the next morning. (Photo courtesy of Clarence and Marie McFadden.)

McFaddens had three children when they arrived on the flat—Mabel and Floyd were toddlers and Clarence was being toted around in a cracker box.

The family swapped their homestead for an acreage on Lick Creek in the late 1920s, and they moved into a two-room frame house. By this time, four more children were born to the family.

The parents slept downstairs, and all six children crowded into the upper bedroom. Clarence said there was never any difficulty getting the youngsters to sleep—his father had a stout razor strap and knew how to use it.

The family didn't own much stock; they survived on deer meat. They hunted year around, which was illegal. Shorty Walton, the game warden, came around the McFadden place once in a while, but since the family needed food, he never reported them.

The McFaddens cultivated a small corn patch, and Mr. McFadden made moonshine for home use. What little cash flow they had came from selling a few extra ears of corn to Si Winkler, a Council grocer.

The kids tried to contribute to the family's finances. Clarence helped a local sheepherder whenever his help took time off. Wages were set at a dollar a day plus room and board. He remembers he ended up with lots of room and very little board.

The family received its final, crippling blow when Mrs. McFadden died shortly after their informal family portrait was taken. The oldest, sixteen-year old Mabel, became a mother to her five younger brothers.

The six children stayed together for a only a short while. The two youngest boys were adopted by families in the southern part of Idaho, Mabel married Barney Camp, and Mr. McFadden sought seasonal work at the Mesa orchard, south of Council. W.W. Whitlow bought the McFadden place, and agreed to hire Clarence. He stayed for about two years, and then joined his father at Mesa.

Another young worker on Mr. Whitlow's ranch was his grandson, Bobby Dunnington. Bobby's mother was Ada Whitlow Dunnington Lynes. Like Clarence McFadden, he spent hundreds of hours digging irrigation ditches. It was haying, however, that sparked his imagination.

In the middle of one of his grandfather's hayfields was an unusual stretch of undulations. Bobby had heard the area was an Indian burial ground, and he wanted to explore the area with a shovel. Mr. Whitlow forbade any excavation, so Bobby had to content himself with intense speculation as he rode various pieces of haying equipment over the swells again and again.

The spot is difficult to locate today. The ground has settled in the last fifty years, and the area is barely rippled.

The Whitlows built their new home above the mysterious hayfield, and the house was several years old by the time Bobby came to live with them. The old log cabin, which served as their first home, was converted into a cooler. Its windows were left open at night, to allow the chilly air to filter through. In the morning, the cabin was shut tight. Its double wall construction insulated against the hottest days.

Stashed in the corner, under thick layers of sawdust, was a

Mabel McFadden and her younger brothers Jim, Floyd, Royal, Raymond, and Clarence pose in the cornfield. After their mother's death, the two youngest boys were adopted by different families. Clarence McFadden began supporting himself when he was eight. It was nearly twenty years before all the siblings were reunited. (Photo courtesy of Clarence and Marie McFadden.)

treasured commodity: blocks of ice cut out of Lick Creek. It did help lower the cooler's temperature, but its most popular use was for homemade ice cream.

In the early Thirties Mr. Whitlow focussed on recreational improvements, which was highly unusual during this era. He had previously developed Soda Spring, which produced naturally fizzy water. A short distance away he built an open air dance pavilion in preparation for a full-blown Fourth of July celebration.

Both local and visiting guests flocked to the event, which lasted all day long. Bellies were filled with delicious potluck offerings, and the new dance pavilion was heartily christened during its only official use. It was the horse race, however, that was the day's highlight.

Bloocher, the area's fastest horse, was favored to win. His jockey, Book Perkins, was married to Wilma Whitlow. The flag went down and Bloocher was off. He thundered through the finish line, but wasn't ready to stop racing. Off through the field the horse and rider flew, until Bloocher found a finish line with more staying power: a beaver dam. The horse screeched to a halt, but Perkins continued to race—head first—into the dam. Onlookers doubted he felt the fall much. He had swallowed a good portion of home remedy prior to the race.

Book's brother, Gene, was always a welcome sight in the community. He was the area's mailman and errand runner, and three times a week he delivered news, groceries, and mail.

He continued his schedule during the winter, even though he had to navigate the unplowed roads which accumulated close to five feet of snow. He solved the problem by building an early-day snowmobile. He pulled the front tires off a Model-T, and replaced them with a set of skis.

His parcel post deliveries weren't always small, neat packages. He was probably glad to get rid of one large, squawking package that arrived for the Whitlows.

He left it at the vacant, white frame house which stood in front of the Lick Creek barn and served as an informal post office.

Mr. Whitlow hauled the crate home, pried off its lid, and introduced the newest member of the family: a green parrot named Barnacle Bill.

Bill's personality and wide vocabulary soon dominated the household. He liked to eavesdrop when the women were talking, and then he rehashed their conversation using three gossipy, female voices. He loved to agitate.

The family left Bill alone in the house one afternoon, and a man from Midvale stopped by to repair a harness. He rapped on the door. "Come on in," he heard.

He opened the door and was confused when nobody came out to greet him. The man walked through the empty house and was startled to hear, "Hello there."

Finally he spied the parrot, and he decided to grab his fishing pole, and wait for the family to return. He heard, "Good-bye," as he closed the door.

The bird became bored when the visitor left, so he started whistling and calling for the dogs. The man felt a little less foolish when he saw a group of confused dogs milling around the yard.

Bobby Dunnington and his cousin, Harold Kelly, taught Bill

some dirty words. He was a sharp old bird, however, and he used them discriminately. Mrs. Whitlow declared that if the bird ever swore, it would have a quick trip to the chopping block. Bill took her at her word.

Barnacle Bill never lost his raucous sense of humor, even in an emergency situation. During the summer of 1940, the Whitlows' daughter, Wilma, and her husband, Book Perkins, were running the ranch operation, while Mr. Whitlow supervised government-employed brush piling crews. When it was time to fix dinner, a fire was started in the cookstove. A spark hit some dry pine needles on the roof, and a hot blaze erupted spontaneously.

The women raced to the upper story, and tried to heave bedding out the window, but it was in flames before it hit the ground. The women immediately abandoned the house. Mrs. Whitlow grabbed Barnacle Bill on the way out, and when she hit the front steps, she slipped and fell. The old bird laughed at her. She later said she was tempted to throw him back in the house.

Mr. Whitlow, who was headed home for lunch, came over the hill just in time to see the barn catch on fire. He scrambled into the barn and managed to release the team and salvage a harness and a saddle before the building was completely ablaze.

It was an hour before the forest fire lookout on Smith Mountain spotted any smoke. By then everything was leveled. For the second time, the family lost everything to a fire. Luckily, no people or animals lost their lives.

Regrouping after the fire's devastation was a tough task. It ranked among the Whitlows' most aggravating ranching experiences, but it probably didn't receive top billing. That honor would have been reserved for Albert Campbell.

Albert received a letter, dated March 6, 1934 that would indirectly launch his tenuous relationship with W.W. Whitlow. George Donart, a Weiser attorney, drafted the letter which read:

> This might just be a blind lead and you may not
> be interested anyway, but the old Lick Creek Ranch
> of 2920 acres has gotten into the hands of a party
> in Portland who seems pretty anxious to sell it. He
> wrote up here asking about a loan. It occurred to

me that you might be interested in buying this
ranch, if you could buy it cheap enough.

If you are, let me know and I'll put you in touch
with the necessary people.

Albert probably spent a few sleepless nights mulling over this
expansion possibility before he fired back his reply:

I am sure that you should loan money on the
Lick Creek Ranch, since it lies in a very good
country and while the neighbors are not too thick,
they are an unusually good class of people.

Now what I want you to do is this. Write this
man a nice long letter and explain at some length
that this land has been leased the past few years to
a sheep man who has allowed nearly all the fences
to topple over and who has undoubtedly thought
that as long as the rocks were left in the fall, the
soil, and grass roots did not matter.

Tell him, also, that you know a man who would
rent his land for five years subject to sale, and that
he might buy, with plenty of emphasis on the
might, should the cow business come out of this
Democratic prosperity we are passing through . . .
Let me know his reactions.

The run-down Lick Creek Ranch bordered much of the
Whitlows' 1,000-acre operation. The two places had overlapping
grazing permits, which created a stressful situation regardless of
the personalities involved.

The first major rub occurred when Albert asked to trail his
herd through the Whitlows' ranch, since it was the most direct
route to his Forest Service grazing allotment.

The fact that Mr. Whitlow allowed the cattle to come through
was amazing. He was even testy about the fishermen who walked
through his fields along Lick Creek, since the hay they flattened
couldn't be harvested.

Mr. Whitlow was silently furious as he watched the OX cattle
slowly eat and trample their way through his hayfields. OX cattle

Albert Campbell had a great deal of respect for Henry Schmidt. Not only was he a top-notch cowhand, he was famous for his sourdough pancakes. (Photo courtesy of Helena Moore Schmidt.)

crossed the Whitlow ranch—with permission—just that one time.

They were neighbors for slightly over a decade. During Albert's first years on Lick Creek, Mr. Whitlow and his crew allocated more time for repairing fences. OX cattle tended to take unauthorized shortcuts and sneak into the Whitlows' upper country on Lick Creek.

Tensions eased in the late Thirties when one of the first logging roads was built. The road cut through both Albert's Lick Creek Ranch and the Whitlows' ranch. Albert started using the thoroughfare to herd cattle to the OX permit.

Disagreements between Albert and Mr. Whitlow never came to blows; the two men respected each other too much. Young Bobby Dunnington couldn't understand the relationship, or his grandfather's pacifistic philosophy. "Keep your mouth shut, if you can't say anything nice," he instructed. There were times when discussions of Albert and his hands were blatantly absent from household conversations.

"Albert looked after Albert, without a doubt," another neighbor remembered, but he wasn't malicious. Albert lived to make his ranch bigger and more productive—a focus his help understood clearly. If helping someone didn't conflict with those goals, Albert and/or his hands were there instantly.

Such was the case when the Whitlows' muley bull, Fred, decided to charge Bobby Dunnington, who was sitting on the hillside. OX cowboy Henry Schmidt knew what was happening almost before the bull did. He grabbed Bobby by the seat of his pants, and pulled the boy onto his saddle as Fred thundered past.

Albert eventually added the Whitlow place to his holdings in 1946. Mrs. Whitlow's health was failing, and a California retirement became more and more appealing. Albert was the only ready buyer, and he paid $25,000 for the 1,000 acre ranch, according to Bob Dunnington. Prior to the sale, Mr. Whitlow sold the timber off his place.

Severing emotional ties was the toughest part of selling the ranch, and Bob Dunnington took it hard. By this time, he was a young man with dreams of operating the ranch himself. He knew his grandparents deserved a comfortable retirement, so he didn't argue the ranch's sale. Even so, he didn't stifle his feelings when Albert asked him to stay on as a hand. "I wouldn't work with you if you were the last man on earth," he said.

A few of Albert's cowboys shared Dunnington's sentiment, but the majority respected Albert for a lifetime, even if they didn't always agree with his decisions. Henry Schmidt fell into this category.

Henry was a long-limbed cowboy who was raised just across the Snake River in Pine Valley, Oregon. When his parents retired, he managed their ranch for them.

Henry met Albert in the mid-Twenties. Albert wanted to buy some winter feed for his cattle, and Henry agreed to feed the livestock as part of the deal.

A short while later, Henry had to make some changes. His

With the Lick Creek scales behind him, Dick Armacost goes after the next group of cattle to be weighed. As a youngster, Dick couldn't wait to become an OX cowboy. Albert required him to finish the eighth grade first. (Photo courtesy of Darline Whiteley.)

marriage and his working arrangement with his parents fell apart simultaneously. When Albert offered him fifty dollars a month to cowboy on the OX, Henry jumped at it.

He joined Dick Armacost, who had since finished the eighth grade, as Albert had stipulated. By the time Henry arrived, Dick had become a highly valuable hand, living up to the impression he made when he rode into the Basin on his soaking wet, one-eyed horse. He was sometimes hot-headed and impetuous, but he was good.

Although Dick was the top man among the cowboys, he learned some life-long lessons from watching Henry. For example, Henry could talk almost any horse out of bucking. If his mount showed signs of bucking, Henry took the slack out of his reins, and retained complete control. Make him walk in a tight circle, and he can't buck, Henry demonstrated.

Dick and Henry usually had different ideas about how to complete their various projects. Once, when they had to swim livestock across the Snake River and trail them to Halfway, Oregon, they argued about herding the horses and cattle together. Dick wanted to finish the task in one trip, but Henry worried the animals wouldn't herd well together.

Dick won out, but they had problems. A horse kicked one of the cows, and the cow decided she would have nothing to do with the integrated herding. She held her ground. Henry tried to get her going by popping her with a rope and spurring her, but she wouldn't budge. It was cold, and Henry was encumbered with a heavy coat and a pair of angora chaps, but he decided to dismount and try some more direct persuasion. He grabbed her tail, and she started moving. She was on the fight now, and trying her darnedest to teach Henry a lesson. Henry and his long legs kept that from happening. Whenever she turned, he followed her rear end around with incredibly long strides. Henry had worked up a good sweat by the time the cow simmered down. She finally returned to the herd on her own.

Henry and Dick constantly argued about procedures, and Henry grew tired of it. He left the OX for Nampa, Idaho, where he became a musical instrument salesmen. It was an unlikely career move for a cowboy, but Henry enjoyed people and they trusted him. He managed to make a solid living, even though he was selling a luxury item during the Depression.

He wasn't a music man for long, however. Albert saw to that. Albert was an excellent salesman himself, and when he finally located Henry, he eventually convinced him to return.

Henry much preferred ranch work, and evidently he and Dick were able to minimize their differences. Before long the Bear correspondent for the *Adams County Leader* began writing about them. This appeared in the March 3, 1933 edition:

> Albert Campbell, the old cattleman, blew into town last Tuesday; he had been down on Slate Creek looking for the bulls that the boys failed to roundup last fall. Luck again with him, he only found the hide and bones of one, which the coyotes stripped. Next year he'll put a bell on each bull so

Henry and Dick won't have so much trouble
rounding them up.

The bulls never wore bells, as the reporter suggested, but Henry
and Dick did get some extra help in a different form. Thirteen-
year-old Bob Whiteman joined the cowboy crew the summer of
1933.

Bob's mother, Carrie Campbell Whiteman, initiated the summer
job. Her husband's medical practice kept the family in Cambridge,
Idaho, so her children had never been exposed to rural living.
What was worse, her boys knew nothing about the cattle
business. Carrie remedied the situation by sending first Bob, and
then her younger son, Don, to their Uncle Albert.

Bob was used to the Campbell work ethic; his mother practiced
it vigorously in their home. "Morning sunshine (particularly that
which comes at dawn) is the *very* best for you," she said
repeatedly.

Nevertheless, he was in for a tough initiation. He knew nothing
about riding horses or working cattle, and his Uncle Albert wasn't
one to give specific instructions. If Bob made a mistake, however,
he heard about it in great detail.

Bob was expected to do a man's work immediately, and his
fledgling skills were tested when he helped Henry and Albert sort
cattle on Bear Creek. They brought the cattle through a gate to
keep them out of the road, and Bob's job was to keep the
independent creatures spread out against the fence. It was a
miserably hot, dry day and the cattle could think of only one
thing: water. Young Bob was the only barrier between the herd
and Bear Creek, and the cattle stubbornly ignored his frantic
efforts to block their path as they jogged past him.

While the cattle were enjoying their hard-won drink, Albert
had a fit. Bob felt terrible; he had failed the crew. Henry boosted
Bob's plummeting confidence when he told Albert, "You couldn't
have held those cattle yourself."

Bob shadowed Albert during his first days on the OX. They
began their day before dawn, and it was almost dusk before they
returned to the cow camp on Wickiup Creek. Henry Schmidt and
his boy, Dan, were there, and after the chores were done, Bob and

Dan started roughhousing and laughing. Albert said they weren't working hard enough if they had enough energy to play at night.

The OX summer schedule didn't allow any time for recreation. The men had filled up on Henry's sourdough pancakes and were working by 6 a.m., unless Albert rolled into camp on one of his regular visits. He came about every ten days to check the cattle and their range, and to get the men started on new projects. Often, Albert's headlights flashed into camp at 4:30, and the men woke up to, "Get a move on it, you can't sleep all day."

Albert once accompanied Dick Armacost and Henry Schmidt on a long ride; they brought a packhorse along and were prepared to spend the night. The sun set just as the threesome was crossing a steep, rocky slope. Albert surprised the men by saying, "Let's camp here." When Henry protested the uncomfortable setting, Albert reminded him that the night wouldn't be a long one.

Normally, the day ended when it was too dark to work, which was well past ten during the summer months. If the "boys," as Albert called them, finished riding early, there were always horses to shoe and fences to mend.

Even though there was no time for planned recreation, there were always unforeseen lulls perfect for hunting arrowheads.

Roping coyotes was another spontaneous sport. Cowboys and coyotes alike enjoyed the long, cool evenings. The most spectacular sunsets colored the sky during the summer; some evenings the hues crescendoed to brilliant reds and oranges, and at other times, the day ended more discreetly with the sky awash in deep magentas and violets. Regardless of the color scheme, it was the best time to try roping a coyote. Several hands who worked during the 1930s remembered watching Dick Armacost in hot pursuit after a rigorous day of work. Dick would no sooner shake out his rope and his horse would break into a gallop. The coyotes invariably charted zigzag courses across meadows and through brush patches. Usually the race was over when the animal darted under a barbed wire fence or plunged into some thick underbrush, but Dick managed to rope at least one.

Henry embarked upon another kind of pursuit at a 1936 Bear schoolhouse dance. He enjoyed dances, and frequently brought his fiddle. This particular evening, however, he was more interested in a lovely, twenty-six-year-old woman who lived on the Starveout Ranch.

The little Helena Moore, who shadowed her father during every ranch task, had grown into an accomplished rider and stock-woman. To appease her mother, she tried teaching in Brownlee, Oregon, for a couple of years. Helena much preferred being the top hand at Starveout, a fact that wasn't lost on Henry Schmidt.

Henry asked Helena to dance several times that night in Bear. She was surprised when he also asked her to the next scheduled dance.

Helena was apprehensive when the day of the dance arrived. She couldn't dispel the feeling that he wouldn't come for her. Nevertheless, she carefully ironed her dress and folded it into a box.

Since there was no road to Starveout, she and Henry had agreed to meet at Johnny and Eloise McClemmons' house, which was also the post office. Before moving to Wildhorse the McClemmons had lived on a picturesque homestead above the canyon on Sheep Peak.

As Helena brushed and saddled her black mare, Dusky, she reviewed her plan one more time. She would casually ride down to the McClemmons' house trailing the packhorse, whose pack would conceal the dress box. If Henry didn't make their date, she would pretend she was just making a social call and picking up the mail. Nobody would be the wiser.

Helena reached the McClemmons' house late that afternoon. She leafed through the mail, and had the customary neighborly chat. Mrs. McClemmons grew concerned, because her visitor was acting strangely. Helena seemed determined to linger, and if she waited much longer, she would run out of daylight on the trail.

Dusk came, and so did Henry's headlights. "I need to get ready for the dance," she announced to the startled McClemmons' household. Within minutes she exchanged her working clothes for a party dress, complete with silk stockings and brown suede shoes.

The couple was married less than a year later, on August 2, 1937. They spent their working honeymoon on Lick Creek, and then moved a few miles west to the cow camp on the old Mackey

When Helena Moore married Henry Schmidt, she automatically joined the OX crew. Since they followed the grazing cattle, their "home" was a series of cow camps. Helena didn't mind roughing it. She always preferred working outside. (Photo courtesy of Helena Moore Schmidt.)

place. Before the first snow fell, they had followed the cattle to Barbour Flat, through the old Rome place and on to Pine Valley. Helena adopted the dual role of cow hand and wife; when she wasn't helping move cattle, she was setting up camp or cooking.

A precarious situation developed that December when an early winter blew in. The 350 cattle at No Business Basin were quickly running out of feed. There were two solutions to the problem: either drive them to Cambridge or take the shorter route to Pine Valley, Oregon, where other OX cattle were being fed.

The trip to Cambridge required a long trip over a frozen road, and that option was rejected because the already sore-footed cattle weren't up to the trip.

Driving the cattle across the Snake River presented its own set of difficulties. Anticipating the danger, Henry sent his bride to Starveout for a visit with her folks.

At the time there were no bridges in the area. OX cattle usually crossed using a ferry boat, but the ferry couldn't handle the river's partially frozen condition. The ice, combined with the river's strong current, made swimming the cattle an impossibility. The OX crew began to look for a crossing on the ice.

The crew found a place where the ice bridged to the other side, and Henry and two other OX cowboys, Slick Taylor and Bill Hinkley, set out to test its strength. The ice was resting directly on the water, which was a good sign. Even though the ice was well supported, some serious fortification needed to take place before the cattle could safely cross.

The men sought help from a company-owned sheep ranch just upstream from the Brownlee crossing, but the men balked, making the excuse that they had too much work piled up.

The three men tackled the job by themselves, alternating layers of hay, gunny sacks, and buckets of water on the bridge. The bitter cold made for miserable working conditions, but the water froze rapidly. When the bridge's depth reached eight inches, the men decided to attempt a crossing the next morning.

Spectators, including the men from the sheep ranch, gathered on both sides of the Snake to watch the crossing. After several minutes of gentle persuasion, the first cow stepped onto the ice. She sniffed the hay scattered on the surface, and the rough surface provided her with enough traction to make it across. The operation ran smoothly until some of the cows tried to double back, searching for their calves. Once the traffic jam was straightened out, the last cows crossed safely.

The 350 cattle joined approximately 450 other OX cattle being fed at Junior and Helen Gover's ranch in Pine Valley. Henry and Helena Schmidt boarded with the Govers that winter, and helped feed the cattle.

Albert regularly purchased hay from various farmers in Pine Valley. Since Albert was the only large-scale buyer, his monopoly enabled him to drive hard bargains. As a result, some of the farmers tried to make up lost dollars by adding a few feet to the haystacks' measurements. "You had to watch the tape when buying hay at Pine Valley,'' remembered Holworth Nixon, whose Dukes Creek ranch adjoined, and later became part of the OX.

Then, as now, large quantities of hay were purchased by the ton. In the days of the loose hay stacks, tonnage was determined using a series of measurements and mathematical equations. First, the distance over the stack was measured by tying a heavy ring to the end of a measuring tape and throwing it over the stack. The ring end was pinned to the ground, the tape pulled tightly over the stack—almost to the breaking point—and the measurement taken. After the length and width of the stack were noted, it was time to whip out a pencil and paper for some figuring. The width was subtracted from the distance over the stack and divided by two. This total was multiplied by the width and then the length. The tonnage was determined by dividing that figure by 512.

Feeding 800 head of cattle kept Helena, Henry, and Junior Gover busy that winter. After a hearty breakfast, the three clambered to the top of the stack and pitched a round-topped load onto the sled below. Helena drove the four-horse team in a

Boo Childers, left, and Toots Rogers, right, shoe horses in time for haying in No Business Basin. In a good year, the Basin yielded almost 400 tons of hay. (Photo courtesy of Darline Whiteley.)

slow circle as Henry and Junior fed from either side of the sled.
On an average morning, they made a total of eight trips to the
haystack, figuring 100 head would eat a load of hay.

When temperatures plummeted, sometimes to fifty degrees
below zero, the herd's appetite increased accordingly. Under these
conditions the threesome worked briskly enough to keep themselves warm without breaking into a sweat. Perspiration on a
bone-chilling day invited sickness.

Some Pine Valley residents seemed impervious to the extreme
temperatures. This is evidenced in the letter W.W. Evans, vice
president of the First National Bank of Halfway, wrote to Albert
Campbell in 1939: "I have said many times that the only reason
Heaven is mentioned so many times in the Bible is because Pine
Valley had not been discovered yet when the book was written."

Albert replied,

> I do not think that you should try to compare
> Pine Valley with Meadows Valley as a cow country
> or with Heaven as a place to live, for I have been in
> Halfway a few winter mornings when the
> thermometer was hovering around the half hundred
> mark, and it was not above zero, and as I remember
> my discomfort, I am wondering if such a Heaven
> would be much to look forward to.

Most Pine Valley residents accepted the harsh winters, but they
eagerly anticipated spring, even though the transition between
seasons was messy. The Gover feedlot thawed into a giant mud
bog. They continued to use the sled to feed, since the wagon
wheels were prone to sinking out of sight.

Henry, who was famous for his adages, told Helena, "When the
blackbirds sing, it means spring." Soon after their song became
commonplace, it was time to move the cattle back across the river
into Idaho. Albert chose to swim them across at Oxbow, Oregon,
that year. The old cows, who knew they were headed to good
grass, didn't hesitate to lead the herd across.

The lush springs were short-lived in the Snake River canyon,
and the cattle were easily drawn to higher elevations and their
milder climates. The same thought appealed to Bailey and Bertha

Armacost, who were renting a ranch on the banks of the Snake, near Brownlee, Oregon. Albert approached them about managing the No Business Basin operation, after his previous manager, Claude Childers, moved to Council to please his wife, Dora.

"Goodness, it was so hot down there," Bertha remembered. "We didn't even have any ice; we had nothing . . .

Claude Childers hauls a load of hay to a stack in No Business Basin. Claude was in charge of the farming operation. (Photo courtesy of Darline Whiteley.)

"We got up there, and it was so nice and cool. We had running water and bathrooms, a refrigerator . . . a gas (carbide) stove, gas (carbide) lights, a gas-powered washing machine, and hot and cold running water."

Bailey, who was Dick Armacost's older brother, had worked for Albert in the Basin during his bachelor days. He needed no orientation to take over the farming operation.

The Basin's steep hayfields were irrigated by a series of hand-dug irrigation ditches, and keeping the water flowing was a constant summer chore. When he wasn't irrigating, there was plenty of fencing to do.

Activity peaked at haying time, when Wildhorse neighbors put aside work on their home places to hire on with the crew. Years before she married Henry Schmidt, Helena Moore was the only woman who worked in the fields.

Haying in the Basin presented some unique obstacles, because some of the fields seemed almost vertical. The men who operated the horse-drawn mowers swore there were spots where the uphill wheel could run over a robin's nest and not break an egg.

"There were always runaways," said Arnold Emery, who earned his first wages from the OX. Mangled pieces of mowing machinery can still be found several hundred feet below some of the most treacherous fields. The number of mishaps was actually surprisingly low, considering the hazardous circumstances.

Most of the haying crew returned year after year, and by the 1930s there was a set routine. Those handling horse teams had to crawl out of bed the earliest; the brushing and harnessing had to be finished before breakfast. For that reason, handling horses wasn't the most popular job, according to Amos Camp, who didn't mind the early hours.

Bertha also had early hours, as she had to prepare mountains of fried eggs, pancakes, and steak for the crew. By seven, everyone had pushed away from the breakfast table, clambered over to the fields, and started working.

Three mowers, which ran simultaneously, were the vanguard of the operation. Once the hay was cut, it was allowed to dry before the next pieces of horse-drawn equipment raked it into windrows.

Buck rakes were used until a Basque from Brownlee, Oregon, suggested they try a rake more suited to the steep terrain. It worked like a platform seesaw. When it was time to start a windrow, the driver shifted his weight to the uphill side of the platform, which lowered the rake's teeth enough to do a thorough job.

Raking served two purposes. First, it gathered the loose hay, making it easier to handle. Second, raking turned the hay, allowing it to dry more thoroughly. Moist hay will become moldy when it's stacked, and hay that's too dry loses nutritional value and becomes harder to handle. The judgment call was made by the men who bundled the hay together in pitchfork-sized shocks.

Hay was carried to the stack site on a slip, which was an eight by sixteen foot platform which skidded on two full length poles. A team slowly pulled the slip, as a couple of men walked alongside, pitching shocks until they formed a high mound. Three slips ran at a time, which gave the people building the haystack a steady stream of work.

Albert used a hay chute on the steepest part of the old Day place, where he started the OX. According to his brother Loyal, the hay was shocked by hand and slid down the chute, which ended just above the schoolhouse.

Three people handled the stacking end of the operation; two of them working the Jackson fork, which lifted hay from the slip to the stack. According to Bob Whiteman, a good operator could empty the slip with five bites of the Jackson fork; two on top of the load and three on the bottom.

After the Jackson fork operator wedged the slightly curved tines into the hay on the slip, he motioned to the person riding the derrick horse. The ropes controlling the Jackson fork were threaded through pulleys at the top of a tall derrick, and the leverage needed to operate the apparatus was provided by the horse, which was once ridden by Helena. She urged the horse forward until the load was positioned correctly over the haystack. After the stacker shouted, "Trip," the fork operator pulled the trip wire, dumping the hay. The stacker had the hot, dusty job of arranging the freshly dumped load in preparation for the next one. When the last load was dumped, a skillful stacker would arrange the topmost layer, insuring that no more than the outside three inches would get wet.

Those working around the Jackson fork were cautious, especially Helena. Her uncle, Jim Nixon, died after a senseless haying accident on his ranch, which was in the neighboring Board Creek drainage.

Jim, who was stacking that day, needed a boost to climb back on the growing haystack. It was customary for the stacker to hitch a ride on the Jackson fork by gripping two tines. Hanging by his arms, he was hoisted until he could drop into position. On Jim's last ride, the derrick horse bolted, which sent the Jackson fork hurtling to the top of the derrick. It slammed into the pulleys, and the impact caused Jim to lose his grip. He landed on the derrick platform, and died the next spring. Although cancer was listed as the cause of death, family members suspected the accident triggered the disease.

Years later, the story occasionally surfaced at haying time, after the day's work was finished. The crew couldn't settle into storytelling mode until they took generous servings from Bertha's heaped supper platters, and they couldn't eat before washing away the day's dust and grime. When they left the fields, they made a beeline for the cold spring above the house, which flowed continuously through a five inch trough.

On the last day of haying, the men had more than clean up on their minds when they headed to the spring. On that day, and that day only, the trough was crowded with cans of ice-cold beer.

The final day of haying also marked the end of an informal competition, in which the OX farmers participated annually. The goal was to break the 400-ton mark in hay production. There wasn't a hope some years, when there was only enough hay to build three large stacks. The chance for breaking records came when five stacks were scattered throughout the Basin. After the measuring tape was thrown over the last stack, the crew gathered for the result. From the time the OX started haying the Basin in 1910 to its peak productivity in the Thirties, some tallies came close, but they were always shy of 400 tons.

There was a slight letdown when the haying crew left, marking the end of the year's biggest social event. Although Bertha was finally able to venture away from the stove, her summer's work was far from finished. She took charge of the abundant vegetable garden and fruit orchard, which produced until the first heavy frost hit, usually in October. Her canning equipment got a steady workout throughout the summer and fall.

The Armacosts' pace slackened in the winter, when feeding was their primary responsibility. Steers were normally wintered in the Basin during the Thirties. In those days, steers fattened and matured for three years before they were sold; steers are now commonly sold as yearlings.

Bailey always had a hired man, who helped with feeding. Elmer Langer played the role for years. Being able to play pinochle was almost as important as being a competent hand. The Armacosts and the hand spent many long winter evenings gathered around the kitchen table, hoping to win with a flourish by assembling a thousand aces in their hands.

"My happiest days were up in No Business," Bertha said during a 1987 interview. The couple had been in the Basin for a little over four years when they decided to start a family. Both had concerns about raising a child in such isolated country.

Underscoring their worries was an incident that occurred the winter after they moved into the Basin. One evening they were startled to hear a rap on their door. A well-bundled Helena Moore explained that her mother, Carmeta, had broken her leg. Helena asked Bertha to stay at Starveout until she returned with the doctor.

On horseback, it took Helena and young Toots Rogers most of the night to cover the twenty-plus miles between Starveout and the nearest phone, which was at the present-day OK ranch on Hornet Creek. They got very little rest before Dr. Alvin Thurston arrived, crawled on a borrowed horse, and set out on one of the most ambitious house calls of his career.

Carmeta was in too much pain to sleep much, so Bertha spent much of the evening reading aloud from the Bible. The emergency ended happily; Dr. Thurston set the leg and it healed completely.

The episode left vivid impressions on both Bailey and Bertha; it clinched the decision to raise their child closer to civilization.

Their son, Vic, was born about the time Albert and Grace had their second daughter, Charlotte. The two were married twenty-two years later in 1958.

When the Armacosts left the Basin, Claude Childers, who was now divorced, couldn't resign from his Council hardware store duties fast enough. He took just enough time to bundle up his clothes, before resuming his old job as farm foreman.

When haying season rolled around, Claude hired Arnold Emery, a young kid who was born and raised on the Wildhorse River. He worked for the OX from 1937 to 1939, and he drew good wages: forty dollars a month.

Arnold was a gifted storyteller, and he had plenty of tales about his growing up years. His family's daily routine had changed little since they first came into Wildhorse in 1892; the modern world was just beginning to creep in, and it had intriguing aspects, like the first radio their neighbor brought into the country. Arnold frequently timed his visits so he could join the crowd listening to the Carter family's show.

Arnold also enjoyed the simpler pleasures. He and a friend once spent the day gigging seven salmon while fishing around the ranch presently owned by Jay and Lori Quilliam. There are no salmon in the Wildhorse River now; the dams on the Snake River block their old spawning route.

When the fish weren't biting, he could always visit the resident stagecoach robber. It was said that Frank Witcraft robbed a stage in the Salmon River country, to the north. He claimed he hid the loot in a cave, and never retrieved it. Witcraft spent his waning years hiding out in Wildhorse, where he is buried.

As he grew older, Arnold went farther afield for his entertainment. He and Bert Warner shared the dubious honor of being the most active outhouse tippers in the country. All the outhouses in Bear were fair game, with one notable exception. Whenever the boys were on the prowl, they knew that Jesse Smith would discourage them with a 30-30 rifle.

Arnold's growing up years were marked by tragedy as well. He was ten years old when he learned that his friend Lloyd Hemminger was missing.

Lloyd's family lived just upriver from the Emerys. One of young Lloyd's responsibilities was taking care of his pet rabbits. That April the rabbit feed looked better across the river, so he grabbed a sack and climbed onto the fallen log that served as a footbridge. He never made it across.

Spring runoff had transformed the normally placid river into an angry torrent. Lloyd lost his footing on the slippery log, fell into the river, and was swept away before any kind of rescue effort could be launched.

The neighbors up and down Wildhorse worried about his mother. Whenever she had a spare moment, she took her younger children by the hand and walked as far downriver as time would permit. Her relentless searching was fruitless.

That fall, a fisherman rode into their yard, balancing a tarp-

Toots Rogers and Arnold Emery display the result of a successful hunt. They were famous for their innovative pranks. (Photo courtesy of Darline Whiteley.)

covered bundle on the front of his saddle. He'd found a small skeleton tangled in some brush.

Lloyd was buried beside the river. Those who attended the burial agree it ranked among the saddest occasions of their lives.

On the anniversary of his death, the spring runoff reached record heights. The water washed over the grave site until the skeleton made its second and last journey downstream.

Arnold eventually found a new sidekick in Tuffy Rogers, and Claude Childers hired them both to help farm the Basin. The working situation quickly became strained, because the boys found themselves trying to please two bosses. Conflicts arose whenever cowboy foreman Dick Armacost spent time there. "Armacost kept us running ragged half the night," Arnold remembered.

They took their troubles to Claude, who settled things by saying, "I'm boss here. You don't have to follow Dick's orders."

A short while later, as Tuffy and Arnold watched Dick ride into the yard on a green colt, a scheme to even the score popped into their heads. They stuck their 45-90 rifle through a hole in the barn's roof and waited for Dick to dismount. Just as he was bringing his leg over the saddle, they shot. "The horse swapped ends, but he stayed on," Arnold said.

Before the boys had a chance to laugh, a dripping form raised up from behind a partition. "What the hell do you boys think you're doing?" Claude boomed as the milk trickled down his face.

"Getting even with Mr. Armacost," they replied meekly.

"Well, O.K. then," was all he said before he sat back down, righted the bucket and continued milking.

Arnold and Tuffy were sure they would be fired, but nothing more was said about the incident. They knew, however, that Dick never forgot.

A rifle blast was definitely not part of Dick's horse training regimen; all his work with horses was marked with calmness and patience. As a result, he always had a string of top-notch horses.

It was a roguish mount that came to mind when Albert and Dick were reminiscing in the late Seventies. The taped conversation was highlighted by the story of their ill-fated horse race from Lick Creek to New Meadows.

Albert's horse, Nick, spent much of the day stuck in a mud bog. By the time Albert coaxed him out, he knew he was out of the race.

Dick's progress wasn't much better. He rode Arkansas Traveler, whom he aptly called "a rough saddle horse." Throughout the course of the day, Dick was bucked off three times, once over a fence. After each tumble, the horse peered back at him and snorted. He never protested when Dick crawled back on; he seemed to be looking forward to the next round.

Neither Dick nor Albert mentioned whether a winner was declared.

Before she met Dick, Erma Watkins had heard "he was a good-looking cowboy who worked for Albert, and was a good hand with horses." They met when a friend of Erma's married Circle C cowboy Brooks Morrison.

Dick and Erma soon followed suit; they were married the Christmas of 1938 in New Meadows. Erma was teaching school in north Idaho at the time, and had to finish the term; so the couple lived apart during their first months of marriage.

Their first home together, which was on the OX, was definitely not an idyllic honeymooners' nest. The point was driven home when Erma slipped into the cellar for some potatoes. She glanced in the direction of some labored scurrying and saw a beady-eyed pack rat raiding the potato pile. He stared at her belligerently until she winged a potato in his direction.

Dick approached Albert several weeks before it was time to move cow camp to Salt Creek. In previous years the bachelor cowboys had made do with Loyal's old homestead shack, but he wasn't about to bring his bride there. Albert hired Fred Meyers to build the replacement, which was always called the honeymoon cabin.

The move took place the day after Christmas, 1939. Dick and Erma parked their car on the Oregon side of the Snake and proceeded to pile their belongings in a rowboat. Erma could see the little cabin across the river, and she couldn't understand why the rowboat had been landed so far up river.

"He (Dick) and Albert were a great hand with a rowboat . . . this was my first experience," Erma explained. "They knew just when to take the current; take it fast or take it slow. We hit the current and shot right over to the other side."

The cabin wasn't quite finished, but it was livable. In a dark corner stood Erma's nemesis: a "God-awful" cookstove. No matter how she coaxed the fire or adjusted the draft, the oven refused to heat. Experience taught her that baked potatoes were an impossibility. Since she was feeding the crew of four, she searched her brain for something different from her usual frying pan fare, something that would cook in the lukewarm oven. Inspiration hit. She carefully sculpted mashed potatoes in a pan, breaking an egg into each indentation. The eggs were still soggy after a lengthy stint in the oven. "I had to take the pretty little things and dump them in a frying pan. The boys were real good; they never complained," she remembered.

She accidentally discovered the oven's problem two days before they were to move from the cabin. It was a beautiful, warm day, so she left the cabin door open. The light reached the wall by the stove, highlighting an open door on the side of the oven. "I could have kicked that stove into the Snake River. I never got to use it hot," she said.

A few years ago Erma's son, Gary, and grandson, Bret, brought her to the cabin in a jet boat. The cabin had since been skidded up the hill, so it escaped being flooded by the Oxbow Dam. The stove was in ruins, but it still stood in the corner of the ramshackle cabin. "I hauled off and kicked it," she said.

"I'd never had exposure to ranching before I married Dick, but I loved horses and the outdoors. I got to ride with him a lot when we were working with Albert, and when we had our own outfit."

For the next year she helped Dick in addition to tackling her other roles of cook, laundress, and surrogate mother. Young Bob and Don Whiteman thought she was wonderful.

She vividly remembers a ferrier who dropped his work long enough to lean against the building and light a cigarette. The act was unthinkable in Albert's camp. He raised a fuss if a cowboy smoked on horseback; it was a waste of time. When somebody told him to get back to work, he explained he was just storing up enough cuss words to finish the job.

Winter found the Armacosts at Junior Gover's place, helping with the feeding. Contracting the winter feeding was working so well that Albert began to practice it more extensively. He started herding OX steers to Baker, Oregon, which was marvelous hay country.

Erma's tenure as a full-time rancher came to an end when the school board at Crooked River begged her to come teach at their logging camp. The one-room schoolhouse had been recently constructed among the worker's cabins. The community was situated just off the OX Ranch, at the junction of the Council-Cuprum and Wildhorse roads.

Dick worried about her living alone during the week, so he left his dog with her. Stubby was a big, black dog who was serious about his work. In fact, he was so conscientious that he probably should have earned a place on the payroll. Dick could send him anywhere with just a gesture and a word. When the boys were gathering cattle, they could bunch them in a corner, leave Stub to stand watch, and take off for another circle through the country. Even if they were gone for half a day, they would return to find Stub had the situation under control.

If Stubby had a fault, it was doing his job too thoroughly. If strays tried to break away from the herd, he could get rough. He once drowned a yearling in Indian Creek by pouncing on its back, breaking its neck.

Stubby was serious about his duties with Erma too, but his new job allowed him to romp and play with the kids. There was always somebody who would play catch with him.

When classes were in session, Stubby sat motionless under Erma's desk, watching as she taught eight grades simultaneously. Each grade level worked separately until Erma started a group activity, such as singing. She also read to all the kids, often from books they brought from home. One day, while the group was quietly listening to a story, Stubby sprang from under her desk, leapt over two rows of desks, and skidded over the last row. He proudly trotted back to Erma with an art gum eraser in his mouth. It took her fifteen minutes to get things settled down again.

Stubby actively pursued his guard dog role only once. Some men working for the Civilian Conservation Corps came into camp, and their leader stopped by the schoolhouse to introduce himself to Erma. Before he could get a word out, Stubby's hair was bristling and a no nonsense snarl was rumbling from his chest. When Erma finally calmed the dog, the man was able to relay his message with conviction: his crew wouldn't be bothering her.

By 1937, the Campbells had been in the cattle business for forty-eight years. Although the OX and Circle C were well known in the cattle industry, most of the general public didn't recognize the two brands.

That promptly changed when both ranches, particularly the Circle C, were shot into the limelight when the Union Pacific Railroad carried a record-breaking shipment of cattle from New Meadows. The feat was the most highly publicized event of the decade. One *Statesman* reporter wryly commented, "I question whether there were more cows than photographers."

According to newspaper accounts, most of the frenzied activity was generated by the visiting dignitaries who participated in "Steer Week" celebrations.

The New Meadows citizens did have major cause to celebrate. Their railroad line had been in jeopardy for several months. The Union Pacific Railroad was in the process of purchasing Pacific and Idaho Northern lines. The ninety-mile stretch from Weiser to New Meadows wasn't as profitable as other routes, and Union Pacific balked at buying it, particularly at $700 a mile. In the end they agreed to buy the line, which restored New Meadows' bright economic outlook.

As a result, the entire community rallied around the Steer Week festivities in an effort to promote local commerce and to reinforce the railroad's decision to maintain the New Meadows line.

"The shipment is attracting romantic interest throughout the west from persons who associate the movement of cattle in such numbers with the days of cattle barons and unlimited range," wrote an anonymous *Statesman* reporter.

Adams County Leader Reporter Lee Highley wrote:

> Pictures taken in conjunction with the cattle movement will be used by Metro Goldwyn for newsreels, *Life* magazine, the Department of Agriculture to prove the value of bunch grass mountain range in Idaho and by the Union Pacific Company to advertise transportation facilities . . . Moving pictures and stills were taken for three days in the fields, pastures, scales and loading pins.
>
> (Sun Valley Rodeo Queen) Miss (Roberta) Bass, nattily attired as a cowgirl and mounted on Marshall Dryden's spirited pinto pony bore the brunt of many 'shots' though she was closely rivaled by Mrs. Caroline Campbell, mother of the Circle C ranch, whose image went to many cameras.

Albert and the cattle buyer, Tim Lydston, stepped out of the gay social whirl in order to orchestrate the shipment. According to the *Adams County Leader*, the most prominent brand was the

Albert Campbell didn't have time for frivolous activities, such as posing for formal portraits. This photograph is the only one of its kind. His daughter, Charlotte, speculates it was taken when Albert was inducted into the University of Idaho's Hickman Hall of Fame for his outstanding contributions to the cattle industry. (Photo courtesy of Charlotte Armacost Campbell.)

OX, which shipped 800 steers and 150 heifers. The Circle C was a close second, with 700 steers and 100 cows. The shipment was topped off with 975 cattle from other area ranchers, bringing the grand total to 2,725 head.

Early in the week the cattle were weighed and brought into concentration pastures, where Brand Inspector J.J. Levengood counted the stock and recorded the brands.

When September 26 dawned approximately twenty-five stockmen, both on horseback and on foot, were ready to roll.

Laws of the time dictated that animals could travel no more than thirty-six hours at a stretch. If the trip was longer than thirty-six hours, the animals had to be unloaded, watered, fed, and rested for twenty-four hours, which was an expensive proposition. The cattle were bound for the George Hanks Company in Denver, Colorado. It was possible to make the trip in thirty-six hours, but only if there were no delays.

The clock started when the first steer clattered up the inclined chute into the box car at 8 a.m. From then on, there was no wasted motion. The sliding door in the last box car slammed shut at 12:45 p.m., and minutes later the three Union Pacific engines pulled the train out of town.

The *Adams County Leader* reported that the 103-car train pulled into Denver with time to spare. As soon as the cattle were unloaded, they were fed beet pulp, as someone suggested the cattle should be fattened on sugar beets to add flavor to the steaks.

The *Adams County Leader* Reporter Highley indignantly responded, "We wonder about the taste of the Coloradoans (sic) that they try at all to add or detract from the flavor produced from the Idaho mountain bear grass which our steers like so well and eat at every opportunity."

The publicity quickly died down, but Albert hardly noticed; there were too many pending deals to look after. After his father died in 1932, Albert's role in the Circle C management intensified. His brother, Rollie, was also actively involved in the Circle C's day-to-day operation, but Albert's shrewd mind handled most of the negotiations and acquisitions.

Between his responsibilities on the OX and the Circle C, the man was rarely home. He spent much of the winter in Baker and Halfway, Oregon, making sure the feeding was going smoothly. The odometer on his Chevrolet spun constantly in the summer; when he wasn't checking the fencing on a Circle C pasture, he was bringing fresh meat and advice to an OX cow camp.

Albert was almost a stranger in his own home. The lonesome, bitterly cold New Meadows winters didn't appeal to his wife, Grace. As a result, she started taking their daughters Alberta and Charlotte to California during the winter.

"Dad was in full agreement that Mom should spend time in California . . . with her relatives . . . He missed his family, but knew we were better off having a few weeks of sunshine in the winter. Dad never discouraged mother when she wanted to travel, as long as he wasn't expected to go with her and she could find someone with whom to travel," said Charlotte Campbell Armacost.

The stress of running two ranches finally caught up to Albert in 1939, when he suffered a serious heart attack. He was first hospitalized at St. Luke's in Boise, and later transferred to a Portland hospital. Throughout the ordeal, he refused to acknowledge his illness, and he never relinquished his ranching duties. Although bedridden and under strict orders to relax, Albert managed to maintain his active role through a continuous stream of letters.

Albert had never tried to capture his ranching operation either with a camera or on paper; he considered such things a waste of time. The letters he wrote during his convalescence reveal some subtleties of his personality and philosophy:

To Vernon Brewer, Hornet District Ranger, Weiser National Forest (currently Council Ranger District, Payette National Forest):

> It keeps me busy keeping up with all the rules and regulations around here. The only time that I can really call my own is the two or three hours I lie awake every night and that is when I buy and sell land and cattle, build fence and (figure out) how the Forest should be run . . .

I know you are pretty busy building roads, fighting fires and trying to regulate the grazing on the Forest, but did it ever occur to you with Hitler taking over Europe with all its armies and equipment, what would happen to a few defenseless rangers if we stockmen decided to take over the forests?

However, the only thing I am worrying about is this, when we got you 11 (Forest Service employees) rounded up and had you swimming the Rio Grande if the tourists and sportsmen following Russia's lead would not step in and claim the spoils?

Now think this all over before jumping on a permittee for getting his stock on the range a little earlier in the spring.

To Tim Lydston, the often anxious cattle buyer:

Dear Panicky Tim,

After reading your letter over carefully I am convinced that in the thirty odd years I have known you, you have not changed a bit with the exception that you have had to let your belt out a trifle.

Rollie can leave Baker Sunday morning if you wire him what to do and whatever . . . you and Rollie figure out will be OK but I want to reserve the right to say, "I told you so," which is not asking too much for a sick man.

Now one more thing, then bed for a few hours. As you probably know, I am also interested in the 1940 Sept. market. If you ever make long range predictions, let me in on it. I will guarantee not to use anything you say or think in the next year's trade. I will even agree to burn the letter if (you) will open up and write just what you think.

To Dick Armacost, cowboy foreman:

Try and figure out some way to make the steers

do good as every pound lost now has to be replaced and a fat steer in Aug. might be worth a lot more than the same steer fat in October and if we have them fat we can always wait but if the other way around, there is nothing to do but fume.

To Carl Swanstrom, attorney, friend and, aggravatingly enough, a Democrat:

> For the last five months one doctor after another has lectured me not to argue or get mad, and I know what would happen before I could set you right on all the political quotations that confront the nation at this time . . .
>
> I'm still content that it will be included in the 25- 30 billion dollar ticket that will be handed our children's children next November just as a reminder that Franklin D. Roosevelt discovered America in 1932 instead of Columbus in 1492 . . .
>
> In closing I want to say that I am still an optimist and believe that with Congress in session, McNutt, Vandenburg, Taft, Hoover and Dewey on the air and in the field and F.D.R. fishing from the rear end of a battle ship somewhere within his 300 mile neutral fishing hole the nation will just rock along somehow.

Doctors refused to release Albert from the hospital until he endured a steady dose of warnings. Topping the list was the suggestion that he sell his land, and opt for an early retirement, at age fifty. He was also instructed to not get angry, eat lighter meals, and lie down after eating. "Yeah, yeah," he muttered impatiently.

When they finally let him go home, he blithely ignored their instructions. He defied everyone by refusing to be sick, and immediately resumed his brisk pace. Contrary to doctors' predictions, his heart carried him through the next forty years.

His return to ranching wasn't without its life-threatening dangers, however. Those came from a pistol-packing ranch hand named Ramey Rose.

Ramey Rose Rogers was named after a
gold mine. She once discouraged a
potential suitor by shooting at him.
(Photo courtesy of Darline Whiteley.)

Five

GLORY DAYS: THE 1940s

"There's nothing funnier than a mad woman."
—*Albert Campbell*

Albert crouched down in the rowboat and paddled furiously as yet another bullet zinged past his ear, barely missing the port side of the rowboat. This shot also hit the water. Albert didn't have to look back to know that Ramey was leveling her .38 pistol for another shot, this time on the starboard side.

The dispute began innocently enough at the Salt Creek cow camp. Albert had rowed across the Snake River to check in with his ranch foreman, Claude Childers, and to spar with Claude's new bride, Ramey. Albert liked to needle Ramey until she was on the verge of throttling him. Usually he had sense enough to retreat before she went over the edge, but he misjudged that day.

The altercation started over a horse Ramey didn't want anybody else to ride. By the end of the discussion, Ramey was seething and she threatened to shoot Albert. He retorted that a woman couldn't hit what she aimed at, so he had no need to worry. That did it. She whipped out the .38, and Albert's route back across the Snake was punctuated by pistol shots barely missing each side of the rowboat. Luckily for Albert, she was a crack shot.

Actually, Ramey was one of Albert's favorite people. She was one of the few who had enough intelligence and grit to win his respect. Some of that respect may have been born of fear, as Albert pushed things too far on a couple of memorable occasions.

One took place on Barbour Flat during branding. The crew had finished eating lunch in the cow camp's bunkhouse, and the women were washing the dishes, which were made from a heavy pottery.

From his vantage point at the end of the kitchen table, Albert began tormenting the ladies, particularly Ramey. He must have hit a vulnerable spot that day, because Ramey responded by throwing a plate, frisbee-style, at the agitator's head. It missed its mark by less than an inch. In the split second it took Ramey to grab another plate, her husband slipped out to the barn and the rest of the crew took cover under the table. Albert scrambled toward the bedroom, but he never made it. The second plate caught him right at the base of the skull. Ramey's daughter, Darline, remembered that Albert looked "like a kid about ready to cry."

"Oh my God," he exclaimed in a high voice. "Bring the needle and thread and sew me up."

Although he didn't require medical attention, the plate left a good-sized welt on the back of Albert's head. His daughter, Charlotte, said a scar marked the spot for the rest of his life.

"Dad figured that he could get out of most any hot spot if he could get the other person to laugh. Ramey came close to not letting him out of a few hot spots," said Charlotte.

Ramey was well-acquainted with the OX country before she married Claude; she had spent much of her girlhood in different locations along the Snake and Wildhorse Rivers.

Her father, Ed Rogers, was somewhat of a nomad. In fact, Ramey Rose was named for a gold mine he had encountered on his travels. Married life and nine children slowed his wanderlust, but he still moved his family regularly. As a result, the children received little formal education; Ramey never attended school past the third grade. Most of her practical reading and math skills were developed from the Montgomery Ward catalog. She was often in charge of ordering the family's clothing, which required her to read the item descriptions and figure the totals.

The Rogers family spent some time on a ranch almost directly across from the OX Wildhorse headquarters on the Snake River. After selling out to Mabel Gordon Ray's father, the family settled along Wildhorse for a time.

The Rogers kids grew up tough, which was probably a survival tactic. Their father was subject to violent rages, particularly when he'd been drinking. Ramey was already married and gone when her mother, Maude, filed for divorce. Maude and the younger children moved back into Wildhorse after she married Dan Bisbee, who had a homestead at the mouth of Bisbee Creek.

Ramey was a widow with a two-year-old daughter when Claude Childers married her in 1936. The threesome made their first home in No Business Basin.

From the start, Ramey and Claude were a study of contrasting personalities. Claude was soft-spoken and rarely swore. Even though Claude was completely loyal to Albert, he was inclined to moan about Albert's instructions, and enumerate the reasons why the strategies would fail.

Ramey Rogers Childers and her daughter, Darline, prepare to mow hay in No Business Basin. Ramey married Claude Childers (left) in 1936. (Photo courtesy of Darline Whiteley.)

Like his wife, he enjoyed an occasional argument with Albert; however, his altercations ended on a much quieter note. According to his step-daughter, Darline, Claude always signaled the end of the conversation by coughing, grabbing his hat, and walking out the door.

As Ramey's conflict resolution methods indicate, her approach often differed from Claude's. At least one difference endeared her to Albert and the crew alike. She never balked when Albert gave orders. While Claude needed persuasion, "Ramey just did it," remembered Albert's nephew, Don Whiteman. "At that time, Ramey was the most valuable asset to the ranch. She was a hard worker."

Ramey wasn't afraid of any kind of work. She pulled calves, dug post holes, mowed hay, and coaxed bulls out of brush patches. She doctored wire-cut horses by slathering honey over their wounds. When branding time rolled around, she was available to throw, castrate, or dehorn the calves. Frank Smith, who helped at brandings as a young boy, was amazed at her capabilities on a cutting horse. Through the years, Ramey was one of Albert's most dependable and skilled hands, yet she was never put on the payroll. Albert's daughter, Charlotte, explained that the Childers were hired as a couple. Nevertheless, the check was always made out to Claude.

When lunchtime rolled around, the crew had a standing rule: Ramey got to wash up first. Whether there were three people or an entire haying crew, she had a meal on the table by the time the last person had washed. Her meals were simple, but delicious. Since there was no refrigeration, ham was the predominant main course.

The menu altered when Albert visited; he always brought fresh beef into camp. Ramey often brought out her huge aluminum bowl and made a wilted lettuce salad for the occasion. Albert always gorged himself on the salad; sometimes he polished off half the bowl.

While the men took a breather, Ramey washed the dishes, cleaned the kitchen, and put away the food. When she was finished, they tromped out together to finish the day's work. By and large, the men respected Ramey.

The No Business Basin haying crew takes a breather. Childers and Rogers family members often brought out musical instruments during the evenings. (Photo courtesy of Darline Whiteley.)

The Whiteman boys, who grew up in civilized Cambridge, Idaho, had never before encountered anyone like her. It was understood that ladies who wanted a profession became either nurses or teachers. Femininity was carefully balanced with professionalism.

Ramey didn't begin to fit the mold. She was direct, often to the point of being crude, and she had a colorful vocabulary which she used freely and naturally. When she drank, she didn't do it halfway. As a result, she pounded her way through a good number of fist fights outside Bear schoolhouse dances. Her sisters were also adept at hand-to-hand combat.

"Ramey never had a cigarette out of her mouth," remembered Don Whiteman. "Ramey wore men's Levi's and men's shirts. She washed and wetted her hair down like a man, and she would comb it straight back. She was rough talking, but she babied her husband," he said.

The "babying" came from Ramey's nurturing side, which surfaced regularly with Claude and Darline, her daughter. On top of her tremendous work load, she regularly baked their favorite

Ramey's caretaker role is illustrated in this photograph. Ramey and Claude Childers enjoy their meticulous yard in No Business Basin. (Photo courtesy of Darline Whiteley.)

pies: lemon, raisin, vinegar, and fresh huckleberry. Since her family loved huckleberries, she made time to pick them. Her favorite patch was at the fork of the Landore and Black Lake roads, and she was always afraid that someone would hit the spot before she did.

Maintaining a spotless home was also a high priority for Ramey; even the dark corners were scrubbed regularly. Darline laughed about the time a colt ran into the house at the Basin. The floors were so waxed that he couldn't stand up.

Yet another household duty was delegated to Ramey: she handled all the hunting. Claude's one and only hunting expedition occurred when he was a young man, and it turned into an ordeal as soon as he shot the deer. The man never carried a pocketknife, which was peculiar for a cowboy. After searching all his pockets, he found only one item that could possibly help him dress out the animal: a buttonhook. The small, blunt hook was designed to button shoes, but Claude was determined to make it do double duty. He poked at the hide for the greater part of the day before the opening was large enough to gut the animal.

Claude did track one other deer, but he had a different mission. This deer was an orphaned fawn.

Darline happened into the kitchen at Barbour Flat as her folks were preparing a bottle for something in the barn. When she tried to trail them to the barn, they sent her back to the house. "Dad didn't believe in girls seeing anything. I rode up after school one day, and they were pulling a calf. I was rushed away," Darline recalled. As a result, she didn't think anything unusual was happening.

When she opened her eyes the next morning, the fawn was standing on her bed. She named her birthday present Bambi.

Darline wasn't given too many responsibilities as a child. She fed the pigs and the chickens, and played outside. "I didn't work inside the house unless I had to," she emphasized.

When work took Ramey away from home, Darline stayed with her grandmother Bisbee, who lived a few miles up Wildhorse. She had a playmate there; her youngest aunt, Lily Bisbee, was just her age.

Darline remembers that most of her mother's days fell into a

Darline Hamilton introduces her pet fawn, Bambi, to a black calf. Bambi was a birthday surprise from her folks, Claude and Ramey Childers. (Photo courtesy of Darline Whiteley.)

comfortable, if rigorous pattern. A tattered, five-year diary with "Ramey Rose Childers" embossed on the cover helps reconstruct her day-to-day routine during the early Forties.

Ramey's day ended as soon as she scrawled one or two sentences in the little book. "Warm!" was all she wrote on an early spring day. Other typical entries included:

> "Rained last night. Put rest of calves and cows (out) and pruned fruit trees."
> "Same old housework."
> "Went down and got Eloise (McClemmons) and groceries."
> "Rode Big Bar to check (for cattle.)"
> "Washed, baked bread at Daggit (Degitz) place."

Anecdotes were hard to detect without interpretive help from her daughter. For example, her December 7, 1943 entry read simply, "I got my eye hurt." According to Darline, Ramey was using a team to drag logs out of the Basin for a community bridge building project. As she approached a recently abandoned fire pit, it exploded. Debris peppered her face, but she suffered no permanent damage. Later investigation revealed hunters had left a live shell in the smoldering embers.

Clear in the back of the diary is a carefully penned notation:

Richard (Brick) H. Rogers went in Army			7-13-40
Ernest	"	"	11-42
Eldon (Tuffy)	"	"	11-19-42

We hope and pray they come home all well as they went in.

World War II was a frightening experience for Ramey and her neighbors. Aside from economic trends, what happened in the

Darline Hamilton and her half-brother, Bud Haskins, gather scrap rubber out of No Business Basin for the war effort. Their mother, Ramey Childers, anxiously listened to radio newscasts. She worried about the fate of her three brothers. (Photo courtesy of Darline Whiteley.)

outside world had never mattered to the remotely located ranchers. After Pearl Harbor, every piece of news became critically important. Democracy was at stake.

Albert was intensely patriotic—the Fourth of July was always his favorite holiday. He turned a concerned ear toward the radio every evening, and encouraged Grace when she focused her attention on numerous war bond drives. A thick stack of commendation letters reveal the depth of her commitment.

The Wildhorse and Bear communities rallied to the cause immediately, even though they were far removed from the war's effects. Almost every family sent someone to fight. Tuffy, the third of Ramey's brothers to enlist, left on the same train as Arnold Emery. OX hands Bob Whiteman, Don Whiteley, and Bub Whiteley joined the effort, as well as Bud McGahey, who left a wife and small daughter in Bear.

The families steeled themselves for personal losses; the war had to be won at any cost. The communities grasped at any project to support the war effort. Ramey wrote a steady stream of encouraging letters and baked cookies for care packages, while Darline and her half-brother gathered old tires, irrigation boots, and any other excess rubber for recycling.

Ramey retained an optimistic outlook throughout the war. Her horse, Clipper, had a white "V" on its neck. Ramey told her daughter that it stood for victory.

Albert and other Idaho cattlemen felt the war's impact years before the United States entered. As president of the Idaho Cattleman's Association, Albert heard that a lucrative government beef contract had been awarded to Tom Carstens, who had a major packing plant in Tacoma, Washington.

The contract was awarded during the Depression, and Albert jumped at the chance to secure a steady market for Idaho cattle.

The beef was quartered, frozen, and boxed before the Army shipped it to its destination in the south Pacific. Part of that beef supplied Pearl Harbor before the attack. The Army also supplied a major storage facility on an island near the Philippines. When the island was later captured by the Japanese, the quartermaster gave orders to ruin the beef by flooding the underground freezer with sea water.

A ranching accident and the resulting broken pelvis delayed Bob Whiteman's entry into the Army Air Corps. Ironically, his cast was removed on Pearl Harbor Day. He fed OX cattle and performed other rigorous ranch work to regain his strength. (Photograph courtesy of Charlotte Campbell Armacost.)

The war brought the nation out of the Depression, and cattle prices leaped. The resulting business opportunities were clouded by one factor: the war was creating a growing shortage of local manpower.

Albert probably felt the tightest squeeze in 1943, the year Dick and Erma Armacost left the OX. Dick sought higher paying jobs until he could afford a ranch of his own. "In those days, anybody capable of operating your ranch was already operating his own ranch. There was no future for a hand. They'd work for an outfit and leave with scars, memories, and a little in their pocket. Guys like Albert didn't get where they were by benevolence," explained Dick and Erma's son, Gary Armacost.

Henry and Helena Schmidt left for similar reasons in 1938. They bought a ranch below Helena's parents' place, Starveout, and eventually put the two places together. The responsibilities kept both of them running.

Both the Schmidts and Armacosts left the ranch on good terms. Although busy with their own endeavors, they jumped at the chance to help Albert during branding, or when he needed neighborly assistance. And Albert reciprocated.

The crew that helped Claude run the Basin was gone too. The summer after Tuffy Rogers and Arnold Emery enlisted, Albert decided to sell the Basin. No doubt it was an agonizing decision; he hated to sell anything, let alone the acreage which launched the OX thirty-three years before.

People have differing views on what clinched his decision to sell. Holworth Nixon, who was a neighbor on Dukes Creek, said the ditches were difficult to maintain. He also mentioned that after a bulldozer broke through some shale, part of the ditch wouldn't hold water. Don Whiteley said that Albert couldn't hire enough guys to watch the irrigated land. It took two or three men to keep the ditches from washing out.

Albert put a $12,000 price tag on the place and offered it to Henry and Helena Schmitt, since the Basin adjoined their ranch. He told them the outfit was worth $20,000. They didn't have the cash, so they had to turn him down.

Ramey and Claude offered to buy the place, and Albert agreed even though it left him with less than a skeleton crew. Ramey's diary noted the date: October 23, 1943.

The Childers had a rough time operating the Basin with their limited capital. In fact, the nation's newly found prosperity never reached the area ranchers with small operations. As a result, the whole Wildhorse community welcomed an unexpected windfall that came on the mail stage one day. The vehicle was crammed with food, blankets, and other essentials, and the driver had instructions from an anonymous source to distribute them throughout the community. Albert was the suspected benefactor, although he refused to accept thanks for the deed.

Albert asked Elmer Langer, who was a good hand with horses, to take Claude's place. Elmer and his brother, Pike, came from Halfway, Oregon, and sometimes their methods differed from Albert's.

One of the longest debates concerned the morning coffee. According to Don Whiteman who worked summers with the

Langers, the brothers couldn't leave a cup of coffee in the bottom of the pot; they liked to enjoy a lingering cup before facing the day. Albert, on the other hand, rarely waited for the sun to rise. He told Elmer there was no time for coffee drinking in his outfit. Elmer said, "Fine. What time would you like us to start?"

"About this time is good," Albert answered.

The conversation took place at six; so the next morning Elmer rousted everyone out of bed a half hour earlier, leaving plenty of time for their indulgence. Albert hit the roof.

Both Albert and Elmer refused to give in, and each time Albert protested, Elmer set his alarm clock a half hour earlier. Don, who had to wrangle horses the first thing every morning, bore the brunt of the argument. He was grateful when the debate was finally settled. As always, Albert had the last word. Elmer and Pike began bolting down their morning coffee.

Elmer, Pike, and Don once spent the day gathering cattle on Indian Creek. It was dark by the time they rode onto Barbour Flat and put the cattle into a pasture below the house. The next morning fourteen head were belly up. A quick check revealed they had eaten the poisonous larkspur plant.

The threesome quickly put the survivors above the fence, and Elmer told Don to change horses and ride to Bear, where he could call Albert. Don, who was just a kid, dreaded his uncle's reaction. It didn't take long for him to think of an answer: "No."

"I've got the dogs and I need to help with the cattle," Elmer reasoned.

Don spent the entire ride to Bear steeling himself up for Albert's reaction. After the operator made the connection, Don explained the mishap and waited for the explosion. None came. Albert just said, "Damn it, Don, you should have checked." He never mentioned it again.

Albert wasn't always so forgiving. He and Don were herding cattle once, and a steer broke away from the herd. Rather than swinging wide and encouraging the steer to return to the herd on his own accord, Don spurred his horse and chased the animal. In a high, agitated voice Albert said, "If I'd of had a .12 gauge shotgun, I'd have blown your head off." He mentioned the incident several times.

Don Whiteman (pictured) helped Pike, Elmer, and Dorothy Langer run the OX ranching operation during the war. Once, when Albert Campbell was late with the groceries, the foursome ate nothing but canned tomatoes for days. (Photo courtesy of Charlotte Campbell Armacost.)

Albert wouldn't tolerate people who were impatient with animals; hands rarely chased, shouted, or even whistled at his herd more than once. Anything that would upset the cattle, even arm waving, was strictly forbidden. When the cattle needed to be moved, it was done with as little agitation as possible, since stressed cattle won't show steady weight gain. "Move 'em slow and let 'em eat," Albert told the crew repeatedly.

His philosophy also covered the riding stock. He told his daughter, Charlotte, "Anyone can make a horse run. It takes a rider to make him walk."

Albert's all-time favorite horse, Nick, liked to walk out. The horse and rider had similar temperaments; both liked to cover a lot of ground and both had a cantankerous side. Nick occasionally came close to gaining the upper hand. When that happened, Albert had to struggle to maintain his demeanor.

Shortly after he was admonished for chasing the steer, Don Whiteman was delighted to watch Albert and Nick in action. As soon as Albert climbed into the saddle, the horse bunched up his tail and was ready to buck. Albert came to anticipate the routine, but that day he ran out of patience. As Don listened, Albert's voice became a high whine, "Nick, if I had a pair of spurs on, I'd cut your heart out."

Albert was particular about stock handling, but range conditions were his top concern. He was always scrutinizing the range, searching for ways to improve its management. Whenever the Forest Service wanted to construct test plots or the University of Idaho developed a new grass variety, Albert eagerly provided the outdoor laboratory.

Albert's hands often viewed the experiments with less enthusiasm. Such was the case when Albert agreed to cultivate a newly-developed rye hybrid on Barbour Flat.

"(Haying) it was a mess," Don Whiteman said. "It would tangle, it was hard to make into shocks . . . and its stems were as big as my thumb."

To make matters worse, the crew couldn't look forward to mealtime. Albert was late with the groceries. "In our pantry we had only Wheaties, condensed milk, and canned tomatoes. He didn't come. Pretty soon we were down only to the tomatoes . . . The whole crew lived on tomatoes for three to four days. Dinner was cold tomatoes. Lunch was stewed tomatoes."

Pike Langer finally decided to buy groceries in Bear. "We saw the cigarette glow over the hill and knew deliverance was near," Don recalled. It was a bleak sort of deliverance, even though he'd bought out the store. The eager hands unpacked three or four cans of vienna sausages and more Wheaties.

A day or two passed before Albert finally rolled into camp. The groceries received more of a welcome than Albert did. Elmer's wife, Dorothy, hustled the groceries inside. The men soon heard wonderful crackling and sizzling sounds coming from the stove;

sounds they hadn't heard in a while. When they eagerly pulled their chairs up to the kitchen table, Dorothy served Elmer, Pike, and Don plates heaped with fried eggs and crisp bacon. Albert's plate came last. It held a forlorn lump of canned tomatoes.

Dorothy also made a chocolate cake with the new provisions. Don was half-ashamed of the hunk he cut. When the three men finished their first helping, only a third of the cake remained on the plate. "If that's all you're going to take," Dorothy admonished, "it will be the last you see in a while."

The OX hands temporarily abandoned their remote posts every fall to help ship the Circle C and OX steers out of New Meadows. Most shipping days lacked the dignitaries and rodeo queens that attended the record-breaking 1938 shipment, but they were always memorable events.

A scheduling conflict made the Union Pacific engines unavailable during loading one year. The resourceful cowboys played two roles that year. While part of them managed the cattle, Don Whiteman and several others used their horses to tow boxcars to and from the loading chutes.

Don was also on hand during the October 3, 1943 shipment, which became another media heyday. Reporter Glenn Balch found the journalists' antics were far more interesting than the cattle. He filed the following page-one story:

> Cameramen were equally as vigilant on the trail as at the pens. For every string had its outflanking fringe of snappers and crankers, all vigorously determined to get "that picture" in whatever position they might have to assume at whatever cost to their dignity.
>
> Herd after herd of these were driven and photographed into the big loading pens and bunch after bunch was snapped and cranked up the runways while sweating cowhands punched and jabbed and swore at cattle and cameramen alike.
>
> This went on hour after hour while back in the dusty ranks late comers scrapped and jockeyed for

parking places. The bawling of the steers sounded over the countryside, drowning the cries and shouts of the drivers, drowning even the click and whir of the cameras.

Among the clickers and whirrers was Dr. Maynard Owen Williams, a photographer for *The National Geographic Magazine*. He and the author, Idaho Senator D. Worth Clark, were preparing a feature on Idaho, which appeared in the June, 1944 edition. Undoubtedly they remembered their New Meadows experience:

> . . . to get photographs of the herd Williams took to the saddle, since a man on foot is liable to 'spook,' or stampede them. The cow pony, sensing a strange rider, turned the stream-crisscrossed pasture into a steeplechase, but the photographer escaped unscathed. Later he sat on a fence and took some closeups.

Needless to say, the photos chosen for publication were obviously "fence shots."

Reports about the number of cattle shipped varied. *National Geographic* set the figure at "about 3,000 head," which concurs with the local belief that the shipment's size broke all previous records.

The cattle buyer, Tim Lydston, clipped a wildly inaccurate account for his files. The yellowed newsprint, which had an Ogden, Utah dateline, reported that 2,200 longhorn steers had been shipped through Ogden by the Albert Campbell Cattle Company. Albert wouldn't have had a longhorn on his place.

The train pulled out of New Meadows bound for Ovid, Colorado. Bub Whiteley, who was working for the OX, rode in the caboose with Tim Lydston.

Once again, the cattle were on a tight schedule. The industry still operated under the law which said cattle could ride no more than thirty-six hours at a stretch. With a twelve-hour stopover in Ogden, Lydston calculated the shipment could reach Ovid within the time frame, if there were no delays.

There were no mishaps on the first leg of the trip; the train

A National Geographic photographer snapped this shot of the Campbell family during a record-breaking cattle shipment on the Union Pacific railroad. From left: Loyal, Rollie, Caroline, Charlotte, and Albert. Charlotte commented that her grandmother was always properly attired; she even wore a hat in the stockyards. (Photo courtesy of Charlotte Campbell Armacost.)

arrived in Ogden at 9 a.m. "The cattle wouldn't eat or drink while they were off; the horses in the stockyards had disturbed them," Bub said. "Tim cried about that."

Lydston was worried about economics. As long as the cattle were without food and water, they were losing weight. And the more weight they lost, the longer they would have to stay on the feedlot.

Like Albert, Lydston lived for his work. This train ride culminated a year of second-guessing the cattle market, countless phone calls, thousands of miles of driving, and haggling prices with ranchers. He loved it all, but this was his moment of glory, particularly since many of the cattle were headed for his own newly acquired feedlot.

By the time the cattle were loaded, Lydston realized his shipment would meet the Portland Rose somewhere around Laramie, Wyoming. The luxury passenger train, which ran between Chicago and Portland, reigned supreme. Her trips were never interrupted; all other trains were sidetracked to let her come through.

Lydston didn't have time to wait. He appealed to Union Pacific's W.A. Harriman, who was a personal friend. Lydston had two factors in his favor. First, he shipped more cattle via Union Pacific than any other individual. Second, Harriman loved the publicity generated by the huge shipment. In an unprecedented move, Harriman picked up the phone and called the chief dispatcher.

"The Portland Rose went in the hole as the cars of cattle went screaming by. The old man was just having a hell of a time," said Tim's son, Hugh Lydston.

The train was thundering through Colorado when news of another delay reached Lydston: President Franklin D. Roosevelt's train needed the track. The conductor was instructed to sideline the train in another two hours.

Although some passenger trains had telegraphs on board, most trains sent and received messages the old fashioned way. Written notes were slipped into special message bags, which were dropped at designated message points.

Lydston dashed off a reply to Harriman which said, "Tell Roosevelt to go in the hole. We can't stop because of the time line." He explained that a delay would push the cattle over their thirty-six-hour transportation limit. That meant the entire shipment would have to be unloaded for the required twelve-hour rest in Greeley, Colorado, which was about two hours from the final destination.

"I've done thousands of dollars of business with you. We've gotta make this work. We can't ruin it now," Lydston wrote. He added one more persuasive point: "These cattle are needed for the war effort."

Harriman telegraphed the message to the presidential train.

Tension mounted in the caboose as Lydston waited for the reply. When it finally arrived he read, "The beef must roll. Roosevelt going in the hole."

OX cowboy Bub Whiteley stayed in Ovid for a couple of weeks, where he helped sort the three-year-old steers that were destined for Chicago.

Every morning Bub watched an interesting routine from his hotel window. German prisoners of war, under their own commanders' leadership, snapped to attention. After another volley of German commands, the group began to sing. Soon afterwards, the prisoners left with area sugar beet farmers. They spent their days in the fields, topping sugar beets.

The war changed the course of Tim Lydston's career twice. When the war started, Lydston was working out of the Denver Stockyards in a comfortable and lucrative partnership with George Hanks. George's wife, Minnie, urged her husband to sell the business as quickly as possible. The couple had suffered through the Depression which followed World War I, and Minnie didn't want to lose their life savings in a similar situation.

George finally decided to dissolve the partnership, and he left the cattle business during one of its most profitable periods. The economic decline that his wife feared never materialized.

According to his son, Hugh, Lydston left the partnership with $800,000 in cash and a ranch in Broomfield, which is now a rapidly expanding Denver suburb. Although forward-thinking friends advised him to keep the ranch, Lydston cashed it in.

He brought his green collateral and a business proposition to Denver First National Bank. Lydston envisioned a feedlot in Ovid, Colorado, which could handle 7,000 head of cattle at a time. He chose Ovid because the nearby Great Western Sugar factory would produce an ample supply of beet pulp, a potent cattle feed. The bank enthusiastically backed his idea, and he was in business.

Lydston sped around the country, choosing the most promising stock for his operation; OX and Circle C cattle lined a good share of the feed bunkers.

The majority of his stock was ready for market when a

shattering announcement was issued from the White House. After a secret meeting with his Brain Trust, President Roosevelt decided to roll back cattle prices to a pre-war level.

Lydston didn't have an inkling of what was coming. "Dad would have given the cattle away for the feed bill. He had no choice but to sell; they were ready for slaughter," said Hugh.

"As a result, Dad went flat broke and Denver First National lost about $700,000. The bank let him have $500, his car, and his furniture."

Thirty days after the cattle sold, President Roosevelt reversed his decision and prices shot back to market levels.

Years after the fiasco, Lydston joked that the President had an ulterior motive. He claimed Roosevelt had issued the price restriction because his train was put in the hole for the cattle cars.

As soon as the bankruptcy proceedings were completed, Lydston loaded his family and belongings into the car, and headed for Seattle. Safeway hired him to buy cattle throughout the western United States and Canada. He was also to run their newly acquired beef packing plant.

The arrangement didn't alter his working patterns; he continued his yearly forays to the OX and Circle C ranches.

Lydston started buying cattle from the Campbells while Albert's father, Charlie, was still at the helm. The business relationship continued for nearly half a century. According to Albert's brother, Rollie, Lydston bought Circle C and OX cattle for forty-eight years. Lydston lost the contract only one year, during the early Fifties.

"He was tough," reflected ninety-four-year-old Rollie Campbell. "As long as a guy's honest, it's part of his business to be tough. We liked him because we thought he was honest, but he did have his enemies."

The Lydston family looked forward to the annual buying trip to central Idaho; the event became a family vacation during the Forties and early Fifties. Since Lydston's wife, Alma, and Rollie's wife, Marguerite, were close friends, the Lydstons headquartered at the Circle C ranch house.

"The adults were at a loss as to how I should treat and address Rollie, Marguerite, Albert, and Grace. I was told, at my earliest recollection, to call them aunts and uncles. I didn't know they were not my real uncles and aunts until I was fifteen years old," Hugh recalled.

Before each buying trip, Lydston spent hours on the telephone trying to amass enough information to predict cattle market activity. He called producers everywhere in the United States, and kept a running tally of how many cattle would be sold and when they would be coming off pasture.

According to Hugh, the Department of Agriculture supplied similar figures, but they weren't dependable. The data came from licensed buyers who weren't eager to divulge information in their competitive business. Most buyers appeased the government by submitting random numbers, and accumulated staggering phone bills while trying to get the real story.

Lydston also kept in close contact with a myriad of feedlot owners and meat packers, who ordered the cattle through him. They, in effect, signed his paycheck. Lydston earned his commission by sizing up a rancher's herd and making a fair offer, based on market conditions and beef quality.

By June or July, Lydston was ready to negotiate an early contract with the Campbells. Over the years, young Hugh watched much of the process from the back seat of his dad's Cadillac. His father's negotiations with Albert were never boring. "I suppose that's one of the reasons I get along well in public confrontations," he remarked. "I grew up around Albert and Tim, who make the worst of anybody I've ever seen look like Grandma Moses."

Albert loved to negotiate with Lydston; it was his favorite time of year. "It was like Christmas, New Year's Eve, and birthdays, all rolled into one for Albert," his nephew Bob Whiteman remembered.

Rollie usually began sale negotiations for the Circle C, but Albert always had the last word. Once a deal was struck for the Circle C, the haggling began for the OX cattle.

The most heated negotiations took place among the cattle. Lydston often drove, jolting his Cadillac over the rough terrain until he reached the cattle. Conversation in the car drifted from personal topics to the attributes of various bulls.

Lydston stopped the car before it reached the herd and he and Albert stepped outside. In the distance, the steers barely acknowledged their presence. That changed when Lydston cupped his hands around his mouth, and emitted a weird assortment of hoots, growls, and squeals. Before long, several hundred white faces were pointed in his direction. A couple of the braver steers stepped toward the car, and the rest formed a crowded semi-circle which curiously approached the strange noise maker. When the steers were close enough, Lydston sized up the herd, checking for quality and size.

After Lydston made his assessment, he and Albert piled back into the car. This time they discussed range conditions, and speculated when the steers would have to be pulled off.

Lydston repeatedly stressed the importance of selling the cattle while they were still gaining weight. Even so, some ranchers hoped to get the best price by keeping their cattle until the last moment. They figured the extra days of grazing would give them heavier animals to sell and, therefore, a better price.

The opposite was true. Lydston would only pay top dollar for cattle that were still grazing in optimal range conditions. Those animals would still be showing a steady weight gain. Once on the feedlot, they would continue to gain and give the feeders the highest margin of profit.

Conversely, cattle that had been subsisting on dry grass didn't show much weight gain when they first hit the feedlot. The extra time and feed needed to put the cattle "on the gain" saddled the feeder with an unnecessary expense.

The OX had little irrigated ground, so Albert usually shipped cattle in late August. The steers were all classified as medium to lightweight, which was a reflection of the shorter grazing season.

Albert's early shipping date did have its advantages. Beef which made it to the packing plants before the fall rush often commanded a higher price. As a result, Albert always pushed Lydston for an earlier delivery date.

After Lydston judged the cattle for size, quality, and availability, he gave Albert a detailed analysis of the current cattle market. Based on that information, he gave Albert an offer and waited for the inevitable explosion.

Tim Lydston tests the cattle scales at Lick Creek, while Claude Childers (right) watches. Tim and Albert Campbell liked to bet on cattle weights. The winner won a fifty dollar Stetson hat. (Photo courtesy of Darline Whiteley.)

"One day's negotiation ended in Lydston storming off in his Cadillac, and Albert leaving in a huff," remembered Bonnie Whiteley Reid, who grew up on the OX. "The next day, he settled for the same price. They seemed to enjoy the argument."

Former OX and Circle C cowboy Herb Mink shared similar memories. "Albert and Tim would call each other anything but gentlemen. They used 'more crooked than a dog's hind leg' to describe some of the dealings," he said.

As colorful as the dickering became, there was one ground rule: they never lied to each other. "They might temporarily withhold information from each other to gain a temporary edge, but in the final analysis, when they had to make the final deal, there was a concession of reality on either side," said Hugh Lydston.

"My dad really liked Albert, but it was rather unrequited. But, I think if Albert liked anybody, he liked my dad," he concluded.

Lydston and Albert had several traits in common: they were driven men who lived for the cattle business, they had ornery senses of humor, and they were stubborn.

Interestingly enough, the two also shared similar backgrounds. Lydston was born in Midvale, Idaho, which is approximately forty miles southwest of New Meadows, as the crow flies. His father, Charles, had dreams of building a ranching empire, and they were coming true. Tim claimed their ranch was larger than the Circle C around the turn of the century.

Charles' aspirations ended abruptly one day when he rode up to a gate on horseback. As he leaned over to open the latch, the horse threw his head, knocking Charles in the temple. He died on the spot. Tim was twelve.

Before long, Tim's mother married again, this time to a man named McCaw. Tim hated him, and later described him as a drunken syphilitic.

Lydston's hatred for his step-father peaked when he was about sixteen. He finally decided to leave home. He saddled a horse, and before he left, he sought out McCaw to give him a token of his esteem—with a pistol.

He found McCaw at the sale yard, and took aim. His first shot missed, and his gun-shy horse started rearing. Lydston kept firing, but none of his wild shots found the target. When the pistol was empty, he took off at a dead run.

Lydston rode the horse to Weiser, which was the nearest community to the southwest. He sold the horse and saddle for pocket money and hired on with the railroad as a stoker. He shoveled coal from Weiser to Santa Fe and from Denver to Seattle. The job launched his life-long fascination with the railroads.

Lydston kept in touch with his mother during this period, and she eventually persuaded him to leave the railroad, and attend a business college in Portland, Oregon. Lydston had completed the fourth or fifth grade in Midvale. Graduation from the business college brought his formal education to the eighth grade level, which was where Albert Campbell stopped.

He made his first cattle deal in Texas when he was about twenty-one years old. ''He bought a bunch of Mexican cattle that were five or six years old and about eight inches wide,'' said Hugh. ''He pulled the hair out of their tails to shorten their tails and make them look younger. Then he took them back to Midvale to sell them to his drunken McCaw step-father to get even with him and to get some dollars off him.''

The transaction caused the final blow-up, and Lydston left Midvale for good. Even after his career was established, he never bought cattle in the Midvale valley.

Lydston ended up in Tacoma, Washington, where Tom Carstens operated one of two giant packinghouses in the west. The other giant, the H.B. Moffet Company, was located in Sacramento, California. The two enterprises virtually controlled the cattle market on the west coast.

Lydston had heard that Carstens was the best cattle judge in the United States. Lydston managed to capture the busy man's attention long enough to make a business proposition. He told Carstens that he wanted to learn the cattle buying trade, and he offered to work for nothing if Carstens would teach him.

''Anytime somebody wants to work for nothing, I'll take him up on it,'' Carstens replied.

From that moment on, Lydston became Carstens' shadow, and his employer loved the arrangement. Not only was Lydston a quick study with a natural aptitude for judging cattle, having an assistant made Carstens' job easier.

Lydston's on-the-job training began in his employer's huge feedlots, where he learned to appraise a live animal's market value using four criteria: fat color, conformation, marbling, and yield.

Fat color became important at the supermarket; housewives preferred the white fat of grain-fed beef over the yellow-tinged fat which distinguished grass-fed animals. Grass-fed beef wouldn't grade prime or choice, the grades that commanded top prices. Those animals were kept at the feedlot until they made the grade.

Accurately guessing a live animal's fat color was a tricky proposition. Carstens taught Lydston to look at the animal's hair. When the hide revealed a combination of oiliness, curliness, and texture, the animal had white fat. Lydston scrutinized thousands of animals, both live and recently killed, before he unraveled the mystery.

Conformation, or the animal's build, was the easiest to judge. Lydston looked for a solid layer of fat over the back and hindquarters.

Marbling, or the amount of fat interspersed with the meat, was also detected by looking at the hair. A hide that was oily and lustrous on the loins, just ahead of the hips, indicated marbling. The quality was much more difficult to judge in the summer, because the cattle were sprayed with an oily insecticide to combat parasites. If that was the case, Lydston watched the animals take a step. A good amount of fat between the back legs or ahead of the knee indicated ample marbling.

The final and most important evaluation was the yield, or the percentage of the animal's weight that produced marketable beef. About the best yield was sixty-three percent, while sixty-one percent was at the lower end of the scale.

All four characteristics had to be evaluated in a few short seconds, as the fat cattle were being sorted. Those that met the criteria were bound for the packing plant. The others went back to the feedlot. Lydston spent hours watching Carstens make the instant judgment calls as the cattle ran in front of him, four at a time. In time, Carstens watched as Lydston made the calls. "In the lead two, by the third and in the hind end," Lydston shouted, telling the men running the gates that the first two cattle were bound for market, the third was to stay at the feedlot and the fourth was also ready for the packing plant.

Mistakes were costly. If Lydston missed on two cattle, the feedlot wouldn't make money. If four graded good instead of choice, money would be lost. With practice, Lydston could sort a constant stream of cattle and never make a mistake.

After six months, Lydston told Carstens he was going to have to leave. Carstens was shocked, "What do you mean you have to leave. Where are you going?"

"I've run out of money," Lydston explained. He was still honoring his part of the bargain by working without pay. "I have to make some money in order to live. But I'll be back, because I'm learning a lot."

"What do you mean you don't have any money?" roared Carstens.

"You don't pay me anything."

"The hell I don't," Carstens shot back. "God damn, I never put you on the payroll, did I?"

"No, and I didn't ask you," said Lydston. "The deal was that I would work for nothing if I could learn."

Lydston went on the payroll that day as an assistant buyer. He worked directly for Carstens until 1928. Even after he left to manage a series of feedlots and packinghouses, Carstens still contracted him to buy cattle, and, as a result, much of the OX beef ended up in Tacoma.

His relationship with the Campbells began shortly after he went on Carstens' payroll, and even early in his career he never failed to make an impression on the ranch hands. He liked to run the show.

He burst into the Circle C kitchen one morning in the 1920s. Bertha Armacost was preparing lunch, and Lydston popped in the door. When he brashly told her how to improve her efficiency, she wanted to pound him.

Lydston also rankled Don Whiteman and Herb Mink on occasion. They walked by his Cadillac one afternoon and spotted a box of fifty-cent cigars setting on the seat. It was the perfect opportunity to settle the score. Both men filled their shirt pockets, and began offering them to the crew. When one of them offered a cigar to Lydston, he took it, smiled appreciatively, and said, "Why, it's my brand," before he realized what had happened. He was furious and he complained to Albert, insisting that the cost of the cigars be held out of their paychecks. Albert thought it was hilarious, because he, too, had fallen victim to Lydston's practical jokes.

Lydston had his eye on one of Albert's favorite mounts; it was a huge animal called Darky Horse. Lydston's repeated offers to buy him were always turned down.

Lydston came to New Meadows one fall determined to bring the horse back to Denver with him. Since Albert again refused to sell, he turned to his second plan of action.

Nearly all the cattle were loaded into the train, when Lydston asked Albert if he could borrow Darky, who was a good yard horse. While Lydston was shouting directions to the men loading the last car, Albert left the immediate area. Without a word, Lydston reined Darky toward the loading chute.

This was premeditated horse thievery. Lydston had figured out exactly how many cattle were being transported and he had ordered an extra railroad car, which could be partitioned in half. The empty partition was conveniently located by the door.

Just before the railroad crew started to shut the door, Lydston rode Darky up the chute. He pulled off the bridle, slapped him on the rump and said, "Get in there."

As the door slid shut, Lydston instructed the crew to wait for him in Council, since he would be accompanying the livestock back to Denver. He also asked the crew to unsaddle the horse and make the animal as comfortable as possible in the boxcar.

The train pulled out, and Lydston went in search of Rollie and Albert. Lydston paid both of them with a draft, the cattle buyer's equivalent to a check, and asked for a ride to Council.

Albert straightened, looked around and asked, "What did you do with Darky? I don't see him around here."

"He's on the train," Lydston said matter-of-factly.

"He's on the train," Albert cried, his voice's pitch rising, "What do you mean he's on the train?"

"I tried to buy that horse from you and you wouldn't sell him to me, but I deserve to have him," Lydston said. "That horse isn't any good to you. You don't know a good horse from a bad one. All you're going to do is break him down, riding him in the snow. This is the best yard horse I've ever seen. He deserves a good home and better care than you'll ever give him; so I just took him. If you want something for him, I'll pay you for him, but you can't have the horse. He's gone."

Albert was almost speechless with rage. "You horse thief," he spat out.

"That's right," said Lydston. "What do you want for him?"

The argument lasted as long as the horse lived, but Darky spent the rest of his life working in the Denver Stockyards.

Lydston didn't always have the last word; Albert occasionally evened the score. At least one year, Albert squeezed a few extra dollars out of Lydston. He had one of his hands step on the scales as his steers were being weighed.

Another one of Albert's carefully planned schemes failed. Albert had about 300 spayed heifers that Lydston was scheduled to weigh and ship the next day. He ran them through the scales early and counted the hours until Lydston's scheduled arrival.

The next morning, as the two men were walking through the heifers, Albert asked, "What'll these heifers weigh?"

Before Lydston could answer, he said, "I'll tell you what. I'll bet you $100 that I can outguess you. And we'll run them through the scale to settle the bet."

The weight bet was an annual event, but Lydston sensed something different this time. For one thing, the ante had been raised. Usually the bet was a fifty dollar Stetson hat. Lydston guessed what Albert was up to, but he took the bet anyway.

Before he made his guess, he talked to one of the cowboys. "Was it clear last night?" Lydston asked, wanting to know if the full moon had shone through.

"It was a beautiful night," answered the cowboy.

"And was it chilly?" Lydston asked.

The cowboy said that it had been a typical, warm summer night.

Lydston mulled the information around in his head before he named a figure. It was ten to fifteen pounds higher than Albert's guess, and he was right on the money.

Albert was disgusted, and his efforts to mask it weren't too successful.

Lydston later explained his reasoning to his son, Hugh. Surmising that the cattle had been weighed in the afternoon, Lydston knew that the cattle had lost weight by the time they hit the scales. There was always some shrinkage, or weight loss, both while cattle were herded to the pen and while they were waiting to be weighed. Hot weather coupled with the lack of either water or feed accelerated the shrinkage.

Lydston knew that the cattle had spent the night eating and tanking up on water under the full moon. The scales reflected the difference, since the bet was settled after an early morning weighing.

Albert rarely lost a battle of wits, and he saved face by recounting a recent exchange he'd had with an Internal Revenue Service auditor. For several days, the auditor pored over the

The Circle C Ranch's first stockholders posed during the annual meeting. Seated (from left): Anna Campbell Organ, Caroline Osborn Campbell, and Carrie Campbell Whiteman. Standing: Loyal Campbell, Rollie Campbell, and Albert Campbell. (Photo courtesy of Charlotte Campbell Armacost.)

Circle C books, and he questioned the annual salary that Albert's mother, Caroline, was receiving. The auditor asked if he could see where Caroline lived.

When they arrived, Albert's elderly mother was sitting in a rocking chair on the front porch.

"What exactly does your mother do," he asked.

"Well now," answered Albert, "she takes care of the chickens and the flowers."

"I see by your books that you're paying her $3,000 a year," the auditor said.

"Yes," Albert replied patiently.

"Don't you think that's a little too much for just taking care of the chickens and flowers?" he persisted.

"Yes, I think it's too much," Albert agreed. "But she won't take a damn cent less."

The auditor let it ride.

Lydston usually traveled solo when he was buying cattle, but he brought both Hugh and his grown son, Vern, on his trip to the OX one summer.

Claude and Ramey were living in a crude, L-shaped house that looked somewhat like an army barracks. While everyone was getting acquainted, Ramey told them about an unwelcome house guest. She was battling a small bear that persistently scavenged around the house's foundation, looking for the treats that she threw out to the dogs.

As was his habit, Albert hit the sack as soon as he finished supper. The rest soon followed suit. Since there was a shortage of beds, Lydston's sons unrolled their sleeping bags outside the house.

Hugh, who was ten or eleven, found the whole situation rather overwhelming. He was used to noisy Seattle nights. Here, the night seemed huge and quiet. When the quiet was interrupted by a creak or a howl, it became frightening. Hugh burrowed into his sleeping bag and waited for sleep. He was about to doze when he heard something sniffing at his sleeping bag.

"Vern, Vern, Vern!" he screamed. His older brother rescued him . . . from some curious cow dogs.

An adventurous lifestyle was also enjoyed by some kids who lived just south of the Lick Creek bunkhouse on Rocky Comfort. Young Dick Parker and his sister, Barbara, were workers. They began earning that reputation as soon as they came into the country with their parents in 1939.

Prior to the move, the family had been living on the Washington coast. Dick's father, Warren, worked in an apple orchard until he was poisoned by the lead and sulphur spray used on the fruit. Doctors told him to change occupations, which was a near impossibility during the Depression. Although he worked sporadically as a logger during the summer and earned a few dollars working for Roosevelt's Works Progress Administration in the winter, the family was barely surviving.

"We're going back to Idaho," he announced one day. "At least I'll be able to hunt enough meat to keep us alive."

Warren Parker was raised on Crooked River, so he was familiar with the Bear area. He asked Charley Warner for a job, and started haying immediately. Charley couldn't pay him much, but he offered Warren room and board in addition to the meager wages. Living space at the Warner ranch was limited, so Warren's wife, Jessie, and the two kids spent the summer camping along Bear Creek.

The Parkers needed to earn enough cash to survive the winter, so Jessie and the kids turned to the only money-making venture in the country: picking huckleberries. Campers and neighbors bought a gallon of berries for a dollar.

Those were hard earned dollars. The huckleberries were tiny; they were rarely as large as peas. Picking was a slow process since the berries had to be picked one by one.

Jessie set the pace. At first she asked Dick to fill a five pound lard bucket daily, but the eight-year-old couldn't muster enough patience. By the end of the summer, a full corn can signaled the end of his working day.

Picking with his uncle, Frosty McConnell, made the time go faster. The old man told amazing stories, but his first priority was picking. He could gather five gallons in a day, but stray leaves and twigs always fell into his bucket. He talked about somebody in Montana who picked huckleberries with a comb. Undoubtedly that method harvested more leaves than berries.

By winter, the family accumulated enough money to rent a small place in Bear. The money crunch, however, was far from over.

Dick and Barbara contributed to the family coffers whenever they were offered an odd job. Charley Warner gave them their first outside job. The Warner's homestead cabin had burned down, and he hired the youngsters to salvage nails from the ashes.

They were hired again to poison ground squirrels. Ten-year-old Dick was given a bucket of oats mixed with strychnine and some advice. "Don't eat any of that," Charley counseled.

Shortly thereafter Charley's grown son, Lawrence, telephoned the Parkers and asked to speak to Dick. "That was pretty important; I didn't get many phone calls," Dick recalled.

Dollars were scarce when the Parker family arrived in 1939. Frosty McConnell (left) helped young Bobbie (Barbara) and Dick Parker gather huckleberries, which they sold for a dollar per gallon. The kids' father, Warren, (second from left) worked for Charley Warner that summer. (Photo courtesy of Dick and Georgianna Parker.)

"My mother did a man's work," said Dick Parker, pictured with his mother, Jesse. "It was just a matter of survival." (Photo courtesy of Dick and Georgianna Parker.)

"He asked if I could come over and help drive their steam engine up to the other place. He needed help. Boy, I was there before I could get the phone hung up."

Dick and Lawrence operated the steam engine together. Dick's job was to steer the engine and blow its whistle. They started at the Warner's home place, and drove about two miles past the schoolhouse to the Elliot place, which Charley had acquired.

"I had to crank that old steam engine back and forth. It had old chain steering on it and it worked me to death. And all the horses on the creek were clear out at the back ends of the pastures. Horses didn't like the whistle at all," Dick said.

Dick and Barbara had a stable full of stick horses which they trained when they had free time. The stick horses, which were all painstakingly named, carried the kids back and forth across Bear Creek, which was full of imaginary cowboys and Indians.

Evenings were spent around the battery-powered radio which perched on a table in the living room. Dick's favorite programs were "The Lone Ranger" and "Sky King."

The war drastically changed the tone of those nightly radio sessions. It was a scary time for Dick. He dreaded the evenings when the newscaster began his broadcast with, "I'm afraid there's bad news tonight . . ."

"I'd think, 'Oh, no. They've landed in San Francisco.' I was afraid the Japs would take us over," Dick remembered.

With their parents' encouragement, Dick and Barbara scoured the countryside looking for scrap iron and rubber tires that could be recycled for the war effort. They earned a penny a pound for everything they salvaged, and each of them used their profits to buy a war bond.

They held the bonds for a couple of years. Dick had to cash his in when the Fordson tractor needed a new radiator. Barbara's bond bought a new tire for the family's Studebaker, which had been converted into a makeshift pick-up.

Dick started drawing a man's wages when he was twelve. He and his father were helping a neighbor hay, and it was an exasperating experience. This particular Jackson fork used nets to lift the hay from the ground to the stack. The man in charge of setting the nets was having difficulty with his job, which delayed the whole

Lawrence Warner used this steam engine to power his sawmill. He called young Dick Parker to help him move the engine—Dick's job was to steer and blow the whistle. The engine is currently on display in Council's city park. (Photo courtesy of Dick and Georgianna Parker.)

Help was scarce during World War II. As a result, Dick Parker (left) started earning a man's wages when he was twelve. Dick watches his father set the nets during a haying operation. (Photo courtesy of Dick and Georgianna Parker.)

Derricks were used to form loose haystacks. (Photo courtesy of Dick and Georgianna Parker.)

Warren Parker uses a buck rake to gather hay. Haying provided one of the few opportunities for outside income. (Photo courtesy of Dick and Georgianna Parker.)

operation. Finally, Dick crawled off the derrick horse and offered to swap jobs with him. Since he did a man's work, he was paid a man's wages: six dollars a day.

The next haying job was at the Whitlow place. Before they started work, his father explained, "Dick draws men's wages too, and he can do a man's work." None of the neighbors balked at the wage increase, partly because help was difficult to find.

"I just turned my wages over to the folks and they used them for what we needed. We needed the money," Dick emphasized.

The Parkers' days fell into a comfortable, if busy routine. Although there were worries about family finances and whether there was enough moisture for a good hay crop, the war remained a major preoccupation. Prospects began to brighten in 1944, and as the months rolled by, the area ranchers grew more hopeful of an Allied victory.

One of the Parkers happened to flip on the radio on August 14, 1945. Excited broadcasters announced that Japan had surrendered. The war was over.

The news spread quickly and a steady stream of gleeful Americans passed the Parker's house en route to an impromptu celebration at the Bear schoolhouse. Dick and his father joined the procession. "I have no idea how many people were there. The dance floor was full all the time, and there were three times that many people outside, drinking, hollering, and shooting at the moon. They were happy."

Many of the celebrants came from Andy Anderson's logging camp on Crooked River. "I never saw such a group of drunk people. They were just completely nuts. They were so glad the war was over. That was a hard war," Dick said.

One logger swallowed the last five inches from his whiskey bottle and shouted, "Oh my God. Fellows, I've been torpedoed." When he passed out, the steadier members of the party dragged him outside, where the other slumbering revelers were stashed. One man never made it that far. He collapsed in the schoolhouse doorway. Occasionally the people stepping over his slumped body were startled to hear him repeat, "I'm a fighter."

Dick and his father left the party early at 3 a.m., since they had cows to milk the next morning. Both slept in, crawling out of the sack at about eight. Judging from the ringing bells and gunshots, the party was still in full swing.

The war had claimed a few casualties from the area, but nobody directly associated with the OX died. Don Mink, who had worked on Charley Warner's ranch, was one who didn't come home. Neither did a couple of boys from Hornet Creek, which is between Bear and Council.

"If you'd have had someone working for you and hadn't saved his job for him, the neighbors would have lynched you," said Dick. "These guys were heroes when they came home. You'd better treat them right. This was a war that wasn't like Vietnam or Korea. This was the war that was fought to save the country. Every man that went was a hero and you'd jolly well better be good to them when they came back."

Dick was with Bud Haskins when a tall, thin stranger rode up the road. After exchanging greetings with Bud, the man asked, "Is Albert down at Lick Creek?"

"I think he is, Don," Bud answered.

The Parker family earned extra cash by selling fence posts. Dick and his father, Warren, felled the trees with a cross-cut saw, commonly known as a misery whip. (Photo courtesy of Dick and Georgianna Parker.)

After the trees were felled, a chain was tied around the log in a half-hitch. One end was placed on a runner, and then the horses skidded the log to its destination. (Photo courtesy of Dick and Georgianna Parker.)

With that, Don Whiteley continued his ride to the Lick Creek bunkhouse. He would become Albert's top hand for the next thirty-five years.

Don's hero status was heightened by the fact that he had been a prisoner of war. The Germans captured him while he was trying to blow up a bridge, and he spent the remainder of the war in Limburg, Germany at Stalag 12.

Albert's nephew, Bob Whiteman, also came home from the war. He, too, returned to the OX, and it wasn't long before an unbelievable rumor reached his ears. "Albert's working on a deal to sell the OX," he heard from several independent sources.

Bob asked Albert if the rumor was true. Albert confided that Gordon MacGregor, a logger, had offered to buy the ranch. He said they were in the process of fine tuning the deal.

"What will happen to me?" Bob asked.

Claude Childers and Gordon MacGregor visit in an unlikely spot: downtown Boise. Most of their conversations took place near the OX, where Gordon started one of the area's first commercial logging operations. He once tried to buy the OX, but a set of copper kettles halted negotiations. (Photo courtesy of Darline Whiteley.)

Albert explained that MacGregor was buying the ranch and a third of the cattle. Albert was going to run his share of the cattle on the OX, annually selling a third of the herd until they were gone.

"When this deal goes through," Albert said, "you can work with my part, the MacGregor cattle, or the MacGregor woods. Think about it and let me know what you decide."

The sale negotiations became serious in 1946. According to the rumor mill, MacGregor offered Albert $275,000 for the ranch, and they were working a separate deal for the cattle.

They were almost to the final handshake when MacGregor reiterated the conditions of the deal. He stressed that the transaction included the land, all improvements, and all equipment. The OX hands would be allowed to take their saddles, clothing, and other personal items, but everything else was to remain.

"That's fine, except for one thing," Albert said. "Grace gave me a set of copper kettles for the line camp last Christmas, and I'm going to have to take those with me."

"No." was MacGregor's flat reply.

In the end, the deal, which probably involved well over $275,000, fizzled over a set of copper kettles.

"At the time I thought all the fuss about the kettles was silly, but MacGregor was right. The 'excepts' would have accelerated, because Albert wasn't 100 percent on the deal," concluded Bob Whiteman.

Losing the buyer didn't phase Albert. His mind was teeming with ideas, and he finally had enough manpower to implement them.

One of his first projects was planting oats on about 300 acres above the Lick Creek barn. Bud McGahey farmed the ground, and when the oats began to sprout, Dick Parker and Del Shelton built an electric fence around the field to keep the cattle out. "Those oats were so high," Dick Parker remembered. "The straw was just getting white and the oats were about ready to combine when Albert turned all his steers in on it."

Dick didn't agree with Albert's strategy. He argued that the oats should be combined first, otherwise the steers would founder.

Albert wasn't worried. The oats were ripe enough that they wouldn't hurt the cattle, he countered.

"I hope every one of them dies, because you're ruining that stand of oats," Dick fired back.

Albert was right. "I never saw anything get fat so quick in my life," Dick recalled. "When those buyers came in they couldn't believe their eyes. And he got the best price he'd gotten for years."

The experiment probably wasn't cost effective, because Albert's crew maintained the oat field for just two years. His unique approach didn't go unnoticed, however. In 1946 he garnered the Grassman of the Year Award. The committee's reasons for selecting the OX ranch were detailed in an accompanying report, which provides the best period overview of Albert's operation and range philosophies.

According to the narrative, the OX ran over 1,300 head and employed three ranch hands and a foreman.

> The success of the operation depends on 110 to 200 acres of oats being planted as part of the reseeding program. Ordinary native rangeland . . . to be reseeded is spring grazed then plowed, leveled and made ready to plant the next spring. Oats are planted for two years without grass seed, then they are seeded down the third year, (for) a continuous seeding program . . . Seeding controls erosion, furnishes feed for cattle, and controls noxious weeds.

The report further summarized the OX grazing pattern:

> Cattle leave winter feeding grounds in March or April and move to higher elevations along the Snake River Breaks until they get to the Lick Creek ranch where they spend sixty days on the Intermediate Wheatgrass pasture. They are topped out on the oat pasture for twenty days and sold as feeders in August.
>
> Three beef animals per acre are pastured this way

for an average gain of 2 1/2 pounds daily. The pasture is grazed to a length of 10–14 inches then stock cattle are turned in to finish off grass and oats (to) 6-8 inches.

Then they are controlled/grazed back to the winter quarters on the breaks of the Snake River. They are kept on privately owned, leased and deeded native pastures on the return trip . . . At all times there is as much grass left when grazing is finished as most ranchers have to begin with.

OX cattle are known by all feeders in the Northwest as gaining as well as any that can be bought. They are never stunted and the careful management of the pastures insures adequate use of the forage with a good reserve for the quick regrowth of the following year.

The report concluded with a quote from Ellis Snow, an eighty-year area resident:

There is no man in this region who has done so much to bring about a proper balance between range and livestock numbers as has Mr. Campbell; even to the extent of procuring additional holdings within the National Forest, without asking for additional numbers on his permit. He has acquired large tracts of devastated rangeland and has restored it to its original condition by protective methods of fencing and deferred grazing.

Albert had plans for expansion. He began by purchasing a 160-acre ranch outside Halfway, Oregon. He continued to winter cattle at Wildhorse and Salt Creek, but the Halfway ranch became his winter headquarters. He bragged that he could drive cattle from Halfway to the Circle C in New Meadows on his own property, with the exception of a few short stretches of Forest Service ground.

During the same time period he purchased the 1,000-acre Whitlow ranch, which adjoined his Lick Creek holdings.

All the neighbors didn't share Albert's enthusiasm for expansion. In fact, when Jack Germer heard that Albert was interested in his place, which was across the Snake River from Homestead, Oregon, he became Albert's most vehement opponent.

Albert and one of his hands, Don Whiteley, stopped by the Germer's house one evening. Albert's attempts to deal on the place were met with angry sputterings from Mr. Germer. Supper time was approaching, so Mrs. Germer interceded and invited the men to supper, and later to spend the night.

After Albert and Don were shown to their room, an interesting conversation drifted through the thin pine walls. "I'm going to kill them," Mr. Germer declared. Albert paid no attention; he rolled over and promptly went to sleep. The ranting spooked Don, who spent the rest of the night devising an escape route out of their room. There weren't many alternative exits.

Much to Don's relief, the night passed without any murders. The growling resumed at the breakfast table the next morning, but with Mrs. Germer's help, Albert and Don parted on civil terms.

Don never forgot that wide-eyed night, and he managed to avoid any future overnight invitations from the Germers.

Albert also had his eye on the Rocky Comfort ranch, which adjoined his Lick Creek property. He had tried to buy it when Herschel Robertson died, but Robertson's widow honored her husband's wishes, and refused to sell to the OX.

The property was repeatedly leased and sold before Dick Parker's family purchased it, shortly after the war ended. It wasn't long before Albert tested his new neighbors.

The most serious confrontation came in the fall, on a day when all of Rocky Comfort was blanketed with fog. The Parkers couldn't see to the road, but they heard Albert say, "I think most of those are Parkers'." They heard their gate creak open and the sound of several animals clattering over the rocks.

The Parkers investigated after the fog lifted. When they reached their pasture, which was across the road, they saw that Albert had been partially right: around ten of the horses belonged to them. Some of the others belonged to Roy Scrivens, who lived in Cuprum. Among the rest of the mismatched herd were eight or nine mules which the Parkers thought belonged to Albert.

All of the animals had been out on the Forest Service allotment. "Back in those days, everyone could run four work horses out on the Forest Service for free . . . We ran more than four sometimes, but there were people who ran twenty head without a permit," Dick Parker explained.

Most of the animals didn't belong on the grazing allotment, but the Parkers resented Albert's solution to the problem. They caught their horses and herded the rest into a nearby pasture, which just happened to hold Albert's steers. The mules immediately went to work; happily chasing the fat steers around the field. The steers had jogged off a little weight by the time Albert noticed the intruders.

He immediately confronted Warren Parker, but the newcomer refused to be intimidated. The conversation quickly escalated into a yelling match. Neither man emerged victorious, but they left with a greater respect for each other.

"I never did quite figure out why Albert accepted my family. I guess he decided it was just going to be better to leave us alone until we got tired of being there. After the argument, (Albert) kind of neighbored with us."

Most of the Parkers' neighboring, however, was with Charley Warner's clan. By the time the war ended, Charley was sixty-three years old. He was still immersed in his cattle operation, although his herd numbers were on the decline.

His son, Lawrence, still lived on the ranch. Lawrence had married Millie Smith in 1938, and the couple started a family, which eventually included six girls.

Lawrence never shared his father's enthusiasm for the cattle business. He loved mechanical things, and preferred to run the haying and sawmill operations.

Lawrence also enjoyed young Dick Parker's company. As Dick grew past the age for blowing steam engine whistles and poisoning gophers, Lawrence noticed that his dad had taken a liking to the boy. Dick eagerly listened to the older man's stories and advice. Besides being a good hand, Dick's presence helped ease tensions between the father and son. As a result, Dick began to work for the Warners steadily.

"Our family never had any range cattle," Dick said. "Dad never

Dick Parker holds the calf steady, while John Camp looks on. Warren Parker is applying the brand and Barney Camp is in the background. Even though the Parkers rarely had over twenty head of cattle, neighbors still gathered to help brand. (Photo courtesy of Dick and Georgianna Parker.)

cowboyed a lot. He didn't ever really teach me about roping or anything like that. I learned all that from Charley."

Since Dick was still going to school, Lawrence and either Slick Taylor or another hired hand handled the winter feeding.

The frigid temperatures around Bear Creek made for heavy losses during calving. The Warners combatted the problem by breeding their cattle later in the summer, so they would calve in mid-April. When March rolled around, Dick helped herd the pregnant cows and heifers to Big Bar, on the Snake River.

The preferred route was over Horse Mountain, but deep snowdrifts often forced the Warners to break a trail through Windy Ridge and under Lime Point. Occasionally, when there had been unusually heavy snowfall, the trail had to be opened with a Caterpillar tractor.

The Warners rented Big Bar, which had approximately 100 acres before part of it was submerged by the Hells Canyon reservoir. They hayed the site during the summer, which provided feed for the herd until the range was ready to graze.

In early April, when the grass was high enough to graze, the cattle were turned loose along the river. They eventually climbed over 6,000 feet in elevation on the Warners' Forest Service grazing allotment, which included the Eckles, Allison, and Kinney Creek drainages.

The cows and heifers calved unattended on the Snake River breaks. "Calving was no problem, because we never did any," commented Dick Parker. As a result, they experienced a high calf mortality rate.

In this respect, the Warner operation contrasted sharply with Albert's. OX calving took place in a variety of locations, including Pine Valley, Albert's newly acquired ranch in Halfway, and the mouth of Wildhorse. All the locations kept the expectant mothers in close quarters, which allowed the cowboys to check them around the clock.

Several things could go wrong during calving. If the mother cow was having difficulty because her calf was either too big or positioned wrong in the uterus, someone was on hand to help. If the calf was either coming out backwards or was unusually large, the cowhand grabbed a pair of calf pullers. In later years, a veterinarian was summoned to perform a Caeserean. If the calf was positioned incorrectly, the cowboy often squeezed a hand alongside the unborn calf and positioned the little head and hooves for birth.

A successful birth didn't necessarily mean the calf was out of danger. Calves are born in a slimy birth sack, and usually the mother's first instinct is to lick her calf clean. Many calves have suffocated in their own birth sack, because the mothers failed to clean their faces first. In a closely monitored calving operation, a cowboy could save the calf's life by quickly clearing the calf's airways.

Another factor critical to the calves' survival was a good dose of colostrum, or the mothers' first milk. Colostrum is high in protein and bolsters the immune system.

The calf could be denied his first meal for a couple of reasons. Some cows, especially first-calf heifers, aren't particularly interested in motherhood. Unless they are physically restrained, they won't let their calves suckle. Other cows never "bag up" or produce milk. Their calves are grafted onto cows that have recently lost a calf. Since a mother cow will reject any calf that doesn't smell like their own, the hands quickly skinned her dead calf, and tied the hide around her new charge. After a few curious sniffs, the cow usually accepted the newcomer.

Scours, or diarrhea, was another calf killer. Current medications such as penicillin, sulfa, and streptomycin weren't available until well after World War II. Although they weren't as effective, Albert and his crew relied on home remedies such as coffee grounds and burnt flour. Many times these unlikely mixtures saved the calves from dehydration and death.

Leaving the cows to calve by themselves took its toll on the Warner herd. In the late Forties, the 350-head cow herd produced only 105 calves, according to Dick Parker, who was on hand during gathering and branding that year. Even during pre-World War II times, before critical veterinary advances were made, a thirty percent calving rate was dismal. But some oldtimers throughout the area reasoned that a cow that couldn't raise a calf on her own wasn't worth having.

Nevertheless, branding was a major community event. "We had such a crew that we couldn't get everybody in the corral," said Charley's nephew, Bert Warner. "That used to be a big deal. Everyone took picnics. We almost had more people than we had calves."

The cattle were gathered in the upper reaches of the Snake River breaks and trailed through Cuprum and Huntley Gulch. Most of the calves were branded at an old set of log corrals near Stockade Spring. A few weeks later, the slick calves that missed the first branding were gathered and herded into a wire corral in back of the Bear Guard Station.

All dry cows, or cows without calves, were destined for market in the fall. While some operations sold the less promising heifers

Dick found Lucky, the horse on the left, when she was a young filly. She was frightened, starving, and standing close to her mother's half-eaten body. Charley Warner gave the filly to her rescuer. The horses are standing in front of the Parker's first Rocky Comfort home. (Photo courtesy of Dick and Georgianna Parker.)

with the steers, Charlie and Lawrence kept all heifers to replenish the cow herd.

Regardless of the season, Dick and Charley spent hours riding the range, which stretched from about 1,700 feet at Big Bar to the summit of Smith Mountain, at 8,005 feet. "Charley could come off that trail when things were pitch black. He knew every trail and wrinkle in that mountain," Dick said.

Since the country was so steep, Charley was particularly careful with his horses. "I was just a kid, and I would want to take my horse all the way up a steep hill without resting it," Dick said. "Charley would say, 'If you do that to your horse this early in the morning, you'll be walking in.'"

The trails leading down to the Snake River were precarious any time of the year, but they were flat dangerous when they were covered with ice and snow. Horses had a much greater chance of misstepping and taking their rider on a 1,000 foot death plunge off the sheer mountainside. As a result, Charley always asked Dick to dismount and lead his horse around the tricky spots. Charley, however, never climbed off his horse. His bum leg made walking an impossibility.

"Charley didn't want to have to walk home, so he had an old form fitter saddle," Dick said. "I thought, 'If Charley likes it, it's got to be really good.' I rode his saddle a little bit and decided I didn't want one of those. That old back hit right above my belt. If a horse would jump with you, it would hurt. And you can't get out of them. They've got them big old swells (which fit over the rider's knees.) Charley would squeeze down in there and sit in it all day long."

Charley taught several area youngsters how to work cattle, including his nephew, Bert Warner. "He never tried to hurry or

The Parkers wintered their cattle on OX ground in Gladhart Gulch, where there was a steady supply of water. "Albert would move all his cattle out in the fall, and he wouldn't care if we used it," said Dick Parker. (Photo courtesy of Dick and Georgianna Parker.)

run the cattle," said Bert. "In that respect he and Albert Campbell worked together pretty well; Albert wasn't a fast cowboy either. You'd get a hotshot cowboy coming around, and it was a problem. Once in a while we'd have trouble, but we had an old dog (to remedy) that situation."

Bert's new bride, the former Tina Edwards, also became Charley's pupil. "Charley was the most infuriating one for a kid to ride with," she said. "He'd ride up on a point and he'd sit there and see a cow. I couldn't wait to get the cow. He'd say, 'Well, where there's one, there's two. And where there's two there's four. And where there's four there's more.' So we'd sit there. Pretty soon the cows would come out. He knew what they were going to do."

Even when the cattle refused to cooperate, Charley never swore. "His worst swear word was, 'By George,'" Tina said.

Although Charley never carried a lunch, he always stopped riding about mid-day, when temperatures peaked. "Well, it's about time to hit the shade," Charley would say. "The cattle are going to stop pretty quick, and we aren't going to move them anyway; we'd just wear our horses out. Let's go shade up someplace."

Sometimes Charley used the slack time to tell stories to Dick Parker. Occasionally he told Dick about the early days, when his family first came into the country. He also loved to talk about his early ranching experiences, when he made regular runs to the Black Lake mining operation. The story about the miner who paid an exorbitant price for a hair-raising ride back to Bear got better with each telling.

Sometimes Charley's thoughts were somber. Although his older son, Toby, had been dead for nearly ten years, Charley still mourned. He continually reconstructed the circumstances surrounding Toby's drowning, trying to find a more conclusive reason for his death.

Dick and Charley frequently stopped at Toby's old camps, which were left intact. The twosome was riding past Toby's old cabin on Windy Ridge when Charley halted his horse. He climbed down, limped over to the cabin and opened the door. He emerged with Toby's hat in his hand, which he nonchalantly handed to

Dick. Oddly enough, the hat fit. Dick wears a size seven and a half hat, which is unusually large.

Although he rarely voiced them, thoughts about growing older also weighed heavily on Charley's mind. His physical limitations didn't bother him nearly as much as being second in command.

"Charley would tell me how he used to do things," Dick said. All of his comparisons had the same theme: his way was better.

Lawrence and Charley had different priorities. Charley had always let his herd calve unsupervised, but he used ranch profits to supplement the herd. As a result, he always ran the ranch at peak capacity, which was approximately 500 mother cows. Lawrence, on the other hand, believed in diversification. Rather than pump money back into the herd, he bought a sawmill and replaced the horse-drawn haying equipment with more modern machinery.

Charley's "old way," wasn't always the best way. New ideas on range management and veterinary advances rarely filtered back to Charley's remote ranch. "There were no vaccinations," Dick Parker said. "Our major form of doctoring was a gun."

Dick remembered one incident in particular. After Lawrence felled some trees in the main hayfield, several pregnant cows wandered through, nibbling on the frozen pine needles. As a result, several sloughed, or aborted their calves. Knowing no alternate treatment, Lawrence killed the two or three cows that had uterine prolapses.

The next summer Dick, Lawrence, and a Bear Creek neighbor, Paul Holmes, found an old roan cow who had prolapsed.

"I'll go get the gun," Lawrence said.

"What for?" asked Paul.

"I've got to shoot her."

"What's the matter with you boy? Why shoot a good cow like that?"

"Well, just look at her," Lawrence replied.

"We can fix that," Paul said as he rolled up his sleeves and began to inch the slimy bulk back into the cow. It was the first time that Charley, Lawrence, or Dick had heard that a cow could survive a prolapse. The procedure wasn't on the cutting edge of veterinary medicine; it had been common practice for well over twenty years.

Although Charley sometimes grumbled about Lawrence's decisions, in the end he usually acquiesced. Even so, Charley allowed himself a few unbendable idiosyncrasies. One involved the milk cows. Both Albert Campbell and Charley shared the view that milk cows were infinitely inferior to range cattle. For that reason, he refused to let them run in the same pasture. Lawrence didn't argue the point; he fenced off part of the pasture for the milk cows.

"Charley had a fierce temper when somebody crossed him," Dick explained. "He'd threaten to shoot them."

"I never heard of him having trouble with Albert. I think Albert was smarter than to cross him. I believe the old devil would have shot you."

Both Millie and Lawrence Warner stressed that they never quarrelled with Albert. He often accepted their invitations to eat supper and spend the night. Lawrence made Millie's round kitchen table, which had a built-in lazy Susan. As soon as everyone found a place at the table, she carried the hot serving dishes in and set them on the lazy Susan. Albert liked that arrangement, he told the Warners. He didn't have to spend the entire meal saying, "Please pass."

The Warners' hospitality went one step further. "If anybody in the country heard that Albert or his cowboys had been through and they hadn't stopped by, they wondered if the OX'ers were mad at them," said Millie's half-brother Frank Smith. "They were supposed to stop in, eat dinner, and make themselves at home. That was regardless of whether anybody was home or not."

Frank and his younger brother, Chall, and their father, Wells Smith, became regulars at the kitchen table in 1941. Wells, who was both Millie's father and Lawrence's first cousin, was born in Bear. He became a widower shortly after Millie's birth; his first wife died in a flu epidemic. Wells left his small daughter with an older brother, and years later he married again. The second marriage dissolved after Frank and Chall were born, and Wells decided to reunite his scattered family in Bear.

The two boys, who were seven and eight years old, immediately became the family's chief fishermen. Wickiup Creek, which ran through the field in front of their house, was the most convenient

Lawrence and Millie Warner posed for this portrait shortly after they were married. OX cowboys looked forward to Millie's home cooked meals. (Photo courtesy of Lawrence and Millie Warner.)

fishing spot. They started casting their lines a few yards from the house and worked their way toward a wooded area, about a third of a mile away. If they didn't catch anything by the time they reached the trees, it was a bad fishing day.

The boys caught three trout which spent the rest of their lives keeping the spring which supplied the family's water supply free of bugs and worms. "One trout was in there for ten years. He was a huge old guy," Frank said.

"Chall and I would go out fishing and catch forty to fifty fish just following Wickiup. We had heard about the game warden, but we didn't know what he was for," Frank said.

Since there was no refrigeration, the boys kept the extra fish in the corral's wooden horse trough. When they accumulated enough, the family hosted a fish fry.

The boys occasionally accompanied their Great-Uncle Charley while he checked cattle. On one such trip, they encountered a

Brothers Frank and Chall Smith feed their pet fawn. When Bambi grew older, he liked to paw at the kitchen door. Millie unfailingly brought him sugar cubes when he gave the signal. (Photo courtesy of Frank and Betty Smith.)

fawn that was barely two days old. Charley helped them catch the little animal and carry it home, where it was promptly christened Bambi.

The boys offered the deer bottles of warm milk, and he soon became a loyal pet. Bambi had a sweet tooth too. When the fawn had a craving, he trotted onto the front porch and pawed until Millie came out with the sugar cubes.

As hunting season approached, the boys spent hours making Bambi look like a pet. They put the deer in a bright vest and fashioned a leather collar, which had a bell and red ribbon tied to it.

Millie was in the kitchen when she heard Bambi paw for the last time. She grabbed some sugar cubes and opened the door just as Bambi fell over. He had been shot in the lung.

The adults agreed that the deer meat shouldn't be wasted, so one of the men carried the small deer to the woodshed and dressed him out. Millie prepared the deer steak, but she couldn't eat it. The boys couldn't stand to look at the meat platter, let alone take a serving. Charley, Lawrence, and Wells were the only ones who braved the main course, but it was a one-time-only affair. The rest of the carcass spoiled.

Frank and Chall had a long succession of wild pets after Bambi died. One was a bobcat that got caught when they were trapping raccoons along the Snake River. After freeing the animal, the boys managed to wrestle it into a gunny sack. They took turns packing the animal, which they named Bob, on the ten-mile hike home. "The trick was to throw the gunny sack over your shoulder," Frank explained. "You knew for sure when the claws were running up and down your back, but he didn't bite." After spending the summer on the ranch, Bob was released.

Two bear cubs, named Teddy and Buzzy, entertained the boys during another summer. While the family was haying on Big Bar, Bub Smith sighted a bear on the Snake River breaks. Bub, who was a cousin, watched the bear for several days. He never spotted any cubs; so he shot her. When he reached the dead bear, he saw that she had been nursing, and he searched the area until he found her den. Inside were two tiny bear cubs with sharp claws. He pulled off his sweatshirt and slipped a cub into each sleeve.

A bobcat aptly named "Bob" joined the family after he was accidentally caught in a raccoon trap. After spending the summer with the boys, Bob was released. (Photo courtesy of Frank and Betty Smith.)

Bub gave the cubs to the Warner girls, but it was Millie who nursed them through their first lonesome nights. The cubs slept next to a quart jar filled with warm water. They frequently woke up crying, so Millie cuddled and rocked them until they went back to sleep.

Frank and Chall eventually took care of the cubs, which soon developed ornery personalities. Their favorite game was irrigating, or, more accurately, irritating. Wells was in charge of irrigation that summer, and as soon as he swung the shovel onto his shoulder, the bears were on his trail. The cubs cuffed each other and played until Wells diverted water to a dry part of the hayfield

Chall Smith and his nieces, Erma and Loretta Warner, play with Teddy and Buzzy. (Photo courtesy of Frank and Betty Smith.)

by building a dam in the ditch. As soon as Wells finished, the bears scuttled in behind him, playing in the mud until the dam broke. When Wells discovered their prank, he threw his shovel at them. It didn't faze them. They thought it was part of the game. On more than one occasion, Wells had to do his irrigating twice.

When the bears began running the ranch, Lawrence decided it was time for a new living arrangement. He rowed the half-grown bears to an abandoned apple orchard which was just opposite of Kinney Creek on the Snake River.

Frank and Chall cautiously befriended the next pet . . . a porcupine. They knew they were making progress when the animal stopped lifting his lethal tail in their presence. Eventually the porcupine recognized all the family members. It was about that time that he became a "royal nuisance," because he liked to go on hikes—if he was carried uphill.

Frank and Chall bottle-fed another set of bears, which they

Jess Smith stops to chat with one of his nephews' bears. Although Jess enjoyed the bears, he didn't always appreciate their contributions. The bears' capers often doubled the work when it came to irrigation. (Photo courtesy of Frank and Betty Smith.)

named Bruin and Bitch. These creatures had two overriding passions: sweets and riding in cars. The cubs were ambling through the woods when they found both treats in one spot: a fisherman's car which smelled slightly of honey and syrup. The bears didn't hesitate. Both climbed into the unattended car and began ripping at camping gear and upholstery until they found their snack. When Frank found the bears, they were sticky and happy. His attempts to get them out of the car were met with swipes and bared teeth.

Jess Smith agreed to keep the bears for the winter. They figured the bears could hibernate in one of his sheds. The bears, however, had different plans. Late that fall a car drove by. One of the passengers opened a door. The bears eagerly accepted the invitation, and nobody saw them again. It was rumored that they ended up in the Boise Zoo.

When winter rolled around, Frank and Chall turned their attention toward skiing. Charley showed the boys how to make

Jess Smith and Wells Smith work on a Snake River fencing project at Big Bar. The two were first cousins. They looked so much alike that many people couldn't tell them apart. (Photo courtesy of Frank and Betty Smith.)

tamarack skis. He explained that tamarack was the ideal material to use; it was the only local wood that would split along the same grain for the length of the ski. Since Charley made skis that were up to sixteen feet long, that was a necessary quality.

After soaking the split tamarack in a five-gallon bucket filled with water, Charley nailed the ski tips to pieces of curved wood. When the ski dried, its tips were permanently curved. After cutting grooves up the center of each ski and making one long ski pole, the boys were in business.

Riding those long skis was a challenging prospect, since there was no way to turn them. Besides crashing, there was only one way to slow down. The boys kept their one ski pole between their legs, and when the scenery started passing too rapidly, they created a makeshift brake by sitting on their poles.

Their main ski hill was located just west of the house. As they mastered all conventional routes down the incline, they tried to create even greater challenges. One of their more ambitious attempts evolved when they strapped a pair of skis onto an old bicycle. They had just pulled their conveyance up the hill, when a neighbor boy, Edward Gallager, stopped by. Since he was the guest, he was given the honors. After a promising start, Edward flipped back and forth over the handlebars, which whacked him in the stomach at the end of the ride. Frank and Chall were howling with laughter until they reached the bottom of the hill, and discovered that Edward had blacked out. Edward recovered, and the all-weather bicycle was permanently retired.

Frank and Chall liked to join forces with Dick Parker, even though he was a couple of years older. The three boys pulled greenchain for Lawrence when he was running the sawmill. "It took all three of us to move a board. We were pretty small yet," Dick remembered.

The threesome also spent time together at the Bear school-house. Dick and his sister, Barbara, usually rode their horses from Rocky Comfort. One afternoon, when the Smith boys were afoot, Dick offered to give them a ride to the cut-off road. They immediately accepted the offer, and Frank crawled on behind Dick. Chall was about to make it a threesome when their teacher, Katherine Fox Clement, told them to stop. "Somebody could get bucked off and hurt," she warned.

Frank Smith, Chall Smith, and Dick Parker were the haying crew on Charley and Lawrence Warner's ranch one summer. Working from June to November, they put up 10,000 bales of hay. (Photo courtesy of Dick and Georgianna Parker.)

Schoolteacher Tina Edwards Warner had her hands full with this class, even though there were only four pupils. Dick Parker's expression (left) tells most of the story. His sister, Bobbie (middle rear), Lawrence and Millie Warner's daughter, Erma, and Bud and Mavis McGahey's daugther, Eva, complete the picture. (Photo courtesy of Dick and Georgianna Parker.)

"Oh no," Dick said reassuringly as Chall hopped on. "This horse can handle all of us." No sooner were the words out, when the horse reared, and the boys hit the ground one by one.

"My argument went down the tubes," Dick remembered.

None of the boys were hurt, and they thoroughly enjoyed the escapade. Mrs. Clement was not amused. Frank and Chall didn't press the point. They walked home.

Mrs. Clement, who had formerly taught in a reform school, taught a record-breaking four years in the Bear schoolhouse. "She was a pretty tough old girl," Dick said. "We never did test her to see how tough she could be. She told us she was tough, and we didn't ask her to prove it. We just took her at her word. She wasn't that hard to get along with."

The teacher's eye glasses proved to be one of her most effective teaching aids. If they were positioned correctly on her nose, she could use them as rearview mirrors. Nobody dared to move when she had her back to the class.

Although she was a disciplinarian, she enjoyed the kids and gave them some flexibility. During the winter months, the prime sledding conditions occurred in the morning, while the snow was still frozen and crusty. Mrs. Clement allowed the children to combine their recesses, so they could take advantage of the best snow.

There were plenty of outdoor games to keep the children occupied when the snow melted. The schoolhouse itself became the center of a game called Anti-I-Over. The kids divided into two teams, which stood on opposite sides of the schoolhouse. One team member threw a soft ball over the schoolhouse roof. If a member of the other team caught the ball before it hit the ground, he or she raced around the schoolhouse to tag an opposing team member. Tagged players had to join the other team.

Tag, Red Rover, Black Man, and softball were other favorite games. Team games were tough when enrollment dipped to its lowest level, at three or four students. The children found that pinecone fights could be just as entertaining.

Mrs. Clement and her predecessors taught from the same set of books that were used in every schoolhouse in the county.

Built in 1911, the Bear schoolhouse produced eighth grade graduates until its 1964 consolidation with Council. The building currently serves as a community hall, where functions ranging from voting to weddings are held. (Drawing by Mary Lorish Jahn.)

Although an Adams County superintendent orchestrated the area's educational programs, school expenditures and serious disciplinary problems were handled by locally elected school boards. It was the teacher, however, that maintained discipline and determined lesson plans. The teachers were also responsible for any additions to the standard curriculum. During the Forties, two different educators lugged their heavy, upright typewriters to the Bear schoolhouse, which gave the kids an opportunity to learn another vocational skill.

Since most of the students worked at different levels, the majority of their school work was done independently, rather than with the class. Effective teachers had to be organized and versatile in order to keep all their students motivated.

There were daily activities which brought all the students together, and singing was a favorite. After handing out the well-thumbed yellow song books, Orianna Hubbard Martin liked to accompany the students on an old player piano.

Orianna was in her seventies when she returned for her last teaching stint in Bear. Decades before she had penned Bear's school anthem, which was sung to the tune of "My Old Kentucky Home." She was very familiar with the Parker sense of humor; she taught Dick's father while he was growing up in Crooked River.

"She was a real small woman. Just like a little bird," Dick remembered.

One afternoon, Dick could hardly wait for the music lesson to start, and it wasn't because he longed to sing about "gladly coming to learn as the autumn days return." His thoughts focused on the piano's unique feature: a small lever which froze the keys and allowed the piano to play pre-punched rolls of music automatically. If someone wanted to use the instrument like a regular piano, a flip of the lever freed the keys.

It took Dick almost an hour to tie a harness that could control the magic lever from a distance. He inconspicuously threaded a control string back to his desk.

Song time eventually came, but Dick's eyes weren't focused on the music book. He waited until the teacher was feverishly working her way into a crescendo, and then he pulled the string. "Every time she hit the locked keys it would bring her right up off of the bench!" he said.

Dick's arrangement of strings allowed him to release the keys, which he did as soon as his teacher was safely earthbound. After a slight pause, Orianna played a few cautious notes and just as she was gathering momentum, Dick pulled the string again.

It happened once more before she became suspicious and found the string. Orianna jumped off the piano bench and started searching for the string's source. Dick knew he was in trouble because she was following the string at a gallop, and the lady only galloped in dire situations. She used body language to express her displeasure. And Dick learned that although she was little, she could pack a wallop.

Distractions occasionally came from outside sources. Tina Warner was speaking to her students, when Archie Bardmas stepped into the classroom.

Tina Warner temporarily left teaching while her family was young. An Easter family portrait shows Tina, her husband, Bert, and their children Gaye, Joe, Pam, and Arlen. (Photo courtesy of the Warner family.)

Archie was an unusual man. He was one of the last surviving bachelors from Barbour Flat, and in a community where local color was taken for granted, Archie was a curiosity.

Tina stopped her lecture in mid-sentence when Archie walked through the door. Without acknowledging anybody or saying a word, he marched to the front of the schoolroom, halted at the wastebasket, and rummaged around until he found a wadded scrap of paper. After smoothing out the paper on Tina's desk, he scrawled a message, which he promptly crumpled and tossed back into the wastebasket. He left the way he came in, seemingly unaware of the other people in the room.

The class was rather stunned after he ducked out the door. Intrigued by Archie's mysterious message, Tina stepped over to the wastebasket and fished out the piece of paper. "Some whales have two spouts," was all it said.

Archie had spent some time in an insane asylum, but even with that detail omitted, he had a fascinating background. After proving up on his homestead, he wandered the United States practicing a variety of professions, including teaching school. His mother, Frances, was the Washington County, Idaho school superintendent in 1904. Bear was part of Washington County at that time, and the schoolhouse was under her jurisdiction. Perhaps it was her influence that prompted Archie to get his teaching certificate.

Besides teaching school, Archie also served with the Merchant Marines and he was a well-traveled hobo. The people who knew him agree that the job title that fit him best was "grub line rider."

Arnold Emery's house in Wildhorse was often his home base. When Archie was in danger of losing his homestead to the tax collectors, Arnold's father paid the thirteen dollar tab in exchange for an informal leasing arrangement.

Although Archie was a little strange, he was brilliant. According to Arnold he could spell any word in the dictionary, and he passed his driver's examination without being able to drive. Pedestrians gave him wide berth.

Archie's choice of reading material was also unique. He subscribed to the *New Yorker*, a publication that is still an oddity in Idaho. Current issues reached him only occasionally, because he rarely paused at a mailing address.

Archie Bardmas was one of the original homesteaders on Barbour Flat. Archie's whims were unpredictable. He once left the house to feed chickens and didn't return for several months. (Photo courtesy of Arnold and Ruth Emery.)

One time, while he was staying with the Emerys, he mentioned he was going to feed the chickens. He left the house with the scrap bucket, but didn't appear again for several months.

Despite his impromptu arrivals and departures, Archie was a full-fledged member of the community. The *Council Leader* reported that he had traveled up Wildhorse to help Albert Campbell as early as 1913.

He was also a regular when the Warners needed haying help. He ran a piece of horse-drawn equipment, and whenever there was a lull in activity, he pulled his current embroidery project out of his pocket and stitched until they were ready for him to roll. The fact that his fancy work was covered with grease and dirt from the haying equipment never fazed him, Bert Warner remembered. Similarly, he never felt the curious stares generated by the weird timing of his stereotypically feminine hobby.

Even more interesting than Archie's samplers were his tales. ''Some of the stories Archie Bardmas told made it seem like he had been kicked in the head,'' Dick Parker said. Archie was particularly fond of telling a familiar fable and putting himself in the lead role. He once told Dick about the time he found a lion with a thorn in its foot. Being a good samaritan, Archie pulled the thorn out. When he encountered the lion later on, they were friends, he said.

There was another unlikely friendship that occasionally livened things up. Dick's uncle, Frosty McConnell, and Charley Warner's nephew, Jesse Smith, were already famous for inadvertently dynamiting their own mining camp.

Since their mining exploits proved to be unprofitable, they decided to accept a caretaking job from Charley Warner. The two men shared a cabin on Big Bar, and one of their responsibilities was to make sure the gate to the property stayed closed. The job was not particularly invigorating, so the men found other ways to amuse themselves.

A pet bull with a sweet tooth helped relieve the tedium. When the bull had a craving for sugar, he stepped up to the cabin's door. The system worked perfectly, until one hot summer day when the sugar didn't materialize fast enough to suit the animal. The door was open, so the bull decided to investigate. Once inside, the huge animal panicked. Jesse managed to slip out the door as the bull was charging around the cabin, toppling furniture. Frosty wasn't so lucky. When Jesse peeked back into the mayhem, he saw "Frosty a screamin' on the back of the davinal." The bull eventually plowed his way back through the doorway, and neither man was hurt in the incident. The bull's interior decorating job kept the men busy for the next several weeks.

Wells Smith decided it was time to leave the Warner ranch in the fall of 1948. His oldest boy, Frank, was ready to start high school. The threesome pulled a trailer house to Myrtle Creek, Oregon, where Wells took a job at a sawmill.

Leaving the relative isolation of Bear for town life created some culture shock for the boys. Two particular changes bothered Frank. He had to make a conscious effort to carry a house key and pull the window shades at night. Door locks and curtains had been unnecessary in Bear.

Dick Parker left the ranch about the same time, just after he celebrated his eighteenth birthday. He was finally old enough to work in the woods as a logger.

Dick's departure amplified tensions between Lawrence and his father. As Charley's physical handicaps worsened, it became increasingly impractical and dangerous for the older man to oversee the range operation. That, coupled with their clashing ranch management philosophies, cemented Lawrence's decision to institutionalize his father in Blackfoot, Idaho.

Charley's unwilling departure upset and saddened several community members, including Dick. Charley's tenacity, ethics, and temper had helped shape most of Bear's younger personalities. It was hard to watch him grow old.

When Charley left the ranch, the area was experiencing an economic boom. Ranchers were profiting from a sustained upswing in the cattle market, and the post-war demand for housing fueled the local timber industry. In addition to the Anderson logging camp at Crooked River, numbers of independent sawmills and logging operations went into business.

The steadily growing supply of loggers and the local cowboys created a loyal clientele for Bear's pool hall. Located approximately one half mile south of the schoolhouse, the front of the building featured a bar with a twenty-foot pipe footrest. The dance floor was in the back of the building.

The pool hall's "his" and "hers" privies frequently fell victim to outhouse-tipping pranksters, who often attaced when the facilities were occupied. One-time OX cowboy Slick Taylor, who managed the bar for a time, found that a few ice-chilled beers could curtail outhouse tipping activities. By the time Bud McGahey took over the pool hall's management, the prank was no longer in vogue.

A good-sized sawmill caused Cuprum to experience its first real prosperity since the Seven Devils mining boom fizzled, over forty years before. Since there was limited housing, mill workers often moved their families into tents. Green lumber produced by the mill was loaded onto Army surplus six by sixes and hauled to the railhead in Council.

Loggers commanded higher wages than ranch hands. The promise of a higher income drew a few of the locals into the woods, including Dick Parker and Albert Campbell's nephews, Bob and Don Whiteman.

Dick's first logging job was with brothers Bert and Clarence Warner. When the Warners first started logging, their only equipment was a set of misery whips, or cross-cut saws, and a D-7 Caterpillar. The rising demand for timber spurred developments in logging technology, and chainsaws soon replaced cross-cut saws. The Warners bought one of the first models, which weighed 110 pounds and was operated by two men. "They were fun," Bert deadpanned.

Dick eventually joined the Whiteman men, who were working for Gordon MacGregor. "I was a log hooker when I worked for Gordon's logging outfit—that's as low on the totem poles as you could get, but he would always stop to talk to me," Dick remembered. "He knew you on the street or wherever. There was nothing stuck up about Gordon MacGregor. Not anything."

Gordon, who also ran cattle near Emmett, Idaho, couldn't drive through the OX without picturing his brand on the Herefords. He had been forced to use hard-line negotiating tactics with Albert when he tried to buy the ranch in 1946. Even though the deal fell through, and future negotiations seemed improbable, he never gave up.

Gordon knew that Dick had worked for Albert when he was a kid. He also knew that Dick was feeding for the OX during the winter months, when logging was at a standstill. "Parker," he once said off-handedly, "why don't you buy that place? Albert won't sell it to me. You buy it and I'll furnish the money." Nothing ever came of the idea.

Albert had no desire to sell the OX. He was riding high. National happenings encouraged his optimistic outlook. Widespread talk of government subsidies and price controls died with President Franklin Roosevelt. Private enterprise was again taking the lead, and the nation's economic outlook had rarely been better.

The cattle market had experienced a steady, upward swing which gave him the operating capital he needed to expand the ranch. His operation was growing, both in acreage and in herd size.

In 1947 Claude and Ramey Childers brought Albert some news that made him both sad and happy. They had been unable to make the No Business ranch pay, and had to renege on their deal. Albert was sorry that their independent venture had failed, but he was delighted to have their help again.

Once again Albert offered No Business Basin to Henry and Helena Schmidt. This time the couple had several years of hard work and a strong cattle market behind them. The deal closed on March 11, 1947.

Claude and Ramey undoubtedly sensed the gradual, but significant changes that were taking place in Albert's operation. Some of the most startling advances could be seen in veterinary medicine. Up until the late Forties, an often fatal disease called Black Leg plagued ranchers. Prior to a vaccination made available during the post-war years, there was no cure for the disease. Don Whiteley remembered an old home remedy that involved slipping a nickel under the diseased animal's skin. "About all that did," he said, "was lose your nickel."

The newly-developed antibiotics also created exciting possibilities. Cattle previously labeled "goners" were making miraculous recoveries.

Albert cautiously began to use some of the preventative

vaccinations that became available. The practice soon became a necessity. When livestock shipping costs became more reasonable, Albert started trucking his recently weaned calves to Baker, Oregon for the winter. The stress of being weaned, combined with the travel, made the calves susceptible to disease.

The most common problems were pneumonia or septicemia, usually called shipping fever. Veterinary advances kept pace with the new difficulties. The first real breakthrough came in the mid-Thirties when sulfa was introduced. Calves with pneumonia responded almost miraculously to the new drug. Veterinary science made another giant leap when penicillin became available in the early Forties.

Affordable transportation permanently changed part of the OX's yearly routine. Albert continued to trail cattle to their winter locations in Halfway, Oregon, and along the Snake River. The annual drive to New Meadows with the market-bound cattle was phased out.

The New Meadows drive had been an annual event ever since Albert first started the OX; he called it "going over the hill." Since the trip caused shrinkage, or weight loss, Albert started the trip well before the cattle were scheduled for shipment. That way, the cattle had plenty of time to round out their weight in a rented Circle C pasture.

The cowboys moved the herd slowly, using three days to arrive at their destination. The crew had to night herd the cattle twice, first at Sheep Creek and then in Price Valley. According to Don Whiteley, the cattle usually stayed together overnight on their own accord.

Lightning storms always made night herding more interesting. On one of the last drives to New Meadows, a tremendous storm blew into Price Valley. "She was hitting close . . . it burned us out of bed," Whiteley remembered. By the time the storm blew through, the cattle were thoroughly scattered. When daylight came, Whiteley, Don Whiteman, and Tommy Clay had a sizable gathering job in front of them. They managed to find all the cattle and make it to the Circle C without a long delay.

According to Darline Whiteley, the last drive "over the hill" too place in 1947. After that, commercial cattle truckers handled the job.

Albert was in his late fifties when the revolutionary changes began to take place in the cattle business. Like most people in his generation, he had a strong sense of tradition, however, first and foremost, Albert was a cattleman. He had spent the last half century watching trends and second guessing the outcome. Albert was not sentimental; if he had to choose between tradition and progress, progress almost always won out.

Albert allowed himself one tradition, which he grasped tenaciously for the rest of his life. While other cattlemen experimented with different breeds of cattle, Albert refused to run anything but purebred Herefords. Angus crosses were becoming popular, because the smaller calves caused fewer problems during birthing, and the breed supposedly fared better in rough country. Albert stubbornly refused to experiment. Herefords, it could be said, were his only sacred cow.

Alberta and Charlotte Campbell didn't spend much time with their father while he was working. Nevertheless, they got a healthy dose of their father's wit and wisdom. "The older I get, the more I realize that he taught by example," Charlotte said. (Photo courtesy of Charlotte Campbell Armacost.)

Six

DOWNSHIFTING: THE 1950s

"All your head's good for is a hat rack and something to keep your spine from unraveling."
> —*Albert Campbell to his younger daughter, Charlotte*

Charlotte sat tall in the saddle and scrutinized the red backs of the Herefords. She was prepared for anything: a break away, or even a stampede. All of her senses were on edge as she scanned the herd for potential troublemakers with a maverick's glint in their eyes.

As usual, her search was disappointing. One cud-chewing cow gave her an empty stare. Charlotte caught a movement out of the corner of her eye, but it was just a young cow, impassively flicking her ears to fend off a fly. Even the half-grown calves, who were potential renegades, were only interested in lunch. The lone cowgirl who would keep the herd together regardless of the danger was, for the most part, being ignored.

Secretly she was glad, because her feet didn't begin to reach the stirrups on her dad's Hamley saddle. Her left ankle brushed the OX brand tooled on the saddle, and her right ankle obscured the Circle C brand on the other side. She patiently continued her vigil, because the chance to perch on her dad's saddle didn't come too often. Today's opportunity surfaced because her dad was moving cattle "over the hill" from Bear to New Meadows, and her mother had arranged a picnic rendezvous.

Charlotte's dad was always on the run, always busy. When Albert wasn't negotiating cattle deals in Baker, overseeing the OX operation, or riding the far reaches of the Circle C, he tried to have supper with his wife and girls at their New Meadows home.

He often started his mornings before the clock struck three, so he was exhausted by the time he got home. He never relaxed by breaking out a deck of cards or pursuing other recreational avenues. Even Albert's after-hours routine focused on business. While drinking a couple of glasses of fruit juice, he revised a list of tasks for the next day.

Charlotte emphasized that fruit juice was always his drink of choice. "He didn't drink because he thought it destroyed life."

Keeping abreast of news developments and market prices was another evening priority. He listened to four different radio broadcasts nightly, and the children had to be quiet during this ritual. Young Charlotte thought that her dad had heard enough news one evening, so she sidled over to the piano and plinked a few notes. "He swatted me once," she said. "I was so startled, as he only corrected me verbally. I ran and hid behind a chair, (where) Mother came to rescue me."

It was usually Grace, her mother, who handled the discipline and other day-to-day responsibilities. "Mother was completely self-sufficient," Charlotte said. "If she wanted something done, she would hire it done. Dad never pulled a weed or mowed a lawn. He joked that he could always tell which house was ours—it was the one with two carpenters hanging off the eaves."

The family rarely had a peaceful mealtime together. Albert delighted in snatching stray pieces of bacon off his youngest daughter's plate, a practice that invariably caused her to scream. Grace always intervened immediately. "Dad knew he'd get a rise out of both mother and me," Charlotte laughed.

If bacon wasn't on the menu, Albert had another favorite tactic. He liked to keep people scurrying by insisting, "Someone's at the door! Go see who it is." The doorstep was nearly always empty, but the exercise served its purpose. Albert wanted perpetual motion, even at the dinner table.

Albert was proud of his girls, even though he liked to joke that he had married a schoolmarm to give his children smarts, while

Grace married a rancher, so that her children would be strong. "Both of us got cut short," he concluded. Albert tempered that thought in later years by telling Charlotte, "The same blood runs in your veins as in mine, and I knew you'd turn out all right."

Grace didn't rely on bloodlines alone; she looked toward the principles set forth by the Methodist Church. The girls regularly attended church with their mother, but Albert rarely accompanied them. "I carry my religion in my wife's name," he explained to visiting ministers while showing them the sights on the Circle C.

Albert strongly supported formal education for his girls, which was an unusual philosophy in that era, especially coming from a practical-minded rancher who was satisfied with his own eighth grade education. "He said education couldn't hurt, and it might make us better wives," Charlotte said, adding that his viewpoint was probably influenced by her mother and her Aunt Carrie Campbell Whiteman.

Teaching the girls about his business was a different matter entirely. Grace never shared Albert's consuming passion for the operational end of the cattle business, and her subsequent involvement in the two ranches was limited to relaying phone messages and expediting correspondence. Her daughters followed suit, and the trio rarely ventured to the OX.

Albert did register two brands in the girls' names, and each fall he selected one choice heifer to carry each girl's brand. When one of his hands had young kids, he picked out a heifer calf for each of them as well. He discontinued the practice when the variety of branding irons complicated the operation. The Campbell girls' brands were later purchased by their cousins, Bob and Don Whiteman.

Of the three Campbell women, Charlotte had the most enthusiasm for the operation. Albert never particularly encouraged her interest, but he did offer her advice as she pursued her interest in horses. "If you ever get lost in the woods," he cautioned, "give your horse his head. A good one will take you home."

As she got older, his lessons became pointed. "You have to know more than the horse before you can teach it anything," he said while watching her training efforts.

Charlotte, who shared her father's independent nature, once decided to buy a horse on her own. After negotiating its price, she proudly brought the animal home and asked for her dad's opinion. After eyeing the gelding, he said, "Well, he'll get you there, but he won't get you home."

"He was right," reflected Charlotte.

Both Albert's pace and his tremendous work ethic created a formidable example for his children to follow. "He wasn't a dictator at all," said Charlotte, stressing that her dad never forced his self-discipline on the rest of the family. "Dad had subtle ways to teach values," she said.

Over the years, he supplemented the girls' education with object lessons. When a distraught Charlotte told her dad she was having trouble getting her classmates to listen to her, he interjected, "If you can't be the bell cow, fall in behind."

Father and daughter did have their exasperating moments. Albert was always in a hurry, and his small daughters had trouble keeping up with his long strides. Maintaining Albert's pace was still troublesome when teen-aged Charlotte started driving and became an eager chauffeur. Almost before Albert could settle into the passenger seat, he ordered, "Kick off the brake! Kick off the brake! Let's get moving." The ritual quickly became irritating for Charlotte, who decided to initiate some subtle teachings of her own. She was behind the wheel and ready one day, when her father slid into the passenger's seat. Before he could shut his door, Charlotte threw the car into gear and mashed her foot down on the accelerator. Her startled father fell into the car seat, knocking his hat off. He chuckled when he had recovered, "I didn't know you had it in you." The event didn't have a lasting impact: "Kick off the brake," remained Albert's rallying cry.

As a general rule, Albert didn't have time for other people's kids, but when he did take notice it was considered a supreme compliment. When he drove by Bert and Tina Warner's place in Bear and saw their eldest daughter, Arlen, pounding fence posts into the ground, he was impressed. He stopped at the house for a visit and jokingly asked if he couldn't adopt both Arlen and their son, Joe.

He also enjoyed Don and Darline Whiteley's young children.

Darline, who was Ramey Childers' daughter, had married Don in a ceremony on the Wildhorse River. Their son, Donny, loved to play "bull" with Albert. Both the stout, older man and the toddler dropped to the floor, and the two butted heads. "The boy got tough and they'd clap heads. When they finished the game, both were sporting large knots," Darline said.

Donny's little sister, Bonnie, also looked forward to Albert's visits. He usually had treats hidden in his pockets. As soon as Albert walked on the place, two sets of little hands searched his pockets.

Albert didn't completely abandon his ornery side with the kids. When Bonnie was a sleeping infant, Albert liked to pull her out of the crib and set her on the double bed, which was in the same room. The move invariably woke her up, and she would start to wail. Like clockwork, Albert's voice would rise above the baby's, "Come get this crying kid."

If it wasn't too cold, the toddlers spent their days in the saddle with their working parents. When bad weather hit, the kids stayed with a neighbor or their grandmother, Ramey.

"It's the only place to raise kids," Darline said. One factor marred the near-perfect set up. Medical emergencies were more likely to have tragic endings in the remote country. "The worst part was worrying about the snakes around the river," Darline added.

The young family headquartered out of a stone house located at the confluence of Dukes Creek and the Snake River.

Albert had bought the ranch from Helena Schmidt's first cousin, Lawrence Nixon. Lawrence's father, Jim, had put the place together; his 160-acre homestead was located on the banks of Dukes Creek.

Jim's enterprise prospered, and he gradually expanded the ranch until it reached the Snake River. His untimely death, which resulted from the previously described haying accident, halted the ranch's growth. After his widow died, their five children inherited the ranch. One of the sons, Lawrence, eventually bought the others out.

Albert wanted to buy the place, which was an ideal location to winter cattle. Lawrence was reluctant to sell, so Albert approached the deal from another angle.

Albert bought the Dukes Creek place from Lawrence Nixon. Lawrence's father, Jim, homesteaded the place. (Photo courtesy of Helena Schmidt.)

Albert had known Lawrence's son, Holworth, since he was a child. Although the young man was ready to launch his own ranching venture, he lacked the financing. Albert promised to loan Holworth start-up capital if he could talk his father into selling the ranch.

"Dad had great faith in Holworth's abilities," remembered Charlotte.

In the end, Holworth was successful, and he and his wife, Marthabelle, bought a place that adjoined the old family ranch to the south. "It took us a long time, but we finally finished paying Albert," Marthabelle said.

OX cowboy Don Whiteley thought that Albert had made a prudent move. "Dukes Creek was good country. It was three times warmer there than in Halfway, so we didn't have to feed as long. When spring came, we just opened the gate and the cattle would take to the hills, up Board Creek."

The milder climate at Dukes Creek enabled Albert to give his first-calf heifers and weaner calves an easier winter. The majority

The Nixons had an extensive haying operation in Dukes Creek. Albert used the ground strictly for grazing. (Photo courtesy of Helena Schmidt.)

of the cow herd, however, continued to winter at the Halfway ranch.

Darline liked living at Dukes Creek, because the stone house was cool throughout the sweltering summers and warm during the winter months. The house, which is now submerged in Brownlee reservoir, had two stories. The bottom floor featured a kitchen, a living room, a dining room, and a bedroom. The unfinished second floor provided additional space for beds.

Ramey took charge of the garden and the orchard, which was full of cherry, peach, and apple trees.

During the early Fifties, Ramey began to have trouble with her throat. After several visits to doctors' offices, they gave her the grim diagnosis: throat cancer. According to Dee Cole, who worked in the Council hospital when Ramey was admitted, nobody was optimistic about her future. Ramey, however, ignored the worried glances. She managed to outpace the disease for almost two decades.

The newly-married Darline Whiteley rides in front of the bunkhouse at Lick Creek. Her mother, Ramey Childers, designed the place, and it's still in use. (Photo courtesy of Darline Whiteley.)

Although Claude and Ramey continued to be Albert's top hands, the younger generation was beginning to hit its stride. The more Albert worked with Don Whiteley, the more Albert liked the young man.

"Don was a really good cowman," Dick Parker related. "He knew every leaf in that country. He would send you to a strange piece of country and he could describe it to you, so that you knew it when you got there. A lot of people can't do that."

Don was also a respected horseman. He spent hours working with his string of horses, most of which he owned. "Albert was a heck of a horse trader. He'd buy the animal and get the seller to throw some hay in. We got a few green horses every year," Don remembered.

"Albert tended to buy horses that were hell for bucking. He would buy them for nothing, he'd get them for half-price, and bring them to the outfit. Them horses was never any good."

Don started stocking his own string for several reasons. First, his ownership guaranteed that he alone would have use of the animals. "There are people who will ruin a horse," he said. "If

Hot, dry weather has long been a frustration for cowboys. Cows are reluctant to move off their winter range unless "the white cowboy" (a snowstorm) encourages them. Claude Childers and "the white cowboy" work together on Barbour Flat. (Photo courtesy of Darline Whiteley.)

you have your own exclusive string, you take better care of it," he added.

Ownership had a dollars and cents value too. Don supplemented his income by transforming green colts into well-trained horses, which always had a ready market.

Don's horse breaking technique was straightforward. "Get on and get going. Put the miles on."

He usually started his colts with a snaffle bit, which is hinged in the middle, and therefore gentler on the horse's mouth. As Don's horses gained experience, they graduated to either a light curb bit or a hackamore.

Don never used a McCarty, a popular type of bridle in the region. Both a lead rope and reins are attached to the bridle, and

Ramey Childers surprised everyone when she survived a bout with throat cancer. Here she stands with her granddaughter, Bonnie Whiteley. (Photo courtesy of Darline Whiteley.)

the rider usually tucks the lead rope under his belt. In the event he is bucked off, he can grab the lead rope and avoid chasing a runaway horse on foot. Don wasn't excited about the concept. "When I'm bucked off, I want to be loose. Otherwise, he might take my britches with him."

The Whiteleys and the Childers spent most of the spring riding the precariously steep Snake River breaks. They made sure the cattle utilized all of the range and prevented over-grazing.

By early June, the mother cows and their calves had worked their way up to Barbour Flat, where branding took place.

The faces around the branding corral varied slightly from year to year. The die-hard regulars usually stayed with the same task.

Having gathered the cattle the day before, the first order of business was separating the calves from their mothers. The bawling calves and their bellowing mothers created a din that lasted all day long.

Fitz Mink, who had worked for Albert in the 1920s, nearly always came back for OX brandings. His uncanny roping abilities created a standard for the other ropers, and as a result, they often challenged each other to impromptu roping contests. Other ropers who helped throughout the decades included Fitz's son, Herb Mink, Helena Schmidt, Dick Armacost, and Albert's cousins, Dick Clay and Ed Clay.

The ropers had a tricky job. They had to cast their loop into a huddled, milling group of calves, and capture an unbranded calf by its two back feet. Accuracy was important, because a series of bad throws made for an idle branding crew and ultimately, a longer day for the stressed cattle.

Ropers frequently caught calves by only one foot, but it was Herb Mink who cast one of the most memorable throws. His loop caught two calves, each by one foot. Herb was proud of the feat, and Amos Camp promised that he'd always verify the event.

Amos kept his word the first time he was asked to verify the story, but he decided to get Herb's goat the second time. Herb was telling the story in Bruneau, Idaho, where a large group of people was gathered for his birthday. Herb skillfully wove the story, giving the audience an embellished picture of his loop, as it tightened around the two calves' hooves. With a storyteller's

Fitz Mink and his horse hold a roped calf steady, while the crew finishes branding. In the foreground, Don Whiteley and Claude Childers castrate a bull calf. (Photo courtesy of Darline Whiteley.)

perfect timing, he called on Amos to back him up. The whole thing went flat when Amos, who was prone to orneriness, said, "You must have me confused with someone else."

Once the roper hit the target, a member of the ground crew sprang into action, toppling the calf so that the roper's horse could drag it over to the rest of the branding crew. The wrestlers were usually younger guys, although there was always room on the crew for an eager, but inexperienced hand.

Gordon MacGreggor, the logger, fit into this category. Albert's nephew, Don Whiteman, was working for Gordon when the two stopped by to watch the operation. Things weren't going smoothly. Five hundred calves had to be branded, but the ropers, who had come up from Weiser, were having trouble hitting their mark. The potent brew they had guzzled during their 100-mile trip to Barbour Flat didn't help matters.

The ropers weren't the only problem. Albert was lacking a ground crew, and before long Gordon hopped off the fence and launched his calf wrestling career. Like most novices, Gordon muscled the calves and used his strength to tip them over. Although he eventually got the job done, his method was slow and exhausting. Many seasoned wrestlers toppled calves by twisting tails or lifting hooves. By catching the calves off-balance, the wrestler could usually complete his task with less time and exertion.

Don continued to watch the show from the fence, and before long, Albert nudged him and said, "Get going."

Don shot a questioning look at Gordon, who answered, "I'm not paying."

"I'll need five dollars an hour," Don told Albert.

"I can't pay you that."

"I'll just sit on the fence and watch then," his nephew answered.

It didn't take long for Albert to give in. "Let's go," he said, nudging Don on the shins.

Don earned his money that day. He ended up throwing over two-thirds of the calves, even though Gordon was working as hard as he could. The crew got a moment of comic relief when Gordon sprinted toward a calf and grabbed it from the front. The calf continued to run forward, with its head between Gordon's legs. The wrestler's backwards ride ended abruptly when the calf lunged forward and kicked all the buttons off his fly.

Ramey thought it was hilarious. She waved her finger at his privates and asked, "What'll it take? What'll it take?" Gordon was too tired to make any retort.

Ramey always handled the vaccinations as Claude applied the brand. Of all the jobs, Claude's was the most exacting. He kept an array of "O" and "X" brands red hot in a nearby wood fire, which he stoked carefully. If the brands weren't hot enough, they wouldn't do the job. On the other hand, if the brands became white hot, they would hurt the animal.

Clear weather was critical to a successful branding, since a rain-soaked hide would diffuse the iron's heat, resulting in a blotchy brand.

Claude also took pains to put a uniform brand on each animal. Putting the "O" brand around the hip bone helped him get the job done.

In the early days, someone with a hot dehorning iron joined the group working around the calf. In later years, Albert waited until the calves were yearlings, and had their horns sawed off.

Heifer calves that had been branded, vaccinated, and dehorned were finished for the day. Bull calves weren't so lucky. Albert usually handled castrations, which were finished in a flash. With a sharp knife, he cut off the scrotum and extracted the testicles, which were sometimes saved for an after-branding feast. The wound was slathered with tar, which provided protection from flies and infection.

Most of the calves were branded at Barbour Flat, but Albert always held a second branding at Lick Creek to catch the slick calves they missed the first time. They also cut out the dry cows, or those who had failed to reproduce. The dry cows were sent to the sale yard, as the cow-calf pairs were herded to summer pastures at Hoo Hoo Gulch, Grouse Creek, Butterfield Gulch, and Fawn Creek.

The makeshift headquarters on Lick Creek were less than luxurious, but they served the purpose. When Albert first acquired the place, the hands stayed in the old stage stop house, which had dirt floors.

Built around the turn of the century, the house had originally been an overnight stop for ore freighters. The two story structure was the setting for a fist fight straight out of a western movie. The altercation started at a dance which was hosted at the house, and the two men climbed to the second story balcony to have it out. One well-aimed punch sent the loser flying over the railing. He reportedly survived his flight.

When the stage stop became uninhabitable, Albert brought in an old Civilian Conservation Corps barracks, which he had purchased from the government. Although it was an eyesore, it did have indoor plumbing and running water.

Del Shelton, who had agreed to do some fencing for Albert, brought his family to the house. His wife, Opal, loved the ranch, although the lifestyle required her to make some adjustments. Learning to stockpile groceries was one of the biggest challenges. The dirt road to Council was long and incredibly rough. As a result, the Sheltons made the trek into town just once a month, on payday.

The long lapses between trips to the grocery store made for interesting menus at the end of the month. Opal was horrified when unexpected guests stopped by for supper. Scanning the empty shelves of her pantry, she found a can of mushroom soup, some flour and eighty quart jars of rhubarb. Opal made the soup into a casserole, and stirred together some biscuits. For dessert, she managed to find enough ingredients to make a chocolate cake with rhubarb sauce.

Sometimes the grocery challenges came during mid-month, like the time Del sauntered in with steaks. He bragged that they came from prime OX beef, but they looked funny to Opal. Her first bite was jolting. The stuff was terrible. Del admitted that it was bear meat. The bear had probably been feeding on an old carcass, since a bear's diet affects its flavor. Hunters prefer bears that have been foraging on berries and other fruit.

Albert soon grew tired of ''roughing it'' in the barracks house, and asked Ramey to design a new bunkhouse for Lick Creek. Her rough sketches were handed to the carpenters when they arrived in July of 1951. They demolished the old stage stop house, which had been built with wooden pegs instead of nails, and whenever possible, they used materials from the old house. The new structure flew together, and crew started using it by the end of the summer.

Downstairs, the house had knotty pine walls. The kitchen and living room shared the first story, and the upstairs housed the bedrooms. The cookstove and the living room fireplace provided the heat. The system was fine during the early days of fall; however, the poorly insulated house became impossible to heat in November and December, when the stragglers were being gathered and herded toward Dukes Creek.

The house had no refrigeration for the first few years; Ramey and Darline continued to keep groceries cool in the spring house. Eventually, Albert purchased a propane refrigerator, and the women appreciated the luxury.

"The house had gas lights in it and was really up town," remembered Hugh Lydston, who visited the place with his dad.

Albert was riding high in 1951. Cattle prices were at an all-time high; fat cattle were selling at an unbelievable forty-five cents a pound.

Since Albert had a few extra dollars, and he had exhausted all possibilities to expand the ranch, he started working on ranch improvements. In addition to the bunkhouse, he bought a 1951 Model A John Deere tractor, a cultivator, and a disk.

All three were loaded onto an implement truck, which tried to keep up with Albert as he sped toward Lick Creek. Albert pulled off the road at Rocky Comfort, and walked around the flat until he found Warren Parker. "I wonder if you could do me a favor," Albert said.

Warren, who was a little leery of Albert's motives, eyed the implement truck and said, "I doubt it."

"I bought this new tractor, but I don't want the boys to run it until it's broken in. If you folks would use the tractor while you're doing your farming this spring, maybe the boys would be able to run it without ruining it."

In those days, new tractors came with a set of start-up instructions. They had to run on half throttle for a specified number of hours, and as the engine became seasoned, the operator had to change grades of oil.

For years, the Parkers used this old Fordson tractor in their haying operation. Frustrations and breakdowns were commonplace. It's no wonder that they were delighted when Albert Campbell asked them to break in his new John Deere tractor. (Photo courtesy of Dick and Georgianna Parker.)

"We had an old Oliver 70 tractor, and we were still doing some of the farming with horses," said Dick Parker. "Albert coming with the tractor was just like Santa Claus coming. A brand new tractor? We'd never had a brand new tractor in our lives. I doubt if dad had ever been on a new tractor, and I know I never had been. And there we were with this brand new tractor—top of the line at that time.

"We sure broke it in for him. I'd run it at night and my sister would run it during the day. And the motor never cooled off on it all spring. But that was one of the best farmings Rocky Comfort ever got. We did take good care of that tractor."

The tractor was headed for Dukes Creek that winter, and Albert wanted Dick to go with it. In the end, Dick ran the tractor, and in exchange, Albert let the Parkers use his equipment for their farming operation.

"I set the cultivator as deep as it would go, put the John Deere in second gear and sat there day after day after day, running that stupid cultivator," Dick remembered.

The high cattle prices also brought prosperity to Albert's cattle buyer, Tim Lydston. Undaunted by his 1943 bankruptcy, he launched another feedlot and packing plant with a partner. No sooner was the business going, when cattle prices plummeted. Fat cattle, that had been selling for forty-five cents a pound, were going for seventeen or eighteen cents a pound. To compound the problem, Lydston's partner died at the same time. When the business sold, Lydston broke even, and he decided to stick to order buying.

Lydston's eighteen-year-old son, Hugh, wanted to learn the business, so his dad gave him a rolling apprenticeship as they bought and sold both fat cattle and feeders throughout Idaho and Oregon.

"It was a hell of a summer," Hugh said. "We drove 13,000 miles in two and a half months. We were driving a '51 Cadillac with a V-8. If I got below eighty miles per hour, the old man would wake up and holler, 'What did you stop for?' Cruising speed was ninety miles per hour. There was no speed limit in Oregon, and that was what we cruised at.

"I drove all night while he slept. We'd get to the sale or wherever we were going and I'd get to sleep in the car. We'd do this for a couple of days, then stop to get a motel room somewhere."

As the Cadillac's odometer whirled, Hugh finally had the chance to get acquainted with his dad and learn his business. Although the business' subtleties eluded him, Hugh thoroughly enjoyed some of his dad's idiosyncrasies.

For example, Lydston loved to have his picture taken. Hugh quickly learned that he could avoid working if he carried a camera around.

Hugh also noticed that his portly, fifty-eight-year-old father had trouble crawling on and off a horse. As a result, Lydston only rode tolerant horses during his later years, because they often had to stand near the strange objects Lydston used to boost himself into the saddle. One horse had to stand over a grain auger's exhaust pipe. The animal never flinched as the warm exhaust puffed directly under his belly.

Hugh received some additional insight into his father's successes and failures that summer, when he ran into John Stringer in McCall. Stringer was a large-scale stockman; his cattle and sheep operations were scattered throughout central Idaho. In fact, one of Stringer's cattle ranches, located between Weiser and Payette, Idaho, was purchased by the OX in 1988.

Stringer had been shipping sheep out of New Meadows, and he had stopped at the Shore Lodge in McCall to wet his whistle. After buying Hugh a ginger ale, he said, "I've known your old man for forty years. He ought to be a multi-millionaire, and he's not. You know why? Well, he always throwed all the dice for himself at once. He was never conservative. He always tried to make a million in one clap.

"For other people, his advice was exactly the opposite. He told them to proceed carefully, an inch at a time, so they'd make a little bit, a solid profit.

"He never followed his own advice for himself. He was always a plunger. And every time he plunged, something happened."

Albert's luck also started changing for the worse in 1952. Although he wasn't happy about the cattle prices, they didn't surprise him. He was used to the boom or bust cattle market. Albert's bad luck came in the form of unforeseeable mishaps.

The first involved Albert's cousin, Ed Clay. Ed had worked for the Circle C before bringing his wife, Loine, and young son, Jerry, to the OX. Ed was a skilled cowboy and roper, but he had a formidable temper.

Ed and Don Whiteley were having a tough time moving yearlings to the spring range; the unusually high spring runoff had washed away all the bridges across Wildhorse. When all but fifteen of the yearlings had crossed, five or six of the animals changed direction in mid-stream, and started swimming for Oregon. The yearlings' dangerous impulse angered Ed, and he plunged in after them.

Ed and his horse were in front of the Wildhorse cow camp

When Ed Clay drowned in the Snake River, his cousin, Albert Campbell, was devastated. Ed is standing by his wife, Loine. (Photo courtesy of Larry and Hazel Clay.)

when Don caught his last glimpse of him. Both Don and Mabel Ray, who lived on the Oregon side of the Snake, watched as Ed's horse clambered up the Oregon bank. The animal was alone.

Ed had been wearing a heavy mackinaw and chaps when he spurred his horse into the river. "I don't know why he and the horse separated," Don said. "Hell, he was probably mad enough not to be using his head. The yearlings were going to come out one side or the other anyway."

Ed's brothers, Frank and Tommy Clay, traveled from New Meadows to join the search party. They found their brother's body several days after the drowning.

Search parties combed the Snake River for Ed's body. His brothers, Tommy and Frank Clay, found the body on a meandering portion of the river called the Oxbow. (Photo courtesy of the Bert Warner family.)

Albert was normally stoic during difficult situations. Whenever he made a mistake or experienced a tragedy, he accepted it, and went on with his life. "Don't cry over spilt milk," was one of his favorite phrases. Ed's death was different. Albert openly grieved over the loss.

A few months later, Albert himself almost became a Snake River drowning statistic.

The advent of the Brownlee ferry gave the OX hands a safer way to transport cattle across the river. Water pressure against open-topped pontoons propelled the ferry, which was guided by a cable strung across the river. The ferry could handle twenty-five head at a time.

Ramey and Claude handled the Oregon side of the operation, keeping the cattle bunched together and loading them onto the ferry. Once the livestock reached the Idaho landing, they were trailed to a nearby OX pasture on Dukes Creek. There was an old storehouse on the property, and the hands stockpiled enough feed to sustain the animals until the entire herd was ferried across the Snake. The process normally took one or two days, but not this time.

It was about noon on April 9, 1952 when Albert and Lovell "Junior" Gover started across the river with a load of cattle. They were halfway across when water swamped the pontoons, causing the ferry to sink. The cattle plunged in and immediately started swimming for shore. Albert and Junior clung to the ferry. Neither man could swim.

The ferry sank quickly. Junior crawled onto a panel, and onlookers watched helplessly as the river spun the makeshift raft and its spread-eagled passenger quickly down the river.

Albert barely kept his head above water by wedging a wooden pole under one arm and a two by six plank under the other. He followed Junior toward a set of rapids.

Albert and Junior had barely hit the water before the rescue effort was launched. Ramey and Claude spurred their horses toward the nearest rowboat, which was owned by rancher Amos Robinette. Ramey jumped in the bow of the boat and Amos took the oars, rowing for all he was worth. They traveled for over an hour before they finally caught up with a survivor. It was Junior. Ramey coaxed him to loosen his death grip on the panel, and inch by inch she pulled his dead weight into the boat.

Albert made it through the rapids, and the river shot him into a series of backeddies, or large whirlpools, that lapped the banks. Albert's cousin, Dick Clay, waded into the water and tried to rope Albert as the eddy's current swirled him close to the bank. Dick's lasso missed and Albert was spat back into the mainstream.

Don Whiteley, who was at Dukes Creek, jumped into his pick-up and raced downstream. He stopped at the next eddy, grabbed his rope and waited for Albert to follow the current. This time Don threw the loop. He missed.

By this time Albert had been in the river for over an hour and he couldn't hold out much longer. Fortunately, the eddy's current caught him again, and Albert looped back toward Don.

Hoping to increase his roping accuracy, Don waded into the water until he was chest-deep. This time his lasso landed around the end of Albert's plank. Don tightened the loop and pulled Albert toward him. He was almost senseless by the time Don hauled him up on the riverbank.

"He wouldn't have made another circle," said Don. "He was so tired when he got out that he couldn't stand. He was just give out, worse than give out."

Both men were taken to the nearest hot shower and put to bed under a heavy layer of blankets. Albert didn't put up a fuss. It was one of the few times in his life that he numbly followed instructions. Before twenty-four hours had passed, he was running the show once again.

Albert Campbell and Junior Gover nearly lost their lives when this ferry capsized. After a successful crossing from the Oregon side, these cattle look forward to green Idaho pastures. (Photo courtesy of Charlotte Campbell Armacost.)

The incident spooked Albert, but he refused to admit it. Friends and neighbors repeatedly asked, "What were you thinking as you went down the river?"

Albert had a stock answer. Before taking the plunge, Albert had tucked a hundred dollar bill into his watch pocket. Someone had given him the money either for earnest money on a deal or to satisfy a debt. Albert insisted his thoughts were on that money as he bobbed down the river. "I figured if I could get close enough to the bank, I'd throw that bill to safety," he reportedly said. For added impact, he also groaned about losing his good Stetson hat during the ordeal.

The Brownlee Ferry's days were numbered, but it wasn't because of the accident. Efforts to tap the Snake River's power potential were launched as early as 1906. Nearly fifty years later the Corps of Engineers and Idaho Power were vying for the right to begin construction. Although the Truman Administration favored federal control, Idaho Power was undaunted. Company officials began preliminary negotiations with private landowners in the canyon.

The 1952 presidential election brought Dwight Eisenhower and a new perspective into office. The Eisenhower Administration favored private utilities, and Idaho Power intensified its efforts to buy the ground which would be flooded.

Albert applauded Idaho Power's plans, although the proposed location of Brownlee Dam would make his Dukes Creek ranch virtually inaccessible. Albert was so sure that the utility company would succeed, that he bought stock in the company. Since Albert religiously plowed most of his profits back into the OX and Circle C, his outside investment was a remarkable vote of confidence. He later told Darline Whiteley that the investment would provide Grace and the girls with a secure future regardless of what happened in the cattle market.

Albert's status as a stockholder didn't thwart his efforts to cut the best deal. Albert left no written record of the negotiation process, but tales abound. Unlike most of his neighbors, Albert avoided naming a price. He wanted to barter instead. No doubt Albert considered the deal from all angles.

It's possible that Idaho Power transactions were on his mind late one autumn night in 1953, after meeting with his attorney in Council. He was about three miles out of New Meadows on a straight stretch of highway when a horse lunged into his path. Albert didn't have time to swerve or slow down. He hit the animal broadside. As the horse's body shattered the windshield, the car crossed the road, slammed through a barbed wire fence and jolted to a stop against a pine tree.

John Goodman, who was working on the highway, found the wreck. The sight behind the driver's window was unbelievably gory. Goodman was sure that the unrecognizable driver had died. Only after he found legal papers in the back seat, did he realize it was Albert.

An Army nurse, who happened to be working at the Pine Knot Cafe in New Meadows, was called to the scene. Although he was barely alive, she prepared him for the thirty minute ride to the Council hospital.

Family members followed the entourage.

The small, country hospital wasn't equipped to handle such extensive injuries. Dr. John Edwards performed an emergency tracheotomy, which enabled Albert to keep breathing. After that, the waiting began. Albert needed the technology available in Boise, but he couldn't travel until he stabilized. Grace and Charlotte spent some of the longest hours of their lives pacing in front of the hospital. Charlotte heard Rollie mutter to himself, "How will we ever manage without him?" Rollie later remembered it as one of the lowest days of his life.

When Dr. Edwards finally gave the go ahead, Albert was loaded on a small plane bound for Boise.

After a brief rest in New Meadows, Charlotte drove her mother to Boise. Neither was fully prepared for the sight that met them in the hospital room. Albert's head and arms were completely swathed in bandages. Charlotte took one look and fainted. The shock made her physically ill, and she was hospitalized for three days.

Albert tenaciously held on to life. As he began to regain consciousness, the extent of his head injuries became apparent. He spent months in a delirious state. His doctor kept him in restraints, which infuriated him during his rare lucid moments.

"Grace!" he would scream. "Get me out of here." The moments of recognition were almost harder to take than the delirium.

Albert's situation was precarious. There wasn't enough medical knowledge about brain injuries. The doctors could do nothing but wait.

The wait was agonizing for Albert's family. "It was awful," remembered Charlotte. "Mom and I spent Christmas in a hotel with a tiny tree. I didn't know whether Dad would live or not.

"Mother's self-sufficiency allowed her to survive the accident. She had been told that Dad might never be all right—that he might become a vegetable or worse. She was under incredible pressure.

"She decided that the boys should keep the (OX) Ranch going regardless. She enlisted the help of Rollie, Claude Childers, and Don Whiteley, and our attorney, Carl Swanstrom," said Charlotte. Grace knew that if Albert survived and she had sold the ranch, the news would kill him.

After several months of hospitalization, Albert showed few signs of improvement. He was thin and had caught pneumonia. It looked like he was losing the battle.

Grace had another tough decision to make. There was a surgeon at the mental institution, State Hospital South, who was willing to try experimental surgery. Grace decided to give it a try.

Albert was readied for the five-hour trip and loaded into an ambulance. His attending nurse later admitted that she had spent much of the trip praying that he'd die before they reached Blackfoot.

The surgeon tried an entirely new approach to Albert's problem. He drilled a hole just above each of Albert's eye sockets. The holes released the pressure on his brain. He finally began to heal.

Recovery was a painfully slow process, for both Albert and Grace. She handled the tragedy stoically, but some of her pressures and worries are reflected in a candid letter she wrote to the family attorney, Carl Swanstrom, in May of 1955:

> I think it was almost too much when I got news
> that (daughter) Alberta had a subarachnoid

hemorrahagel ruptured blood vessel between membranes that cover (the) brain. She has recovered as completely as one could hope for, the blood vessel that ruptured being so small the doctors were unable to find it and surgery was found to be unnecessary with only the admonition that she should not lift.

Dr. Fredman was not very helpful when he cautioned should Alberta drop dead, Albert was not to be told.

He also repeated over and over that Albert must not bump his head which increases our apprehension about driving Albert about in a car, but it was the only thing he enjoyed all last winter since he had to be kept in the dark about his business and we felt that we had to take chances rather than let him stare at the floor.

I cannot be sure that this letter is coherent now that barbituates add to my befuddlement. I am faithfully following Dr. Edwards prescribed treatment for an ulcer and am responding to his nostrums, bless his heart.

Albert is doing fine. Dr. F. cut him off his sedative medicine gradually and I am glad. If they (sedatives) effect him as they do me it would be hard to judge his recovery while taking them.

After Albert was released from the hospital in Blackfoot, he was sent home to New Meadows with round-the-clock nursing care.

"He had lost a year of his memory," Charlotte said. "He came back asking about things that happened at the beginning of his life. He was in great pain, as he hadn't used his muscles, and he was weak beyond belief."

After six months of home recovery, Albert agreed to do something that was completely out of character: he said he'd go on a vacation.

Albert, Grace, and a nurse left for the British Isles on the

Queen Mary. Itinerary revisions showed that Albert was on the mend. For example, when Grace suggested they go see the crown jewels, Albert flatly refused. Instead they trekked to Scotland, where Albert could evaluate the country's grand champion bull.

Albert was ready to go home when he happened to see a minor story in a British newspaper. The Federal Power Commission had finally granted Idaho Power permission to construct three dams along the Snake. The event marked an abrupt end to the vacation.

Albert desperately wanted to wheel and deal like he had before the accident. He just couldn't. His mind had lost its sharp edge. Both his wit and his judgment had dulled, and he keenly felt it.

His role in the family had changed dramatically during the two years following the accident. Before, Albert had called all the shots on both the OX and the Circle C ranches. When he was hurt, Rollie took over both operations for the better part of three years. The OX crew assumed many management responsibilities, making the situation workable.

When Albert was well enough to manage the OX again, he had to work with several restrictions. Since he could no longer drive, he had to depend on a variety of hired drivers. Sleepless nights had previously given him an early start on the day's business. Now they remained just sleepless nights.

The drivers often experienced off-road adventures. Albert was partial to abandoned logging roads and even cow trails, particularly after the fall rains. "He was always getting people stuck," remembered Bertha Armacost. "He always preceded the trip by insisting, 'You won't get stuck.'"

The accident curtailed Albert's way of doing business. Grace quickly quelled any of his expansion ideas, urging him to manage what he already owned.

"The accident took a lot out of Albert," reflected Larry Clay, Albert's cousin and a long-time Circle C cowboy. "He was very resistant to changes in the business after the accident."

His daughter Charlotte offered an example: "Dad always sold two-year-olds because he wanted bigger beef. It caught up to him. After he was hurt he kept it up, even though it wasn't cost effective."

His handicap was also reflected in his cattle herd. "Albert . . .

Meeting Scotland's grand champion bull was the highlight of Albert's vacation. (Photo courtesy of Charlotte Campbell Armacost.)

always had good cattle and good bulls. After he got hurt so bad in the wreck, the cattle went way down hill. You could see it. Albert always had uniformly big cows. After he was hurt, there were more small, bad-looking cows," Dick Parker said.

Although Albert's personal business decisions were sometimes skewed, he still had an uncanny grasp of the big picture. He could still predict economic trends and changes in the cattle market, and younger ranchers often sought his advice. Albert's young cousins, Darrell Campbell and Dorsey Campbell, consulted Albert frequently when they were launching their ranching operation.

"People were always coming to him to ask advice," remembered Vic Armacost, Albert's son-in-law. "He was always glad to share information. He never smugly kept it to himself."

Guests couldn't just "drop by" Henry and Helena Schmidt's place in Starveout Basin. Driving to the ranch requires a minor expedition. The guests who snapped this picture caught Henry and Helena repairing their barn. Helena quickly donned a dress for the occasion. (Photo courtesy of Helena Schmidt.)

Seven

TRANSITIONS: 1960–1982

"I never want to go through a summer like that again. It sure makes you spooky at fire."

—Helena Schmidt

No Business Basin and the breaks of the Wildhorse River were miserably hot places to be in the summer. The craggy rocks surrounding the cabin at No Business absorbed the sun's rays, and threw the heat back into the Basin. It didn't take long for the lush, green spring to succumb to the heat. Among the thousands of steep, grassy acres on the Wildhorse River breaks, only the irrigated hayfields remained green. The place was ripe for a wildfire.

On July 22, 1960, Henry and Helena Schmidt had pretty well finished their haying. They were in a deep, exhausted sleep when Junior Walton pounded on their bedroom door and shouted, "Fire!" It was 2 a.m.

Junior had been helping them with their haying operation in the Basin, and he had been asleep in the cabin's front room. He was probably roused by the fire light reflecting through the cabin's windows.

As soon as Henry pulled on some clothes, he strode to the wooden phone set and reported the fire. The trio saddled their horses, grabbed shovels, and quickly covered the mile between the barn and the fire.

The fire was in their hayfield, dangerously close to a huge stack of loose hay. One thing saved the stack, according to Helena. They had accidentally created a fire barrier around the stack when they were putting it up. Any loose hay that would have spread the fire was buried in a thick layer of dust.

A hay stacker had been left in the middle of the field. It was a tall, iron structure, and Henry figured their saddles would be safer there than in the barn. They unsaddled the horses, turned them loose, and slipped the saddles over a metal cross bar, which was about ten feet off the ground.

The Schmidts' young dog, named Tim, watched the whole operation. He decided to protect the saddles, and no amount of coaxing would get him to leave. Helena worried that he would be hurt if the fire flared up. Hours later, when they returned to the stacker, they found Tim stationed under Helena's saddle. He had kept the saddles safe.

The trio spent the rest of the night trying to contain the fire. They threw dirt on the flames and built a fire line on the uphill side of the fire.

Their work was dangerous. "The steeper the terrain, the faster the fire runs," explained Jim Fry, the Forest Service fuels specialist on the Council Ranger District. "The canyon acts like a chimney—the fire gets to running faster and spotting ahead." Staying uphill of a fire like that is a good way to get burned alive.

The Schmidts had their animals and the winter's feed supply to protect. Their home in Starveout Basin was also in danger, should the fire escape in a southwesterly direction. Luckily they had the benefits of night firefighting: cool air moves down steep slopes at night, which keeps the fire from spreading rapidly. They took advantage of the situation, and worked throughout the night and the cool morning hours.

Junior, who was in his late thirties, had a history of heart trouble. Henry worried that the continuous exertion might kill him, so he insisted on a slower pace.

The Forest Service hand crews arrived early that afternoon, and their efforts were fortified by an old military plane, which dropped plumes of retardant at the head of the fire.

The trio took a break, and rode to the ridge which separates No

Business and Starveout Basins. They watched the C-119, also known as a flying boxcar, dump its load of fire retardant. Before the ship could gain elevation, an engine started missing. The pilot apparently decided to land in the wide, grassy strip in front of their cabin. Before he could get the plane turned around, it crashed.

"It sounded like a bomb," Helena said.

Henry's colt, Carrot, whirled around on the ridge top. Somehow Henry managed to stay on.

The plane exploded on impact. Its crew consisted of three Montana men, who were killed instantly.

Pieces of the wreckage were strewn all over the Basin, and spot fires started and spread in all directions.

The riders urged their frightened horses down the steep slope to the house and barn, where two calves and six work horses were corralled. "They were so scared," said Helena. The horses crowded around Helena, silently asking for help. "I couldn't do anything but take care of the horses," she said.

Several firefighters focused their efforts on saving the house and the barn. Before the fire, Helena had faithfully irrigated the land around the buildings. That effort saved the house right after the plane crash, but it wasn't out of danger. One firefighter poked a hole in the irrigation ditch, and set up a portable pump. They saturated the house and barn with streams of water.

The wind shifted, and it looked like their efforts were in vain. Helena watched as they started bringing her belongings out of the house, in an effort to save them. Several tables and her radio were sitting on the lawn before someone said, "The wind's shifted again. We can probably save the house."

About that time, a low-flying aircraft dropped several smoke-jumpers on the ridge around the Basin. The smokejumpers were a big boon to the firefighting effort. The highly trained men could parachute into inaccessible spots quickly, and they could contain the spot fires while they were still relatively small.

A helicopter was dispatched to the scene a short time later. It shuttled the fire crews from the Basin to the ridge. "The helicopter could take three men at a time," said Helena. "It had a turnaround time of three minutes."

The fire was contained three days after it started. A skeleton crew stayed in the Basin for nearly a month afterward, watching for smokes and flare-ups.

Miraculously, the Schmidts lost no animals in the fire. Of three haystacks in the Basin, only the smallest one, containing about twenty tons of hay, burned. It made for a tight winter, but they were thankful. Things could have been much worse.

The cause of the fire was never fully determined, although Helena suspects it was started by some disgruntled fishermen from Ontario, Oregon. Even after Henry warned them, they continued to leave the Schmidts' pasture gates open. Henry had asked them to leave right before the fire started.

Three years after the fire, the Schmidts decided to sell No Business Basin to old-time OX cowboy Dick Armacost and his wife, Erma, in 1963.

The Schmidts had plenty to keep them busy on the home ranch and were far from retired. They hadn't yet settled into their new routine when a tragedy occurred. Henry suffered a stroke while repairing the barn. Helena wasn't quite sure what was wrong with him, and she grew concerned enough during the middle of the night to call Fred and Ruth Cole.

Ruth Cole handled the telephone exchange out of her home on Hornet Creek Road. The people who lived in Bear, Cuprum, or along the Wildhorse River could contact each other on their old-fashioned crank telephones, using a different combination of long and short rings to summon each person on the line. One long ring summoned Ruth, the operator. She could patch the callers into Council or other long-distance locations.

Outside phone calls could only be placed from 8:00 a.m. to noon, unless there was an emergency. Helena's long ring came at 2 a.m., and more than one person on the party line picked up the receiver to see what was wrong.

Helena explained the emergency, and said she didn't feel confident about her driving at the moment. Ruth said she would send her husband, Fred, immediately.

Fred worked for the county, and had plowed and graded all of the area's roads. The Schmidts' place was so isolated, however, that he'd never been on their road. Afraid that he'd get lost, he

Helena Schmidt and a calf simultaneously milk the Guernsey cow. (Photo courtesy of Helena Schmidt.)

asked OX cowboy Don Whiteley to meet him at the Wildhorse Road cutoff, which was about forty minutes from Council.

Following Don in his outfit, it took Fred more than an hour to navigate the International Scout to Starveout. Henry Schmidt had just recently used his crawler to punch a road up the nearly vertical hillside. Fred was a little apprehensive as he had to back up and inch forward repeatedly to make the hairpin curves. His headlights often caught nothing in their beams. It was like they were shooting off the edge of the world.

Helena was anxiously waiting at the house. Fred had taken out the passenger seat, so Henry was able to lie flat in the Scout. Helena crawled in beside him.

The trip was exasperatingly slow once they passed the switchbacks. Twenty miles per hour was the fastest possible speed on the Wildhorse Road.

They made it to the Council hospital, and Henry lingered for four days before dying. Helena never left his side.

Fred Cole and Don Whiteley cooperated on another venture with a happier ending. Fred was running the county road grader, near the Speropulous Ranch, when he spotted Don flagging him down. "I can't get this bull to do anything," Don said, gesturing toward the obstinate creature. "He won't lead. He keeps breaking my rope and I can't feed him here all winter."

After Fred agreed to help, Don dug a hole in the snowbank and backed his pick-up in. They tied a rope around the bull's horns and cranked up the road grader. The rope broke, so they dug out a chain and tried it again. The bull set its feet, but he wasn't as strong as the heavy equipment. He basically skied his way into the back of the pick-up.

Fred logged thousands of hours behind the controls of the county's D-6 Caterpillar tractor. He kept the road between Council, Bear, and Cuprum clear of snow from 1952 to 1973.

There were years when the snow banks were twelve feet deep. "Sometimes Ruth was lucky if she got to see me four hours out of the day," Fred said.

He thoroughly enjoyed his job, but admitted that, "sometimes the fumes and the noise in the open Cat' got to be a bit much."

Roy Moritz, who carried the mail to Bear and Cuprum, often followed the snowplow on his route. He was following Fred at a good clip when the plow hit a hidden stump. Fred, who had been running the plow while standing up, had an ugly gash across his forehead.

"He had a hunk of hide in his eyes," Roy's son Norval Moritz recounted. "Both of them being as tough as they were, Dad tied

Ruth and Fred Cole linked the OX Ranch and its neighbors to the outside world. Ruth was the telephone operator and Fred kept the roads plowed. They posed for this picture during a skating party shortly before their 1931 marriage. (Photo courtesy of Carrie Cole.)

Fred's head together with a rag, and they kept going until the job was finished."

"In the hospital, two doctors told me that I would become paralyzed," Fred said. "It did hurt, but you don't believe all you hear." Fred proved the doctors wrong.

Ruth Cole also provided Bear and Cuprum with a vital link to the outside world. When Council received a dialing telephone system in 1960, her job was created. "Fred volunteered me for the job," she said. "He went to the telephone meeting, and I didn't."

She put the switchboard in her kitchen, and was on duty from eight in the morning until noon. "Occasionally an emergency call would come in and I'd connect it after hours," she said.

"One guy from Portland would call and say it was an emergency. I got to listening to the conversation. It wasn't an emergency, so I cut them off."

The toughest part of her job was connecting the bad news calls, particularly those that brought word of death. At those times, she almost regretted her job.

Sometimes the constant ringing during her "off" hours was irritating. Calls made on the crank phone system rang in every house on the line. This was especially annoying at five o'clock in the morning, when two ladies on the line regularly liked to exchange recipes. Ruth got fed up one time and turned off her system's ringing envelopes. She regretted it. Someone died that night, and there was no way to get word through.

Ruth was once alarmed by a call from the OX bunkhouse. Herb Mink needed to make an outside call. He was having trouble getting his message across, because he started to stutter. Finally, he got so frustrated that he let a few barnyard words slip out. Ruth promptly disconnected him.

After that incident, she wasn't too eager to answer calls from the OX. About three months after the abrupt disconnect, Herb called her again. He explained that he'd had a flat, and he needed to call the OX for a replacement.

"How far are you from the OX?" she asked.

"Ten miles," he answered.

"Try walking it, and maybe it will be harder to cuss out the operator next time," she said before the phone went dead in his ear.

Dial phones made their debut in Bear and Cuprum in 1978. "I missed the operator business awfully," Ruth said. "I would always visit a little bit before putting the call through."

A lot of Bear residents, including Paul and Ruth Ernst, were sorry to see the party line go. Keeping current with the community news became a conscious effort.

There were some, however, who rejoiced. Bonnie Whiteley Reid was frustrated with the system, even though she grew up with it. She, too, was fed up with the early morning recipe exchanges. "Calls placed outside the immediate area could hardly be heard," she added. "You had to stand there and scream."

Bonnie's family had experienced drastic changes after Albert's accident. Her grandparents, Claude and Ramey Childers, had led both ranch and family activities since the 1930s. Ill health forced them both to retire in the mid-1950s. They moved to a small house in Council.

"You can't find people like that anymore," commented Frank Smith, a former neighbor. "The Childers were just as devoted to Albert and that place as if they'd owned the place."

"Granddad had emphysema and pride," Bonnie said. "Albert and Grace gave them meat, different kinds of food, and they carried some medical expenses, but they never gave so much that they would hurt his pride."

After Claude's retirement, Don and Darline Whiteley took over. Ranch dynamics had changed so much, that it was almost like going to work for a different outfit. In the past, Albert had been the one in control, the one with the master plan. His employees knew what was expected of them.

The Whiteleys saw their role in the operation change. Albert gave them sporadic bursts of direction, but they had lost their consistency. "After Albert was hurt, Don was pretty much his own boss," observed Bob Whiteman, Albert's nephew.

Ranch life was complicated further when the Whiteleys' teen-aged son, Donny, was killed in a car accident near Halfway, Oregon. His death devastated the family.

"I'd do anything for Albert," said Donny's sister, Bonnie. "When Donny died, he took care of things."

The Whiteley marriage didn't survive the tragedy, and they divorced in 1962. A short time later, Bonnie dropped out of school and went to work for the ranch.

She married Stuart Reid, and the couple sometimes became frustrated with Albert's tight-fisted ways with money. Bonnie was shocked when he readily agreed to buy a clothes dryer for the house in Halfway, Oregon. The tune changed when he got the bill. "Jeeesus Christ," he reportedly bellowed. "I didn't think it would be over ten dollars." Apparently he had pictured a folding rack, not an electric model. Nevertheless, he paid the bill.

Albert provided their housing, and he bought all their food, whether it came from a grocery store or a cafe. Even so, their monthly paychecks seemed scant.

"We made less money, monetarily, but were ahead financially because we were provided with food and a house. We can appreciate that now, more than at the time. When you're young, you expect more than you'll ever get. We can see now that we had it awful easy," Bonnie reflected.

Herb Mink joined the OX ranks in 1967. Since his father had been an OX cowboy, Herb spent much of his childhood and adolescence on the OX and the Circle C.

"Kids nowadays need someone like Albert Campbell," he said. "I learned that the easiest way isn't always the best way. For example, when I was learning to drive (fence) posts, he made me drive off the ground. When I asked why I couldn't drive them off the cart, he said that if you learn how to drive them from the ground, you've learned how to drive them anywhere. Sometimes you'll be stuck outside without a cart."

Herb had worked for the Circle C between 1945 and 1955 before coming to the OX. Having experienced the working atmosphere at both places, he said he preferred the OX. Working for the OX was simpler, he explained, because there was only one boss.

He readily noticed the changes that had taken place. "The pace . . . slackened," he said. "Things weren't as well organized, and it took longer to get things done."

Albert's interest in the ranch's day-to-day operations hadn't waned. Herb remembered: "He stayed at the OX as much as he could after the accident. He just paced the floor. The longer he was in the house, the more he became like a caged lion. And the harder he was to get along with.

"People didn't understand why Albert stayed at Lick Creek during the fall all the time. But it was the only time he could see ninety-five percent of the herd together, while we were feeding them hay at the feedyard. He could see the year's accomplishment before they were weaned on the river. At any other time, he had to look from a moving vehicle, and he couldn't see that much."

Herb held one of the most important posts at the ranch: he was the cook. "I never could cook a meal to suit Albert," he said. "Albert said that examples of ruined food were cabbage with vinegar and rice with raisins. But he still ate it.

"One time I baked an apple pie. I never could make a crust. Albert asked if there was any of the crust left. I said, 'Yes.' He asked me to save it. I thought I had done a good do on it, and I thought he wanted another pie. He just wanted to wrap his stirrups in the crust."

Albert normally went to bed right after supper, at about 6 p.m. "Everyone was in bed one night, and I stayed up with a book so I could put some wood on the fire," Herb said. "At about 8:15, Albert came down the stairs. 'What the hell are you doing reading a goddamned book?' he asked. 'Everyone ought to be up eating breakfast by now.'" Some things hadn't changed. Albert still wanted to start the workday during the middle of the night.

He couldn't get ranch expansion out of his mind either. His longtime neighbor Warren Parker was about ready to give up ranching on his Rocky Comfort place. Albert had wanted that particular place for over thirty years, but none of the previous owners would sell to him. It looked like Warren might cut a deal with him, but there was a major hitch: Grace.

Albert stewed on the problem for some time before he figured out a way to deal with Grace's stubbornness. Somehow he acquired a ranch about fifteen miles closer to Council on Hornet Creek. He traded the ranch for the Parker's place, increasing the OX by 755 acres. It was his last acquisition.

Shortly before the Parkers left, they got a visit from Bear's self-appointed urban renewal chairman: Millie Warner. "Millie was a big frog in a little puddle up there. She liked to get things going, organize things," said Dick Parker.

This time, Millie wanted to bring electricity to the area. Before too long, Idaho Power would have three dams generating electricity just over the hill. She wanted to seize the opportunity.

Idaho Power wouldn't consider the project unless every resident decided to hook up. The cost per home was $2,500. "I doubt if we made $2,500 in ten years," Dick said. "We wouldn't have had that much to put out for power in twenty-five years."

Nearly all of the residents had propane appliances and/or electrical generators. The only television on Bear Creek belonged to the Bud McGahey family, and the light plant frequently sputtered off during "Gunsmoke's" climactic moments. Although it was sometimes frustrating, the residents were adept at coping with such emergencies. They enjoyed most of the modern conveniences.

Millie didn't let that daunt her. She left a piece of paper with Warren, and asked him to list all the appliances the family would use if they had power. She was hoping that Idaho Power would reduce the subscription rate if they realized they would be selling plenty of power.

"We couldn't have afforded any electrical appliances," Dick emphasized. "There were a lot of years where $800 to $900 was gross income off that old ranch. You don't go buying electrical appliances like that."

Nevertheless, the paper was filled out when Millie returned. Warren Parker had written, "electric razor," on it.

"Millie went stomping out to the car and left. She never even argued," Dick remembered.

"I could just see old Dad crawling up the light pole with an extension cord for his electric razor. He'd have done that."

Millie's efforts were about two decades early. Her cause came to the forefront again when the Silver King Mine brought power as far as Cuprum in 1972.

"We could live without it and it looks like we may have to," Georgia Stinnett explained to Doug Peeples in a 1978 interview for the *Idaho Statesman*.

"We shouldn't have to haul water every time a generator breaks down. The only time we use our electric lights is when company comes, because we don't want to have to make the 320-mile trip to Boise every time something goes wrong with the generator.

Mavis McGahey and Beth Warner were Bear's post-masters at varying times. The post office was housed in the McGahey's front room until it closed in 1974. (Photo courtesy of the Bert Warner family.)

"Most of the time we eat, read, play cards, or whatever with a gas lantern. When we use the TV set, I usually hook it up to a car battery—and I feel like I spend most of my time charging batteries."

According to Bear residents Bud and Mavis McGahey, Idaho Power was reluctant to pay the $118,000 necessary to bring power to Bear. They asked residents to pay $4,400 up front, and guarantee to pay a monthly power bill of at least $37.50 a month for seven years. Power finally came to Bear on November 19, 1979.

Like the OX Ranch, Charley and Lawrence Warner's operation experienced drastic changes in the late Fifties and early Sixties.

Many of those changes were evident at Charley's funeral in

1957. He died in Blackfoot, Idaho at the State Hospital South. Lawrence had his body shipped to Bear.

Charley's funeral was one of the best-attended events in Bear's history. Approximately fifty people attended the memorial service, which was held in Millie and Lawrence's newly constructed home. His death marked the end of a generation—he outlived nearly all of the area's original homesteaders.

The ranch began to reflect Lawrence and Millie Warner's interests and priorities. After Lawrence's boyhood home burned to the ground, the couple designed and built a new house. They had two criteria for the home. First, they wanted each of their six daughters to have a room. According to Tina Warner, the second criterion had to do with size. Millie wanted a home that was bigger than the Circle C ranch house in New Meadows.

They met both objectives. Their home had approximately 6,348-square feet of space. The upper story housed the daughters, who hung blankets to partition their rooms. The main floor had a spacious living room and kitchen.

The full basement held the home's heating system, which was evidence of Lawrence's love of mechanisms. He installed a sawdust burner, which recycled a waste product from his sawmill. The home was also heated by cordwood. Millie's brother, Frank Smith, remembered that it took an intimidating amount of wood to heat the house. The family nearly filled the 2,116-square foot basement with wood each fall.

Interesting machinery abounded on the Warner place. Lawrence was the first stockman in the country to stack his hay with a Farm Hand loader. The equipment stacked hay much more quickly than the age-old methods.

The Warners' cattle business suffered several blows during the late Fifties and early Sixties. Their faltering relationship with the Forest Service took its toll; the Warners' Forest Service grazing permit was reduced. Hornet District Ranger Phil Cloward documented the rationale for the reduction:

> Because of the delicate economic nature of the
> established year-round operations in this climate
> . . . any change in their system of use has had

considerable adverse effect on the permitees. Consequently suggestions for change have been bitterly fought . . .

Through the lease of the only available arable land on the Snake River as a mid-winter base, and by using the forests as early and late as weather permitted, the Warners clung tenaciously to their original system of year-round use.

The continued use of the Snake River country by cattle, in the extreme early spring and late fall, coupled with poor cattle distribution because of the severe slopes, resulted in a downward trend (in resource conditions) and depletion of areas of heavy concentration. Following the Eckles Creek Fire of 1960, the Snake River portion was closed to grazing. The Warners' season on the higher range was adjusted to May 15 to October 31.

The substantial permit reduction, coupled with a weak cattle market, encouraged Lawrence to pursue a favorite venture: his sawmill. He logged and milled wood from the ranch, but the economic picture still looked grim.

He finally decided to start selling land. Wanting to keep the home place intact, he sold the satellite acreage that his dad had accumulated over the years.

When that didn't solve the financial crisis, Lawrence and Millie made a tough decision. They decided to sell.

Lawrence listed the place with Council Realtor Ferd Muller. He gave Ferd one stipulation: the ranch could not be sold to Albert Campbell. "Dad wouldn't have approved of it," he explained in a 1988 interview.

Holmes and Gretta Gabbert purchased the ranch in November of 1966. A year later, they deeded the property to their son, Dwight, and his wife, Jane.

Ranch life is a tough adjustment for most people who are used to the pressures and conveniences of an eight to five job.

Nobody in the Bear area had witnessed this transition before the Gabberts came; most area newcomers had come from other agricultural areas. Both the Gabberts and the locals experienced culture shock.

The locals warmed to Jane, who had a friendly, easy-going disposition. Dwight, however, displayed a few idiosyncrasies. "Gabbert was a strange one," said Bonnie Whiteley Reid. "Gabbert was book smart, but knew nothing about animals."

Bert and Tina Warner remember having an unexpected visitor at ten o'clock one winter morning. When they opened the door, they found Dwight dressed in his slippers and robe. He told them he was searching for some lost cattle, and wondered if they had seen them.

Community branding took on a different flavor at the Gabberts' house. Usually the OX crew came to help out. Year after year, Dwight would start checking his watch during the afternoon. He left the branding crew promptly at five o'clock, whether or not the task was finished. According to Bonnie, he fixed himself a highball and turned on the evening news. The neighbors stayed until the task was done, often completing it with more efficiency.

Dwight and Jane called their place the Seven Devils Cattle Company. Dwight had graphic design talents, and he was proud of the brand he designed. It looked like a devil's pitchfork, with the number seven forming the handle and the pitchfork's middle prong. Locals dubbed it the broken pitchfork.

"Gabbert got into debt so far that he didn't have a Chinaman's chance," said Bonnie.

The ranch sold again in June of 1976. Californians George and Dorothy Gillemont and John and Jeanne Dyer participated in a fifty/fifty partnership.

The Dyers both came from military families, and John spent six years as a captain in the Special Forces. After a tour of duty in Vietnam, the couple returned to California where John finished his college education at Humboldt State University.

The ranching lifestyle beckoned, and the Dyers leased a place adjacent to a wilderness area in northern California. They had initially planned to turn the rundown compound into a boys' camp, but it developed into a unique dude ranch. In addition to running 300 head of cattle, the couple hosted flying seminars. "We were teaching backcountry survival," John said. "If you're

Actor George Kennedy was among the pilots who sharpened their back country flying skills at the Dyers' California ranch. Kennedy is hugging Jeanne Dyer. (Photo courtesy of John and Jeanne Dyer.)

over the wilderness and your engine stalls, we taught you how to walk away from the landing. That was one part of it. The other part of it was how to survive."

Several of John's Special Forces cohorts attended the seminars, and word-of-mouth advertising brought a continuous stream of newcomers.

"We had a lot of people there and we had a lot of fun," said John. "George Kennedy, the movie star, used to come all the time."

Their business was five years old when they learned that their landlords had gone bankrupt. With Gillemont, who was a former ranch guest, the Dyers tried to purchase the ranch. When that failed, they began searching for another ranch.

"We looked all over the western part of the country for a place that was remote, had lots of National Forest surrounding it so

that subdividers couldn't come in and divide the land," he said.
"(We looked for) a pretty, pleasing setting with a possibility of
recreation as well as agriculture."

They had one final criterion: the ranch couldn't have many
improvements. "We couldn't afford it," he explained. "We didn't
have a lot of money in those days. As it was, we had to take a
partner to invest in the Seven Devils."

An exhaustive search followed. "Every time I saw an ad in the
newspaper, I called the Realtor. We probably screened 200–300
ranches in the western United States, and personally visited about
150 of them . . . We looked all over Colorado, Oregon,
Washington, northern California, Nevada, and a little bit in
Utah."

They found the Seven Devils Ranch in May, and the deal closed
a month later. "After we got the place, it took about a month and
a half to get it fit to live in," John remembered.

The huge home that Lawrence and Millie Warner had built was
now infested with rats. John's wife, Jeanne, and their six-year-old
daughter, Amy, went to visit relatives until the house was devoid
of unwanted roommates.

"Rather than have a clean piece of ground to start with, we had
to pick up all the trash and clean up the old buildings and
garbage," John said. "That's probably what added more work to
that ranch than anything. It was strictly cleaning it up. We were
proud of the place. It began to show. The fences started going up,
corrals got changed so that they would work. We were proud of
the place. It was our life."

"I still don't know how we did it," he said. "Without Jeanne,
none of this could have happened."

Working capital was in short supply. With the general clean-up
completed, the Dyers focused on their guest operation. The
house, now called "the lodge," was completely refurbished. The
previously unfinished top story was divided into 5 large bedrooms
and three baths. A separate heating stove was installed upstairs.

On the second story, they constructed a spacious deck that had
spectacular, sweeping views of the ranch and Cuddy Mountain. In
the summer, the deck was a perfect spot for entertaining hordes
of guests; in the winter, snow shoveling provided Jeanne with
vigorous aerobic workouts.

Amy Dyer pets a newborn calf. During the short winter days, Amy was rarely home during the daylight hours. She often watched the sun rise and set from her school bus seat, since the ride was over an hour long each way. (Photo courtesy of John and Jeanne Dyer.)

John Dyer (foreground) takes a break from clearing hayfields on the Seven Devils Ranch in Bear. Jeanne Dyer's visiting uncle, Lowell Newton, enjoyed the working vacation. (Photo courtesy of John and Jeanne Dyer.)

When the ranch's dirt landing strip was completed, they were ready to accommodate guests. The paying guests generated the ranch's working capital.

"The pleasure of a dude operation is that you get to meet a lot of people," Dyer said. "On the down side, it takes a lot of supervision.

"It was hard to entertain, to help (the guests) along in their vacation when we had work to do . . . sometimes it would make for a twenty-hour day.

"Most people who come to a ranch operation want to help. And most are good help. But if you spend all your time teaching someone how to do something, you could have had the job done in half the time without the frustration. For example, take building a fence. People don't know what is supposed to happen. Take people out of their element and they can have all the desire in the world and not be a hand.

"(Eventually) we got squared around so we didn't need the

Feeding with a horse team has at least one distinct advantage: the horses always start, no matter how cold it is. Diesel engines are much more temperamental. (Photo courtesy of John and Jeanne Dyer.)

John Dyer brings yet another load of firewood into the Seven Devils Lodge. (Photo courtesy of John and Jeanne Dyer.)

dudes and we got rid of the (guest) operation. When you get busy doing your thing, your livelihood is first, and people have got to come second," he concluded.

The Dyers met Albert Campbell and many of their other neighbors during a water rights meeting. Albert greeted the Dyers by announcing, "You can have all the water that I own in that country, because I don't even own a shovel. If I did own a shovel, I wouldn't know how to use it, so just go ahead and take all the water you want."

During the course of the conversation, Albert mentioned that the best summer grazing in the country went with their ranch. He explained that for years he'd tried to get Charley Warner to let loose of the ground up Little Bear Creek and Smith Mountain.

"Do you have a good wife?" Albert asked abruptly.

John tried to introduce Jeanne, who was standing by them, but Albert ignored him, and never even cast a glance toward Jeanne.

"Well," said Albert, "if you've got a good wife, get her a good

Seven Devils Partners George and Dorothy Gillemont try their hands at ranching. (Photo courtesy of Helena Schmidt.)

tent and a grub hoe. Maybe in a year or two you'll get all the poison (larkspur) off that mountain. Then, without a doubt, you'll have the best range in that part of the country.''

Eventually the Dyers were included during the OX brandings, which took place in early July. Although Albert could barely see, he stayed close at hand, leaning on a fence.

By the time the Dyers arrived in Bear, Albert was beginning to recognize his own mortality. He often declared he'd live to be 100.

His acquaintances teased him about his lifespan and his wealth. ''What are you going to do with it all when you die, Albert?'' they asked.

Albert had two standard replies. The first was, ''Well, they say I can't take it with me, so I'm not going.'' At other times, he insisted he'd find a way to take it with him.

Roy Moritz had an alternate plan. The postman was bringing both the mail and Albert to Bear when he made his proposal. If Albert would draft a check for his net worth, Roy said he'd be glad to pocket it until Albert needed it. Albert declined the offer.

At age eighty-seven, he was still a dominating presence at the cattle auctions. Cow boss Don Whiteley spent much of his time driving to weekly auctions in the vicinity. As each bunch of cattle was driven into the auction ring, Albert demanded, "What is their size? How much do they weigh?"

Leo Braun, who worked for the OX in the early eighties, remembered watching Albert at the Weiser sale barn. Albert wanted to run the show, and after bossing several people, he announced, "I'll only bother you people twenty-one more years, and then you can do what you want."

Albert's last years were frustrating in many ways. He had long since relinquished his role in Circle C operations, but his interest never waned.

Tensions mounted when several family stockholders suggested selling the ranch. Their collective investment wasn't bringing an adequate return. By that time, forty-two of Charles Campbell's descendants owned the ranch, most having left the home place to pursue other interests.

Many of the younger family members wanted to sell the ranch

The horses hauled hay in the winter and people in the summer. John Dyer takes a group of visitors on a hayride. (Photo courtesy of John and Jeanne Dyer.)

Don Whiteley (left) and
Albert Campbell (right) visit
with an unidentified man.
Albert's canes could be
treacherous, especially if he
caught people chasing his
cows on motorcycles.
(Photo courtesy of Charlotte
Campbell Armacost.)

for a couple of reasons. First, their investment was losing money.
Second, the inheritance would help them further their own
dreams and ambitions.

Selling the Circle C was unthinkable for the older generation.
They had spent their lives shaping and being shaped by the Circle
C. Their identities and senses of accomplishment were tied to the
ranch.

In the end, when the final tally was taken, the majority voted to
sell the ranch.

Three partners bought the ranch in 1972, right before land
prices skyrocketed. The partners included two cattlemen, Val C.
Stiefel, Jr. of Fullerton, California and Eugene Schwertner of
Austin, Texas. The third partner was an attorney, Robert L. Lewis
of Palo Alto, California.

Their investment, which totalled slightly less than 3.5 million dollars, bought a piece of ground forty-two miles long and between ten and fifteen miles wide. The ranch consisted of 29,191 acres of deeded land and 105,436 acres of leased land. The purchase price included 6,112 head of cattle and all equipment and improvements.

The partners retained Rollie's son, David Campbell, as manager.

Idaho Statesman Reporter Bob Lorimer wrote, "Lewis and Stiefel stressed they were not in the land development business, 'recreation or otherwise'—but they would continue basically as a cow-calf and steer operation."

Albert was not directly involved in either the negotiations or the sale's closing. Consequently, he had never met the men who purchased the Circle C. A few years after the sale was finalized, Albert accompanied Dale Smith, the New Meadows veterinarian, into the local Pine Knot Cafe. Dale noticed one of the buyers at a table and said, "Look, Albert. There's Bob Lewis."

Albert's failing eyes couldn't see the individual, and the name didn't ring a bell. Dale explained who Lewis was, and introduced him to Albert.

"So you're the son of a bitch who stole the Circle C," was Albert's only comment.

Lewis countered, "You're right."

The partners eventually divided and sold the Circle C Ranch. Some of the ground continues to be ranched, but much has been subdivided for homesites.

About that time, Albert moved into the nursing home facility in the Council hospital. "Dad was ill, and he needed more care. He went willingly—he still had his driver," Charlotte said. The move eased the chore of day-to-day living and made Albert's commute to the OX Ranch shorter.

The hospital routine sometimes rankled him. Once Charlotte placed an inconspicuous tape recorder in the car, and Albert made some observations of hospital life. "Nurses in the hospital have the idea to take a shower once every day or two, and by damn you can't take a shower without getting your feet wet, and can't do that without getting your hair wet, and that's how to catch a cold!"

Albert Campbell's cousins, the Clay brothers, move cattle through the Circle C corrals. The Campbell family ranch was sold in 1972. (Photo courtesy of Larry and Hazel Clay.)

Losing weight was another sore spot. Albert tipped the scales at 275, and his doctor urged him to lose weight. The cattleman's response was, "I'm not going to lose it. It's taken lots of dollars to put that weight on."

The days he spent in Council developed a pattern. After a ham and eggs breakfast in one of Council's two cafes, he did his banking. He often cashed his checks at Maxine Nichols' window. After scrawling his signature on the twenty-five dollar check, he asked Maxine to give him fives. "That way Grace won't get all my money at once," he quipped.

It was about that time that Albert decided to sell the timber off his ranch. Several loggers had tried to purchase the timber in past years, but Albert took a special liking to Glenn Stout. The younger man shared many of Albert's philosophies and his work ethic.

Grace enjoyed a similar rapport with Glenn's wife, Barbara.

When the two women visited, Grace's stories became unusually candid. Grace talked of her engagement to Albert, and how she would settle for nothing less than a one-carat diamond in her engagement ring. She had stood her ground, even though Albert argued and predicted that the luxury would bankrupt the ranch. The ring materialized after she promised it could be sold if there was a ranch-threatening crisis. More than a half century later, the conversation piece was still glimmering on her hand.

One day Glenn asked Albert if he could buy a piece of Albert's ground between Bear Creek and Steves Creek. There were nearly forty acres of land, which lay on the edge of the ranch. Albert gave his standard reply, "I've always been in the business of buying land, not selling it." But a few months later Grace rapped on the Stout's door. Grace's message surprised everyone: Albert decided he wanted to sell the parcel.

Albert's word was still the law and he continued to manage the OX Ranch. As the years passed, it became increasingly evident that he could no longer do an adequate job. Even the casual observer noticed that his cattle herd and portions of his range were deteriorating.

Forest Service records from the 1970s reflected the changes. A range conservationist, charged with creating a longterm range management plan, decided to delay the effort. He predicted the plan would be useless in a few years, when Albert died. He speculated the ranch would be divided and sold.

Documentation of meetings Albert had with the Forest Service are also telling. One read, "Albert was unusually lucid today." Another stressed that the resulting agreement should be carried out immediately, "before Albert forgets."

Eventually the ranch was put in a trust, managed by John Byerly of Idaho First.

Even with this turn of events, Albert refused to sell. "I'll be damned if I'll sell it. I'd give it back to the Indians first." Potential buyers began courting him in the nursing home, spending hours listening to tales of his exploits.

John and Jeanne Dyer were among the visitors. Encouraged by high cattle prices and Council's bank manager, Ed Kesler, the

Albert and Grace Campbell survey the OX grazing ground on the Snake River breaks. (Photo courtesy of Charlotte Campbell Armacost.)

Dyers tried to lease the ranch. "Son," Albert said, "I put that ranch together and I'm going to run it until the day I die."

Albert and Grace enjoyed the company, but one woman went a bit far when she sent Grace a basket of fruit from Florida. "That woman's trying to buy me!" Grace said indignantly. As a result, that relationship came to an abrupt end.

Albert never did abandon the ranch. "Getting this or that done on the ranch was almost Albert's last thought before he died," said Albert's sister, Carrie Whiteman.

Albert died on August 5, 1979. He was ninety.

His daughter, Charlotte, tackled the formidable task of condensing his life into a few, short paragraphs. "His life has been full and vigorous," the obituary read, " . . . he often expressed the great attitude that he needed to get more things done each day. God is now giving him a rest."

Grace kept the thick stack of sympathy cards that poured in. "Albert Campbell was really a hero of mine," wrote Logger Gordon MacGregor, who had tried to purchase the ranch years before.

Another life-long friend, Inez Wilson, wrote, "Albert was a great man. No other can fill his footsteps—only follow them and humbly so."

After Albert died, John Dyer and George Gillemont located additional partners who were interested in the OX. They tried to purchase the ranch from the estate, but the deal didn't jell.

After some deliberation, Grace and her daughters, Charlotte and Alberta, decided to solicit sealed bids for the ranch. Charlotte kept the 160-acre place in Halfway, Oregon, but the remainder of the ranch was to be sold in one piece.

Advertisements in the *Adams County Leader* inventoried the ranch as follows: 13,900 acres of deeded land, 7,835 acres of state lease, 780 cattle plus the 1980 calf crop and eight horses.

Sealed bids were to be received by May 1, 1980. It was to be a cash deal.

The sale was the major conversation topic in local coffee shops. Speculation ran wild about who would bid and how much the ranch would bring. Several prospective buyers spent time going over their balance sheets. Gordon MacGregor was among them.

Grace Campbell and partners John Dyer, George Gillemont, and Al Dietsch sign the OX Ranch purchase agreement. The ranch had been in Campbell hands for seventy years. (Photo courtesy of Charlotte Campbell Armacost.)

"I thought Gordon would end up with it," Charlotte remembered.

When bid opening day arrived, there was only one envelope. The Dyer partnership, which had added two partners in anticipation of the sale, submitted a bid below the minimum.

A month and a half of contemplation and negotiation followed, and on June 17, 1980, the bid was accepted.

The transaction created an ironic historical twist. For years Albert had tried to buy Charlie Warner's ranch. In the end, it was Charlie's old ranch that swallowed the OX.

After all of the planning, dreaming, and scheming the partners were elated. Although the Dyers were excited, they had first-hand knowledge of the work ahead.

Before long, the partners' euphoria over owning the OX waned. When they began to understand the financial commitment necessary to bring the ranch up to speed, they began to balk. Money pressures increased as the interest rate soared; at one point the prime rate reached twenty-two percent. Cattle prices were equally dismal. Within a year, the group decided to sell. The partners began searching for a buyer.

Al Dietsch contacted Hixon Properties Inc., a San Antonio-based holding company formed by the Hixon family in 1914. Brothers Tim and Joe Hixon flew to Boise, where they met Dietsch and John Dyer. The foursome took a small plane to the ranch, and they took an aerial tour.

Both brothers were surprised at what they saw. Joe had expected to see a "desert-looking wasteland." As they flew over the pastures, Joe thought, "This looks more like a golf course."

Tim was awed by the ranch's beauty, but was skeptical that the ranch's steep, rugged terrain was practical for a cattle operation. That's when John Dyer stepped in with the business figures. The men were impressed with his ambition.

Tim Hixon and his brother, Joe Hixon, spend extended periods of time at the ranch. Both take active roles in ranch operations. Tim helps the crew hay and gather cattle. Joe also enjoys moving cattle, and his specialty is organizing trail cleaning expeditions. (Photo by Heidi Bigler Cole.)

The driving tour brought the Hixons to Windy Ridge for the first time. "This is absolutely gorgeous," Joe said, as Tim recorded the views on film.

Family members Irene Whitney, Bill Geiger, and George Turpin traveled to the ranch later that fall. With their influence and recommendations, the family agreed to purchase the ranch. The deal closed in December of 1982.

"We bought the ranch with the understanding that we were buying it for the next two or three generations. It's for our grandchildren and beyond," Joe said.

The family agreed it would remain a working ranch rather than evolving into a dude operation.

"It took lots of hard work to make that ranch . . . like it is today," Dyer reflected. "And I'm sure if Albert could see it today, he'd be proud of it, because it's working.

"It's down to dollars and cents today. Because Granddad did it that way, doesn't mean that Sonny's going to be able to do it

Restoring the Lick Creek barn was a major undertaking—there wasn't much left to work with. Using the original timbers, the Dyers reconstructed the barn. (Photo courtesy of John and Jeanne Dyer.)

today and survive. People are just going to have to pay more attention to economics to survive.''

"A lot of the old styles are still there, and a lot of the new management practices are there. I'm sure that if Albert had been alive today . . . he would have probably changed his ways. By the time his health and mind were failing, there were a lot of changes in the industry. I'm sure if Albert had been able, he would have made the changes necessary to be a survivor.

When the partnership bought the OX, many buildings were in disrepair. The Lick Creek barn topped the list. It had been built in the early 1900s for Lewis Hall, the railroad promoter. (Drawing by Mary Lorish Jahn.)

Epilogue

THE OX RANCH TODAY

"Albert always used to say, 'If I could just come back and see what you kids do with this place,'"

—Bertha Armacost

Chris Anderson was doing a welfare check on expectant mother cows when his horse slipped and fell, crushing his leg. He was taken to Dr. Gary Bills, an orthopedic surgeon famous for "fixing busted up cowboys." The injury didn't keep Chris from branding the next spring. Using a little ingenuity, he fashioned a makeshift spur, created a stirrup out of an old garden hose, and protected his bare toes with a work glove. (Photo by Heidi Bigler Cole.)

Winter feeding can become a monotonous chore. OX hands liven things up by dropping hay in the shape of the brand (above). Winter feeding has shifted from the Wildhorse Headquarters to the Sand Hollow Ranch. This ranch, which is between Weiser and Payette, Idaho, was purchased in 1987. Abundant grass and milder winters make it an ideal spot for calving. (Photo courtesy of John and Jeanne Dyer.)

When the steep breaks of the Snake River begin to green, it's time to begin putting out salt. Don Page (above) packs 200 pounds of salt on Henry, the mule. Don designed and hand-stitched the ranch's packsaddles. Ranch Manager John Dyer launched an intensive salting program which improved herd health. Tests showed the cattle were missing vital nutrients. Adding supplements to the salt boosted their health, and interestingly enough, their interest in motherhood. (Photo by Heidi Bigler Cole.)

Albert Campbell liked to use the Wildhorse Headquarters (right) for calving, and the tradition continued under John Dyer's management. The milder winters along the Snake River gave the calves a needed boost. The feedlot's proximity to the river caused some environmental concerns. As a result, the calving operation has been moved. (Photo courtesy of John and Jeanne Dyer.)

Doug McKinney (left) and his daughter, Kerri, ride the ranch's "red mule," a Honda four-wheeler. The family lives on the Snake River during the winter months, where they take care of first-calf heifers. The first-time mothers often have difficulty calving and mothering their new-borns. As a result, they are checked every four hours—day and night. The red mule makes the chore easier. (Photo by Heidi Bigler Cole.)

Don Page (below) and his dog, Rontu, share lunch near Salt Creek. Don is especially popular at lunchtime, since his wife, Kay, always packs homemade cookies. Kay wasn't pleased when she learned that the dog was also enjoying her cookies. As a compromise measure, she now packs store-bought cookies for the dog. (Photo by Heidi Bigler Cole.)

Tony Cole, Chris Anderson, Jody Hawhee, John Dyer, and Doug McKinney gather the cattle for a branding at Barbour Flat. The cow/calf pairs are herded into a large corral. (Photo by Heidi Bigler Cole.)

Brandings at the OX have become less of a neighboring event; between the cowhands, their families, and the Hixon family, there is always plenty of help. Members of the 1987 branding crew (below) gear up for a steak dinner near Indian Creek. (Photo courtesy of John and Jeanne Dyer.)

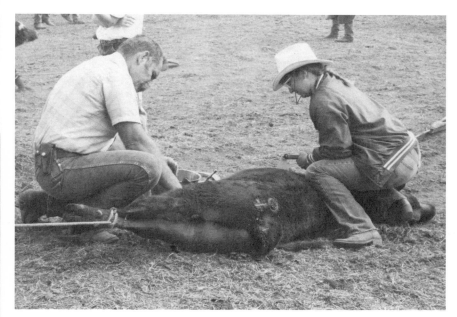

Cow Boss Frank Anderson (above) castrates a recently branded calf, while Lori McKinney prepares to insert an ear tag. The ear tag will discourage disease-carrying insects from bothering the calf. (Photo by Heidi Bigler Cole.)

Dr. Paul Sherman caught the branding ferver while studying Idaho ground squirrels on the ranch. He made this squirrel forever famous by "branding" it with liberal dose of dye. Sherman, who hails from Cornell University, and Dr. Eric Yensen, from the Albertson College of Idaho, spend much of the spring studying the endangered species. The squirrels have been found in only two areas; one of which is on the ranch. (Photo courtesy of John and Jeanne Dyer.)

Branding with the Quilliams is one of the year's most anticipated social events. Wildhorse and Hornet Creek neighbors form the branding crew. Here, Hornet Creek Rancher Butch Snorgrass holds a roped calf steady. (Photo by Heidi Bigler Cole.)

Lori Quilliam (left) reheats a branding iron to a red-hot temperature. She's picky about her branding irons. If they're too cool, they won't brand properly. Brands that are too hot will harm the animal. Lori and her husband, Jay, own the last self-sustaining ma and pa operation in the country: the X-Cross Ranch. (Photo by Heidi Bigler Cole.)

Lunch is one of the highlights of a branding. Dee Cole, Dodie Brown, and Iris White (below) ready cool drinks for the grubby branding crew. (Photo by Heidi Bigler Cole.)

OX Cow Boss Frank Anderson (left) is famous for his stout coffee and wry observations. Frank owned the Lazy Valley Ranch in Rough and Ready, California, before coming to Bear. (Photo courtesy of John and Jeanne Dyer.)

Haying keeps Farm Boss Dean Adams and his wife, Janee, busy for months. Hixon family members pitch in too. Timo Hixon and his father, Tim, are haying crew regulars. This mechanized haystacker has alleviated much of the back-breaking work. (Photo courtesy of John and Jeanne Dyer.)

Jeanne Dyer and Karen Hixon enjoy a cool drink after a morning in the blackberry patch. First-time pickers are advised to wear long-sleeved shirts and heavy-duty boots to guard against the merciless thorns. Rattlesnakes are casually mentioned after the buckets are full of berries. One bowl of blackberry cobbler is worth the risk. (Photo by Heidi Bigler Cole.)

Tim Hixon, Amy Dyer, Chris Anderson, and Frank Anderson (above) prepare to gather cattle off the OX Forest Service allotment. (Photo courtesy of John and Jeanne Dyer.)

Frank Anderson and his son, Chris, once decided to compile a photo album featuring notorious cows. Beulah (left) tops the list. She is the last of the old longhorn-crosses from the Seven Devils Ranch. "She's a thinking cow, if that's possible," Frank reflected. He had been gathering cattle off the summer range, but Beulah hadn't appeared yet. "She's probably been watching me from the brush. She'll come home when she's ready, thank you!" (Photo by Heidi Bigler Cole.)

Jeanne Dyer's parents, Alda and F.B. Elstad (above), enjoy a front porch view from the cabin in No Business Basin. Tim Hixon, Joe Hixon, and John Dyer bought the Basin in 1989. They were almost as excited as Albert Campbell was when he'd started his ranch on the site seventy-nine years before. (Photo courtesy of John and Jeanne Dyer.)

Sisters Kerri, Kendra, and Kayla McKinney (below) are often recruited to help brand and gather cattle. Ranch life often affords unexpected situations. During calving season, the girls occasionally share their bathroom with cold, newborn calves. As they get ready for school, the chilled calf gradually warms in a tub of lukewarm water. (Photo by Heidi Bigler Cole.)

Neighbors still gather around OX corrals when Ray Hunt (above) teaches a clinic. He shows professional and amateur riding enthusiasts how to work with animals, rather than against them. His philosophy works. A veterinarian once watched as OX hands loaded a bull into a stock trailer. A job that could potentially last hours was accomplished in a few minutes. The veterinarian joked about the ranch's "trained" bulls. (Photo by Heidi Bigler Cole.)

Trailing cattle during a droughty fall is dry, dusty work. Cowboy Chris Anderson (right) enjoys a swig of cold pop. (Photo courtesy of John and Jeanne Dyer.)

OX hunters (above) join the scores of "flatlanders" who want to bring home an elk. Joe Hixon (on grey horse) and Tony Cole head out across Barbour Flat as Don Page leads the mule string: Brandy, Henry, Casey, and Myra. It was the mules' last pack trip together. (Photo by Heidi Bigler Cole.)

Doug McKinney (below) takes the Kleinschmidt Grade down to the river. The road isn't as treacherous as it used to be, but it is still avoided by people who are afraid of heights. (Photo courtesy of Doug and Lori McKinney.)

OX hand Mike Campbell (top) leads the packstring during a chilly hunting trip. (Photo courtesy of John and Jeanne Dyer.)

Fall is a busy time for OX cowboys. Calves are weaned from their mothers, and their protests can be heard for miles. Cows and heifers are run individually through a squeeze chute, where they are given vaccinations. Pregnancy testing also takes place at this time. One year a young female elk joined a herd of heifers. Frank Anderson (pictured) named her Wonder, and she obligingly followed other members of the herd through the chutes. They gave her an ear tag, and set her free. However, Wonder had other ideas. The next morning she had jumped over a fence and into the feedlot with the original group of heifers. (Photo by Heidi Bigler Cole.)

Although Fred Cole (far left) no longer plows the road between Bear and Council, he is still a pillar of the community. There are no wallflowers when Fred is at a Bear schoolhouse dance; he dances with all the ladies, young and old. During the winter months, he rises at 4 a.m. to feed hundreds of wild turkeys. The turkeys know where Fred's property line is, especially during hunting season. (Photo by Heidi Bigler Cole.)

Bob and Eva Bureau (left) twirl around the floor during their wedding dance, while Clarence Warner cheers them on. (Photo by Heidi Bigler Cole.)

Leo Braun (below) began playing at Bear schoolhouse dances when he was an OX hand. Bud McGahey (second from right) and his grandchildren Terri Turner and Dale Lake are also regulars. During the winter months, musicians grow scarce. The dance was once cancelled at the last minute and a pinochle game was held in its place. Dale, who was Council's veterinarian, was called away to perform an emergency Cesarean on a cow. (Photo by Heidi Bigler Cole.)

During the writing of this book, I stayed on Charley Warner's old homestead site. This was the view out my front window. While piecing together the history, it wasn't difficult to picture Charley Warner bringing home his new bride, Frank and Chall Smith trotting down the road with their fishing poles, or Albert Campbell riding by, dreaming of owning the place. Sometimes, more modern pictures came to mind. I could see Bryan Hixon jumping in every

puddle as we walked up the road, or little Sam and Ben Warner running from imaginary bulls. Right now, I envision the many miles I walked over the pastures, wondering how I'd ever be able to capture this history on paper. None of us were ever able to possess the land. But for a short time, it possessed us. We were lucky.

An OX heifer weighs her options. Whichever direction she chooses, she'll be on her home range. (Photo by Doug McKinney.)

Azurite Gulch. Named for its abundance of bright blue copper ore, the gulch was used by Indians as a summer encampment.

Barbour Flat. Homesteaders Bobby and Anthony Barbour lent their name to this site, which was originally called Bachelor Flat. Other single homesteaders included William Reynolds, Harry S. Gum, and Archie Bardmas.

Bear. The community was named by Amos Warner when its request for a post office was granted. The area was heavily populated with black and grizzly bears at the time.

Bear Tree Gulch. Well over fifty years ago, a bear raked his claws down the trunk of a pine tree located on the breaks of the Wildhorse River. Horseback riders immediately notice the deep gouges, which are at eye level. A favorite trick is to show an uninitiated rider the claw marks, and while he is examining them, someone shouts, "Why, he's still up there!" A reaction is guaranteed.

Bill Gulch. Area natives and Forest Service maps published prior to 1960 refer to Nigger Bill Gulch and its neighboring Nigger Jim Gulch. Both Jim and Bill were unusually reclusive homesteaders who arrived before the turn of the century. It is rumored that they were escaped slaves obsessed with the fear they would be captured and returned. Another story said they were on the lam from the law.

Circle C. Prior to the ranch's 1920 incorporation, cattle were marked with a square cross on the side. That brand ruined too much leather, so the Campbells chose the smaller Circle C branded on the left hip. It was easier to make a clear, uniform brand with the circular shapes.

Cuddy Mountain. Named for John Cuddy, who owned and operated a flour mill near Salubria.

Degitz Creek. George Degitz, a Homestead, Oregon bartender, homesteaded along the creek's banks. Degitz commuted to work until he begrudgingly sold his place to Albert Campbell.

Dora Mountain. Located above No Business Basin, it was named for Dora Childers, who married and divorced OX Ranch foreman Claude Childers.

Eckles Creek. John Eckles grew prize-winning fruit on his Snake River homestead. The life-long bachelor had plenty of company during the winter months when itenerent miners would come to stay.

The *Council Leader* printed a graphic account of his death in its July 4, 1912 edition.

> . . . he was taken by a violent coughing spell when a few feet from the house. His brother-in-law and sister, Mr. and Mrs. Kilgore, rushed out to find him with the blood gushing from his mouth and by the time they could carry him in the house and lay him down he had expired.

. . . he was known far and near for his
hospitality and many kind acts, in fact, the latch
string of his cabin always hung out.

Garnet Creek. It flows by the Blue Jacket mine where hundreds
of garnets were unearthed.

Horse Mountain. Two early miners, Frenchie David and Charlie
Walker, started wintering their horses on Big Bar on the Snake
River. The animals grazed both Horse and Smith mountains,
and gathering them could become a day-long task. The men
regularly shot cougars and coyotes for fear they would stalk the
horses.

Hoo Hoo Gulch. Albert Campbell and his "boys" were trying to
move cattle with little success. Every time the herd was headed
in the right direction, the cattle would hear huckleberry pickers
talking and spook. Finally, Albert lost his temper. The pitch of
his voice got higher as he shouted, "You tell those so and so
pickers to stop their hoo hooing."

Injun Gulch. During his bachelor days in Utah, Amos Warner
swapped a bag of flour and a sheep for his oldest son, Frank.
The boy, who was the son of a Shoshone chief, grew up to be a
schoolteacher and Mormon missionary. He didn't accompany
his family to Bear, so his occasional visits were an anticipated
event. He helped the family gather wood in the gulch, and it
was named in his honor.

Jim Gulch. Although reclusive, this black homesteader contributed to two noteworthy events. He reportedly constructed
the Huntley/Speropulos barn and he barbecued beef during
"southern style" the area's first and last subdivision promotion
at Ogemah. In the late 1960s, a photograph of an elegantly
dressed black woman was found under the floorboards of his
homestead cabin. Who she was and why her portrait was kept
hidden remains a mystery.

Lick Creek. Natural salt licks along its banks attracted deer and other animals.

Lockwood Saddle. Edward Lockwood was an early day miner and Weiser businessman. According to the 1900 census, he was born a New Yorker in 1826.

Lost Creek/Basin. As the creek winds down the mountain, it disappears. It resurfaces at Little Bear.

Lynes Saddle. Collis Lynes (pronounced lions) mined in the 1910s, so he was a relative newcomer to the area. Leaving one's name on a landmark was a privilege reserved for the old guard, and they grumbled about a youngster receiving the honor. Lynes later married Ada Whitlow. His father, Charlie, was also a miner, and he built the Lick Creek barn in 1902.

Mickey Creek. Named for a miner.

No Business Basin. Jim Hazen Summers, an avowed Indian killer, lived above the basin on Cuddy Mountain. Indians steered clear because they had no business going there.

Ogemah. Around 1910 Johnnie Rogers and a partner known only as "Fox" platted a townsite on Indian Creek, a mile downstream from A.O. Huntley's place. They promoted the site while hosting a Fourth of July celebration. Promises of free "southern barbecued beef" and coffee drew several wagonloads of people who were more interested in the party than the property.

As the would-be investors approached Ogemah, they were greeted by a nauseating stench. The barbecue beef had been slow cooking . . . since July 1st.

Pepperbox Hill. When reports predicted the location had a hundred-year supply of copper, throngs of people sunk their picks into the formation. The resulting pockmarks inspired the name.

Rocky Comfort. Freighters hauling supplies and machinery to Landore named the flat. They dreaded springtime roads, especially the area around Crooked River, which became a boggy mire. When they rolled up onto the "comfortable" rocky flat, they knew danger of becoming stuck had passed.

Salt Creek. The name was inspired by the hot mineral springs located near the creek's mouth. People used to bathe in the springs, which relaxed tired muscles, and reportedly killed lice.

School Section Gulch. When the land was originally surveyed, each township had a section was set aside for a school. A school was never built on this site, but any money generated by the land is to be spent on education.

Seven Devils Mountains. Two Native American legends explain the name's origins. The first involved a brave who became lost during hunting trip. He zigzagged the country trying to get his bearings, but his efforts were futile.

When he was nearing exhaustion, he felt something watching him. He turned and found himself face to face with a devil. He immediately forgot his exhaustion and continued his flight across the country. Every time his energy seemed gone, he would turn, see another devil, and somehow find the strength to continue. The brave saw seven devils before he reached his companions.

Another legend claims the area was plagued by seven giants who terrorized the population. The tribe dug seven huge holes, and when the giants stumbled into the holes, the tribe members were ready with vats of acid, which turned the giants into stone.

There are two less colorful claims on the name. Noyes B. Holbrook said he named the mountains in 1862 while he was prospecting.

The History of Idaho, published in 1899, gave Hudson Bay Company explorers credit. The starving explorers barely survived their journey through the mountains, which must have left a formidable impression.

Sheep Peak. When the Emerys settled in Wildhorse, eight or nine bighorn sheep lived on the sheer bluffs above their house. The local population call the formation Sheep Rock. Forest Service cartographers altered the name to avoid confusion with another Sheep Rock, located to the northwest.

Sheep Rock. When the first settlers arrived they sighted mountain goats and bighorn sheep on its upper regions.

Smith Mountain. Crazy Horse Smith, a prospector, once came out of Black Lake on skis . . . his navigation hampered by a dense fog settled over the mountains.

After traveling for a couple hours, he found another set of ski tracks which he followed for several more hours. When the fog lifted, he realized he'd been following his own tracks, and he had circled the mountain three times. The mountain has been called Smith ever since.

Soda Springs. Located above the Lick Creek barn on the old Whitlow place, the site was originally named Deer Lick Springs by W.W. Whitlow. Ailing deer sought out the naturally carbonated water, and after convalescing in the vicinity for two or three weeks, they chased back into the forest.

In later years, humans sought the water's medicinal qualities. Council's Dr. Alvin Thurston created a tent camp where rheumatism patients stayed for weeks, taking daily baths.

Generations of children have brought root beer extract or Kool-Aid to the spring so that they could make their own pop.

Efforts to carry the water home were futile, as the water loses its fizz almost immediately.

Joe Hixon financed the spring's redevelopment in 1988. Excavation revealed planks from the original boardwalk and stays from a submerged fifty-gallon-barrel.

Starveout. When the Emerys and Meyers homesteaded along the Wildhorse River in 1892, there wasn't time to plant and harvest a hay crop. They improvised by cutting wild grass with a scythe. The Emerys agreed to feed during the winter, if the Meyers would periodically supply them with food. The Emery's food supplies dwindled and there was no sign of the neighbors. When the larder was completely empty Ed Emery said, "Well, I guess we starved out," and the family packed their belongings and headed back up the river.

Steves Creek. Steve Robinson was one of the first homesteaders in the Bear area; he arrived after his wife and two children died. He had fought in the Civil War and loved to pick fights with northerners.

Robinson died at age eighty-six in 1920. His obituary in the February 13 *Adams County Leader* read,

> The deceased will be remembered as a representative of a care-free type early pioneer, the active years of whose life had been spent in the great outdoors at a time when there was no limit to elbow room—at a time when no game laws prevented him from bringing down a deer and the native trout sought not the protection of a fish warden. In the lore of the wilds, he was rich. Of worldly possessions he had none.

Summers Creek. Named for Jim Summers, of No Business Basin fame, the creek was possibly the sight of a bloody confrontation.

Summers was an avowed Indian killer; his hatred was said to

have stemmed from an incident in California, where he and his cousin were prospecting. After his unsuspecting cousin was killed on their claim by a roving band, Summers set out to get even. He eventually wound up on a Cuddy Mountain homestead, where his last major altercation took place. Long-time Bear resident Jesse Smith told the following unsubstantiated version in a 1971 interview with Jim Camp:

> It was right in the bottom of Summers Creek where the war started. I guess that was about one of the easiest ways to the river, course ol' Jim Summers run onto their tracks between there and Wildhorse . . .
>
> Old Jim Summers, Rattlesnake Jack, and I think there was three or four of them went down by Sheep Rock in a gulch that runs down . . . Summers Creek. There was about thirty Indians camped in there and the damn Indians buckled right into them when daylight come . . . The Indians just shot the hell out of them, they shot old Jim in the hip . . . (The others) kept the Indians off old Jim 'til he got to the river and got on his horse and could swim across. He went to Pine Valley, and it was about a year before he could get out and hunt Indians again. They packed the (dead Indians) back by Sheep Rock (now called Sheep Peak) and buried them on kind of a flat place (on the south side of Summers Creek) . . . Their graves are there, I don't know if they packed them all out there or not. There was about thirty of them down there, and he just buckled into them and they come out with their guns.

Towsley Spring. Towsley was a prospector whose claim had a spectacular view of the Snake River Canyon. When he built his outhouse, he didn't bother with a door. It would have only blocked the view.

Wesley Creek. Named for a miner.

Wickiup Creek. Sheepeater Indians favored camping spots along this creek.

Wildhorse River. One story says horse thieves used the drainage to pasture stolen horses. After a couple years, when the rightful owners had given up the search, the horses were gathered and sold.

Doug McKinney cuts a calf from the herd at the Lick Creek corrals. Before coming to the OX, Doug worked on his family's ranch in Rye Valley, Oregon, and earned a ranch/range management degree at Treasure Valley Community College. (Photo courtesy of John and Jeanne Dyer.)

BIBLIOGRAPHY

"A Statement of the Operation of the OX Ranch Contest Entry of Adams Country Grassman of the Year," unpublished, 1946.

Accounting Ledger of the OX Ranch, recorded by Albert Campbell, 1917.

"Allen Uncovers Peacock Copper Mine in 1862," *Idaho Statesman*, October 30, 1927.

Anderson, Chris. Interview. Sand Hollow, Idaho. March, 1988.

Anderson, Frank. Interview. Sand Hollow, Idaho. March, 1988.

Armacost, Bertha. Interview. New Meadows, Idaho. January, 1988.

Armacost, Charlotte Campbell. Eulogy for Albert Campbell, 1979.

Armacost, Charlotte Campbell. Interview. Walla Walla, Washington. January, 1988.

Armacost, Dick and Albert Campbell, tape of discussion in late 1970s.

Armacost, Erma. Interview. Weiser, Idaho. December, 1987.

Armacost, Gary. Interview. Homestead, Oregon. April, 1988.

Armacost, Vic. Interview. New Meadows, Idaho. January, 1988.

Beckman, Joy, "Steers from Idaho's Circle C Trucked to Yakima Valley," *Washington Farmer*, November 7, 1963.

_____ "New Meadows Ranchers Ready Cattle Shipments," *Idaho Daily Statesman*, September 26, 1963.

——————— "Dance Ends Tourist Season at Bear," *Idaho Daily Statesman*, December 1, 1964.

Borah, William E., Western Union Telegram to Albert Campbell. From Washington D.C., March, 1934.

Bradshaw, Lloyd. Interview. Weiser, Idaho. February, 1988.

Braun, Leo. Interview. Council, Idaho. April, 1988.

Bridges, T. Ray. Interview. San Antonio, Texas. May, 1988.

Camp, Amos. Interview. Emmett, Idaho. February, 1988.

Campbell, Albert. Written agreement dissolving partnership with Arthur Campbell, December 12, 1914.

——————— Letter to Vernon Brewer, November 30, 1928.

——————— Letter to William E. Borah, March 6, 1934.

——————— Letter to Tim Lydston, August 23, 1937.

——————— Statement of range conditions, late 1930s, unpublished.

——————— Letter to Vern Brewer, September 20, 1939.

——————— Letter to W.W. Evans, October 30, 1939.

——————— Letter to Tim Lydston, November 24, 1939.

——————— Letter to Dick Armacost, February 7, 1940.

——————— Letter to Vern Brewer, February 15, 1940.

——————— Letter to Carl Swanstrom, 1940.

——————— and Grace Campbell. Interview by Joe Bennett and Doug Jones. New Meadows, Idaho. April, 1976.

——————— Charlotte Campbell Armacost and Carrie Whiteman. Tape of discussion. Summer 1977.

Campbell, Charles A., Letter to Editor, *Meadows Eagle*, December 23, 1911.

Campbell, Darrell. Interview. New Meadows, Idaho. May, 1988.

Campbell, Loyal. Interview. Boise, Idaho. March, 1988.

Campbell, Rollie. Interview. Boise, Idaho. January, 1988.

"Claim Peacock Richest Copper Mine in World," *Idaho Daily Statesman*, late 1930s.

Clark, D. Worth, "Idaho Made the Desert Bloom," *The National Geographic Magazine*, Vol. LXXXV, No. 6, June, 1944.

Clay, Larry and Hazel. Interview. New Meadows, Idaho. May, 1988.

Cole, Fred and Ruth. Interview. Hornet Creek, Idaho. January, 1988.

Cole, Lee and Dee. Interview. Hornet Creek, Idaho. March, 1990.

"Come to the Land of Pleasure," *Council Leader*, May 2, 1913.

Cuprum Precinct, Washington County 1910 Census. F.B. Morrison, Enumerator. April 26-30, 1910.

Degitz, Chuck. Interview. Payette, Idaho. March, 1990.

Donart, George. Letter to Albert Campbell. March 6, 1934.

Dunnington, Bob. Interview. Bear, Idaho. September, 1988.

Dyer, John. Interview. Bear, Idaho. March, 1988.

Ellis, F.W. and Harry L. Crane, "The Story of Council, Idaho," *The Idaho Magazine*, December, 1905.

Emery, Ruth and Arnold. Interview. Wildhorse, Idaho. November, 1987.

Evans, W.W., letter to Albert Campbell, October 17, 1939.

Felt, Margaret Elley, "During 66 Years of Ranching Campbell Faced Danger, Hard Work," *Idaho Statesman*, May 22, 1976.

_____ "The Indestructable Albert Campbell," *High Country*, Vol. 1, No. 8, April, 1978.

"Great Idaho Copper Mine Will Operate," *Boise Capitol News*, August 1, 1935.

Hamley, L.H., letter to Albert Campbell, April 1, 1936.

Harding, Glen F., *Amos Warner Family Book*, Ogden, Utah: Brigham Young University Printing Service, 1972.

Highly, Lee, "Ten Timber Wolves," *Adams County Leader*, undated.

_____ "Circle C Cattle Are Shipped Sunday According to Schedule," *Adams County Leader*, October 1, 1937.

_____ "Some Untold Stories About Early Mountain Mail Service," *New Meadows Eagle*, undated.

"Historic Notes of the Seven Devils Country," Idaho State Historical Society, undated, author unknown.

History of Idaho: Personal and Family History, Vol III. New York: Lewis Historical Publishing Company, Inc., 1959.

Hunt, Ray and Caroline. Notes from horsemanship clinic, Bear, Idaho. July, 1988.

Huntley, Arthur O., untitled *Idaho Statesman*, January 21, 1934.

_____ Letter to Albert Campbell, March 5, 1927.

Husak, Frank. Letters to Adams County Tax Collector, August 2 and August 9, 1969.

"Idaho's Copper Boom Brilliantly Shows on Horizon," *Boise Capital News*, October 18, 1935.

Johnson, David P., "Saga of the Circle C," *Spokesman-Review Sunday Magazine*, February 25, 1973.

Jones, Louise, "Cowhands, Families at Spread Near Council Need Muscle, Teamwork, Stamina in July Branding Jobs," *Idaho Statesman*, July 24, 1969.

Kelly, Zoe Whitlow. Interview. Astoria, Idaho. March, 1988.

Lindgren, Margaret. Interview. Council, Idaho. April, 1988.

Lindsay, Winifred B., "Seven Devils Minings District," series of articles in the *Weiser Signal* through May 22, 1966.

Lloyd, W.W., "Destruction of the Bannock or Sheepeater Indians," unpublished, undated.

Lorimer, Bob, "California Stockmen by Circle C. Ranch," *Idaho Statesman*, undated.

Lydston, Hugh. Interview. Boise, Idaho. February, 1988.

Lydston, Tim. Letter to Albert Campbell, November 21, 1939.

Martin, Orianna Hubbard. *Ballads of Idaho, It's Scenes and Citizens*. Weiser, Idaho: Commercial Printers, 1952.

McFadden, Clarence and Marie. Interview. Council, Idaho. March, 1988.

McGahey, Bud and Mavis. Interview. Bear, Idaho. January, 1988.

McGuiness, Ruth. Interview. Homestead, Oregon. April, 1988.

McKinney, Doug. Interview. Smith Mountain, Idaho. September, 1988.

_____ Interview. Brownlee, Idaho. February 2, 1988.

Mills, Nellie Ireton, "An Empire of Free Grass," *The Idaho Reader* (by Grace Jordon).

Mink, Herb. Interview. Bruneau, Idaho. February, 1988.

Moritz, Norval. Interview. Council, Idaho. December, 1991.

"New Operations in Seven Devils Make Old Miners and Prospectors Wonder If Their Dreams are Becoming Reality," *Sunday Capital News*, November 14, 1926.

Nichols, Maxine. Interview. Fruitvale, Idaho. July, 1991.

Nixon, Holworth. Interview. Weiser, Idaho. January, 1988.

Old Timers Column, *High Country*, Vol. 2, No. 2, August, 1978.

Page, Don and Kay. Interview. Homestead, Oregon. February, 1988.

Parker, Dick and Georgianna. Interview. Fruitvale, Idaho. February, 1988.

Peeples, Doug. "Bear Runs on Diesel Oil, Propane and Batteries," *Idaho Statesman*, September, 1978.

"Pioneer Cattle Owner Finds Ideal Idaho Home," *Idaho Statesman*, undated.

"Plans for Exploring, Testing of Peacock Diggings Brings Back Memories of Early-Day Explorations," *Idaho Statesman*, June 4, 1965.

Pope, Senator James A. Letter to Albert Campbell, July 23, 1935.

Quilliam, Jay and Lori. Interview. Bear, Idaho. October, 1988.

Ray, Mabel and Phylis Cranor. Interview. Oxbow, Idaho. April, 1988.

Reid, Bonnie Whiteley. Interview. Cambridge, Idaho. February, 1988.

Schmidt, Helena. Interview. Starveout Ranch, Idaho. June, 1988.

"Seven Devils," *Weiser Signal*, July 21, 1983.

Shellworth, Harry C. Notarized letter of August 21, 1917.

Shelton, Opal. Interview. Council, Idaho. September, 1987.

"Silver King Mine," *High Country*, Vol. 1, No. 10, June, 1978.

Sinclair, Vern and Helen. Interview. Bear, Idaho. June, 1988.

Smith, Dale. Interview. McCall, Idaho. July, 1992.

Smith, Frank. Interview. Council, Idaho. April, 1988.

Speropulos, Heitho. Interview. Weiser, Idaho. January, 1988.

Stout, Glenn and Barbara. Interview. Council, Idaho. February, 1989.

Swanstrom, Carl. Note on Campaign Poster to Grace and Albert Campbell.

Taylor, Dixie. Interview. Homestead, Oregon. April, 1988.

Taylor, Suzanne, "Noted Kleinschmidt Grade Opened Area for Ore Removal in Seven Devils Land," *Idaho Evening Statesman*, June 7, 1965.

United States Forest Service, correspondence on OX allotments.

Walker, Eugene H., "The Geologic History of the Snake River Country of Idaho," *Idaho Historical Series*, No. 8, September, 1963.

Warner, Bert and Tina. Interview. Bear, Idaho. December, 1987.

Warner, Joe. Interview. Bear, Idaho. April, 1988.

Whiteley, Bub. Interview. Halfway, Oregon. November, 1987.

Whiteley, Darline. Interview. Ontario, Oregon. December, 1988.

Whiteley, Don. Interview. Halfway, Oregon. January, 1988.

Whiteman, Carrie Campbell, "Charlie Campbell, Cattleman," *The Idaho Reader* (by Grace Jordon). Boise, Idaho: Syms-York, 1963.

Whiteman, Carrie Campbell. Interview. Council, Idaho. February, 1988.

Whiteman, Bob. Interview. Council, Idaho. November, 1987.

Whiteman, Don. Interview. Riggins, Idaho. January, 1988.

Youngblood, Frank. Interview. Boise, Idaho. February, 1988.

Dusty boots mark the end of the trail.
(Photo courtesy of Howard and Leigh Hultgren.)

INDEX